Chance and the Modern British Novel

Related titles in the Continuum Literary Studies series:

Character and Satire in Post War Fiction
Ian Gregson

Iris Murdoch: Philosophical Novelist
Miles Lesson

Marginality in the Contemporary British Novel
Nicola Allen

Since Beckett
Peter Boxall

Chance and the Modern British Novel

From Henry Green to Iris Murdoch

Julia Jordan

continuum

Continuum International Publishing Group
The Tower Building   80 Maiden Lane
11 York Road   Suite 704, New York
London SE1 7NX   NY 10038

British Library Cataloguing-in-Publication Data
A catalogue record for this book is available from the British Library.

ISBN: 978-1-4411-2531-6 (hardcover)

Library of Congress Cataloging-in-Publication Data
A catalog record for this book is available from the Library of Congress.

Typeset by Newgen Imaging Systems Pvt Ltd. Chennai, India
Printed and bound in Great Britain by MPG Books Group Ltd

Contents

Acknowledgements

I would like to acknowledge my gratitude to the Arts and Humanities Research Council, who gave me a Doctoral Study Award which supported me through the initial period of research for this book. A slightly different version of Chapter Three will be published by The Cambridge Scholar's Press in a forthcoming collection of essays, and I thank them for their kind permission in letting me reproduce it here. I would like to thank Colleen Coalter and everyone else at Continuum Books for making the publication process so enjoyable. Mark Ford has been a constant source of help and generosity, and I would like to thank him, as well as all of the staff at the English Department of University College London. I owe Rod Mengham and Derval Tubridy a significant debt for their guidance and kindness, and I would like to thank Nuzhat Bukhari for her enthusiasm and support. It was as a student in the Classics department at King's College London that I first developed my interest in chance, and I would particularly like to express my gratitude to Carlotta Dionisotti, Michael Silk and Alessandro Schiesaro for giving me an early sense of the pleasures of academic study. I would also like to thank the peers and friends with whom I have discussed my ideas in various seminar rooms and pubs in London and Glasgow: David Gooblar, Adam Rosenthal, Alex Von Tunzelmann, Ruairi Patterson, Samantha Lawrie, Paul Vlitos, Brian Doherty and Brian Hammond. My thanks also go both to the contributors to TSW and to the staff and regulars at the Barony Bar in Edinburgh, without whom this book would no doubt have been finished a year earlier, but to whom I owe a degree of sanity. Finally, I would like to thank Janet Langdell and Tim Maggs for all their support and love; my sisters, Lucy Jordan and Anna Simon; and of course my parents, Claire and Michael Jordan, for everything. And most of all – as always – I thank David McAllister.

Preface

Human arrangements are nothing but loose ends and hazy reckoning, whatever art may pretend otherwise in order to console us.

Iris Murdoch

Our modernity . . . was constructed upon the systemic denial of chance.

Thomas Kavanagh

The idea of chance bears a unique, and contradictory, relationship to human life. It represents reason, as an acknowledgement of chance as the organizing principle of events denies superstition, and delivers a fatal blow to the possibility that events are fated or known by a higher power. And yet it also represents the rebuttal of reason: chance is incomprehensible and unpredictable, by definition, and as such it is allied to the rebellious, the whimsical, the nonsensical and the subversive. Between these two paradoxical understandings stands the modern self: defined, to some extent, by chance – that we are uncertain, fitful, inconsequential, aware of our own insignificance in a random universe, has been the twentieth-century realization *par excellence*. As Richard Rorty argues, the modern individual is modern precisely because of the impress of chance; he must make 'an effort to achieve self-creation by the recognition of contingency' (Rorty, 1989, p. 25). This recognition of our essential contingency has perhaps altered our very mode of perception, as Gerda Reith states:

> Chance infiltrates and suffuses modern life; not only as gambling and games of chance but, far more generally, as an 'orientation' to reality or, rather, as the fundamental category of reality to which we must orientate ourselves . . . social life has become increasingly and openly randomised. (Reith, 1995, p. xvi)

The overwhelming variety and unpredictability of modern life, or its contingency, and the recalibration of our place in relation to this that took place in the twentieth century, inculcates a sense of man as no longer the lightning rod of meaning, but just another contingent cog in the wheel. We are not, in any sense, necessary. We are very much products of chance as well as experiencers of it.

And yet the cultural history of chance in the twentieth century has also been the story of a slow smothering of its unpredictable, rebellious, incomprehensible aspects beneath the new sciences that sprung up to categorize and to classify it. The century of Freud was one where the entire notion of accident was questionable: with new knowledge of unconscious intention, does chance become a means of self-deception to cover our true desires? Similarly, and working in a sort of pincer movement from the other side of culture, the new mathematics of statistics and probability theory were, by the beginning of the mid-part of the twentieth century, the dominant modes in which chance existed in rational discourse. They tamed chance, in Ian Hacking's excellent phrase, and this taming can be understood as the absorption of chance into a dull taxonomy of experience that recasts all human endeavours as examples of or deviations from the average. The beginnings of the 'taming' of chance had originally happened in tandem with the birth of the modern novel in the eighteenth century, which similarly circumscribed the boundaries of chance's operations by the introduction of larger causal explanations of why things happened. This co-nascency contributed to the marginalization of chance throughout the novel's history: the novel is the vehicle for causal and psychological explanations for events *par excellence*. The resulting eccentricity of the position of chance in relation to the novel, illuminated by analysis of one specific period in literary history, is the subject of this book.

As such, I am interested in one specific type of chance. Attitudes to chance throughout its modern history could, very broadly, be said to fall into two categories. First, simply put, there is 'true' chance, otherwise referred to as randomness. Secondly, there is fate masquerading as chance. It is common for writers to use 'coincidence' to portend a hidden order or knowledge within the plot. From the perspective of the reader chance does not 'appear from the heavens'; it is embedded in the predetermined narrative structure of the text. Therefore it cannot be re-created with mimetic truthfulness; in its own representations it always contains the knowledge of the impossibility of that representation. Chance is usually, in narrative, revealed as or assimilated into spots of determinism. Creating a story in the very simplest sense fashions the unpredictable stuff of life into a determined order, and it is this basic problem, chance's inimicality to narrative, that transforms most seeming instances of chance in the novel into their opposite: what appears at first to be pure chance is revealed to be, as it is assimilated into, fate. As a corollary to this narratological tension, the inherent discomfort in the relation between chance and narrative finds an echo in the wider human relation to chance: chance would, given full rein, render a life into a meaningless concatenation of random, disconnected events. Therefore an unavoidable corollary to the human urge to tell stories is the extinguishing within those stories of chance's true operations. Iris Murdoch, who will form the subject of my fifth chapter, describes this primary and often overlooked problem eloquently, as 'our tendency to conceal death and chance by the invention of forms. Any story which we tell about ourselves consoles us since it imposes pattern upon something which might otherwise seem intolerably chancy and incomplete. However, human life is chancy and incomplete' (Murdoch, 1970a, p. 85). Leland Monk, in his book *Standard Deviations* (1993), comments:

> The novel has always been of (at least) two minds, evidencing in its realist mandate a fidelity to experience in all of its contingency and, at the same time, being a generic imperative to structure its material in an aesthetically autonomous and unified representation. A novelistic concern with chance is then always engaged in a simultaneous affirmation and denial of its existence. (Monk, 1993, p. 153)[1]

The tension between our attraction to forms that seek to counter life's meaninglessness with narratives, and our contradictory desire for art to be as close to reality as possible (and so to tell us something about this, the most central aspect of reality as it is experienced), amounts to chance's 'unrepresentability' in narrative.

This book examines the ways in which selected writers represented chance in the mid-part of the twentieth century, explores the problems that they encounter and seeks to discover the forces and motives that inspired and shaped these representations. Chance bears a particularly pressing relationship to the mid-twentieth century: the attraction to disorder was perhaps greater during the age of possibility that followed the Second World War, and therefore this period particularly fertile for the scholar of chance and the novel. However, this tension became pressing in the mid-twentieth century for various reasons: chance had secured its dominion, scientifically, by the 1940s, and, philosophically, once the existentialists' ideas had become common currency in intellectual and literary circles of Britain and Europe. These developments, of course, coincided with the Second World War, and all of my writers are in this sense 'post-war', although the later ones would perhaps not have defined themselves as such. It is indeed possible to argue that my chosen period represents a high point of chance: deterministic modes of thinking are again perhaps on the rise, and chaos theory and its influence on the systems novel of the 1980s and 1990s is perhaps symptomatic of a new attitude to chance, one which I do not have space to explore here. A preoccupation with accidents is one way in which the representation of chance in the novel has developed in the postmodern era. The subject's collision with the object, and with the material world, is a constant reminder of our contingency in a world of technological onslaught. But this book will stop short of these interesting developments, and will instead concentrate on examining the period in which the writers I am most interested in produced their work. I have tried to seek out texts that, in differing ways, show signs of strain at the fault-line that chance offers to the critic; a fault-line that may yet prove insuperable.

The structure of the book is broadly chronological, though there are, inevitably, some moments where the careers of the writers I discuss overlap with each other. My first chapter examines the idea of chance, the intellectual, theological and philosophical history of the idea, and the associations it sustains. It is vital to take the long historical view, here: there are clear dangers in conceptualizing chance as a stable concept that flits through history, unchanged by any given social, political or philosophical context, and it is possible to detect significant change in the relationship between chance and humanity's conception of it. Throughout its pre-twentieth-century history, I argue, it has been associated with ignorance, passivity and evil, and it was not until the twentieth century that the final break with determinism occurred and afforded chance a neutral status. Although neutered by its absorption into statistical mathematics and probability theory, chance in the mid-twentieth century was still associated with negative ideas, as I go on to argue in my third chapter. My second chapter centres on the post-war novels of Henry Green, and argues that the Second World War had a contributory effect to the obsession with chance in my period. The fragmentation, disorder and uncertainty of the time created a fecund environment in which anxieties about chance were able to flourish. Life itself, for many people, seemed more sensitive to possibility: people were living under the rule of probability, where the chances of dying were hastily calculated and recalculated according to whatever limited information was available. Green echoed this cultural preoccupation with chance and dealt with it as a question of the author's ability to represent freedom in the novel, and thus to represent a world ruled by chance. To this end Green was interested in the retreat of authorial omniscience and I will examine both his stated aims, and his success – or otherwise – in achieving his desire to act as a recorder, rather than controller, of his material.

My third chapter examines Samuel Beckett's 1953 novel *Watt*, the legacy of Existentialism, and its effect on chance. Beckett was writing in an intellectual climate in which the existentialists on the continent had drawn new associations between chance and existential freedom. In *Watt* though, as I argue, the horror of infinite possibility meant that chance retained its negative connotations the sentences of *Watt* are infected with, and paralysed by, paralysed by possibility, and an inability to decide on any one course of action becomes both a critique of the traditional limitations of the novel and of the horrific implications of the absolute randomness of a world suddenly open to pure chance. My fourth chapter looks at the liberation of chance in the 1950s and 1960s by the rediscovery of the Dadaist trope of radical aleatorism, and I argue that this is a serious response to the recognition of the problems presented by chance in relation to narrative: indeed, perhaps the only way to let a work be experienced as 'chancy'. I use B. S. Johnson as the paradigmatic, and perhaps only, example of a truly aleatorical novelist in Britain in my period. My fifth and final chapter looks at the ways in which the idea of chance was rehabilitated after the radical experimentalism of the 1960s, identifying and discussing its transmutation into a philosophical and literary preoccupation with contingency. The writer, I suggest, who best expresses this transformation, and who takes it most seriously, is Iris Murdoch, and I examine some of her novels of the 1970s to glean an understanding of how this philosophical belief in contingency is able to sit happily with the novel form. I suggest that it is her insistence on the importance of the contingency of character, and the belief that lies at the heart of her novels that contingency is related to goodness, that eventually saves chance, in Murdoch's oeuvre, from its age-old associations with ignorance and paralysed passivity. In Murdoch's writing an acceptance of contingency, and an accommodation between free characters and the 'crystalline' perfection of form, transforms the workings of chance in the novel into an analogy for the operation of grace in a secular world.

Chance, as we shall see, manifests itself in the novel in various ways. In an essay on that other great unknowable and unrepresentable literary obsession, death, Elisabeth Bronfen points out that the unknowability of death means that 'every representation of death is a misrepresentation' (Bronfen and Goodwin, 1994, p. 4). I would argue something approximating this for my own topic, that 'every representation of chance is a misrepresentation'. Monk makes a similar point in his study of chance and the modern novel, when he suggests that 'Chance is the unrepresentable Other of narrative'

(Monk, 1993, p. 10). Where my project differs from existing studies of chance is that, in contrast to Monk and others, I suggest that chance *has* managed to be represented at various junctures, usually by writers who seek to disturb the form that is such a representation's greatest hurdle. Bernard Bergonzi said in 1970, 'Art must essentially be the impression of form on flux' (Bergonzi, 1970, p. 210). There is, I contend, an alternative artistic tradition, one that has tried to let the flux, in all its haphazard glory, represent itself. Chance is an endlessly variable subject that sheds light upon the motivations of writers according to how they use it; in its very ambiguity, as well as in its power, it threatens and disturbs us. When one writes about chance, one is never really writing about chance itself, but what chance can tell us through its refracting, distorting lens. I will attempt to keep this in mind during the book, while all the time trying to give chance its due: not mistaking it for something else, or wishing it away, or effacing or marginalizing its operations. As Henry James famously points out in his preface to the New York edition of *Roderick Hudson*, 'Really, universally, relations stop nowhere, and the exquisite problem of the artist is eternally but to draw, by a geometry of his own, the circle within which they should happily *appear* to do so' (James, 1934, p. 5). The writers I have chosen to study in this book all believed that the proper role of the novelist, to a greater or lesser degree, was to lever open this neat Jamesian circle, so that the contingency of the universe could be allowed to impose a geometry of its own.

Chapter One

A Fine Thing: A History of Chance

[T]he details, whether good or bad, [are] left to what we may call chance. Not that this notion at all satisfies me.

Charles Darwin

Richard Ellmann recounts a story about one of the few occasions when James Joyce, engaged in the massive task of writing *Finnegans Wake* (1939), and with his eyesight beginning to fail him, employed Samuel Beckett to act as his amanuensis. One afternoon '[t]here was a knock at the door which Beckett didn't hear. Joyce said, "Come in," and Beckett wrote it down. Afterwards he read back what he had written and Joyce said, "What's that 'Come in'?" "Yes, you said that," said Beckett. Joyce thought for a moment, then said, "Let it stand." He was quite willing to accept coincidence as his collaborator' (Ellmann, 1982, p. 649). Ellmann tells us that Beckett was fascinated by Joyce's method, which to him was characteristic of his tendency towards an expansive inclusivity in his approach to his writing. In a recent newspaper interview, Stephen Montague recounted an anecdote about his fellow composer John Cage: 'When I first met John in 1975, he had given me his phone number and told me to call if I was in town. When I was next there, I did. "Am I interrupting you?" I asked. "Of course," he replied. My heart sank. But then he continued: "I regard telephone calls as unexpected pleasures. I like to remain open to things I can't predict."'[1]

Cage's policy of remaining open to all things unforeseen is an entirely prosaic and everyday reaction to chance and the unpredictable, and characteristic of how they function in the late twentieth and early twenty-first centuries. Uncertainty can be anxiety inducing, or it can be exciting; in the second half of the twentieth century we seem comfortable enough with either interpretation of the idea that the fundamentals of the universe rely on random precepts. For Cage, who is happy to allow chance to decide the internal plot of his day, and to interpret the unexpected as pleasurable, chance has its own narrative to impose on us. For Joyce this was extended to its logical conclusion: if chance can have authorship over a life, why not a work of art? If it is, after all, how we live, why not let it in to the text? For both, chance has, as the scholar of chance Gerda Reith puts it, 'become radically autonomous, an ontological category in its own right' (Reith, 1999, p. 14). In other words, chance is allowed to have its own existence, one whose autonomy we respect, and to which we happily submit. This equanimity in the face of randomness brings with it a sense of permissive, limitless possibility. Indeed, in this way, the unpredictable can be seen to work as an eroticized channel of the imagination[2] – there is something undeniably exciting in the thought that anything at all might happen.

For reasons I will explore in this chapter, chance has in its history more frequently been seen as threatening to and subversive of our sense of a happy life. As Monk comments, 'the history of thinking about chance is in general a history of its marginalization' (Monk, 1993, p. 13), and a universe ruled by chance is an idea that mankind has historically struggled with. The biologist Jacques Monod, in his book *Chance and Necessity: An Essay of the Natural Philosophy of Modern Biology*, articulates this very human urge to minimize the arbitrary when he concludes: 'We would like to think ourselves necessary, inevitable, ordained from all eternity. All religions, nearly all philosophies, and even a part of science testify to the unwearying, heroic effort of mankind desperately denying its own contingency' (Monod, 1972, p. 44). We might like to extend this to other aspects of culture that, in the secular West, have latterly fulfilled some of the same needs: the novel, films and stories in general; astrology; luck and superstition; or a popular belief in coincidence or synchronicity – all can be recast as agents of reassurance, relentlessly conspiring to place us as subjects at the centre of the world. Narrative – whether fictional, historical, religious or the sort of narrative that we internally rely on to make sense of our own lives – acts to construct a version of experience where meaning is made, given and hungrily consumed. By this process, it necessarily evades the task of constructing a version of reality that would faithfully re-create the operations of chance, and in this way we are existentially placated: reassured that we are protagonists of a story, that we are subjects at the centre of our own lives.

Chance, of course, has a rather different story to tell: if we accept that the universe is run on random precepts, then we are inconsequential beings who matter little, if at all. Indeed, if everything is arbitrary, then the urge to form narratives that place us at the centre of the indifferent world around us, or to select points of external happenstance and deem them meaningful in the stories of our lives, start to look like grossly egotistical and self-deluding acts. A chance event, one that occurs for no apparent reason, or is not the predictable outcome of a detectable cause,[3] is therefore peculiarly hard to assimilate into a view of our surroundings that places us at their centre. Narrative tells us that there is a story to be told; that it will disclose its meaning to us; that the world makes sense. Chance tells us we are contingent, replaceable; it tells us that nothing, anywhere, happens for any reason whatever.

Monod's book, while diagnosing this large-scale resistance to the arbitrary, was also part of the twentieth-century scientific and cultural vanguard which helped to challenge the reasons for, and conditions of, that resistance. As I will argue, Quantum Physics, Dada, the collapse of what tend to be called the Grand Narratives: each of these seemingly disparate cultural phenomena represents a development in the gradual erosion of the domination of chance by appeals to meaning. As we might expect, with this shift in our understanding of how chance operates in life came a correlative shift in the ways that chance operates, and is represented, in the twentieth-century novel. In a spirit similar to that with which John Cage was happy to let chance decide the plot of his day, some twentieth-century writers, following Joyce, began to play with the idea of letting chance collaborate in the construction of literary texts – started to let it, sometimes in apparent contradiction to the god-like powers of the author, decide things, and thereby to instigate what Leland Monk has called the 'undecidability of pleasure' (Monk, 1993, p. 152): an alternative, chance-based novelistic aesthetic, and one more reflective of our uncertain, contingent, accident-prone ways. Joyce's refusal to throw away his throwaway comment has proved to be significant for this reason; it stands as an emblem of the ways in which the alternative narratives that chance is able to impose begin to intrude on that most deterministic of cultural forms – the novel – and radically subvert the previously dominant narrative of the author.

Brian Richardson has argued that 'causal connection, however intermittent, deferred, or oblique, is a necessary condition of narrativity' (Richardson, 1997, p. 37). An exception to this, he suggests, is the characteristic rejection of causality that develops in the novels of the mid-twentieth century. He argues for three types of causation in fiction: supernatural (as in Milton's *Paradise Lost*), naturalistic (as in Flaubert's *Madame Bovary*) and 'the chance universe found in modern works like Borges's "The Lottery of Babylon"' (ibid., p. 38). These differing types of aetiological explanation reflect the wider cultural approach to causality, determinism and chance at any given time, as he points out: 'In the nineteenth century the different deterministic systems of Marx, Darwin, and Freud jostled for explanatory supremacy of the social world with the confines of naturalism' and 'the same is true of character motivation . . . conscious and subconscious desires are pitted against biological forces and the logic of history' (ibid., p. 39). He quotes Walter Scott from the Preface to *The Monastery* (1820) ('it is part of the author's duty to afford satisfactory details upon the causes of the events he has recorded, and, in a word, to account for everything'), and reflects that 'The rise of nineteenth-century realism led to the suspension of providential teleology and the marginalization of chance' (ibid., p. 41).[4] An emphasis on causality, or a concentration on an explanatory structure for represented events, evidently marginalize the opportunities in the novel for a true depiction of the random. Causality is in this sense firmly opposed to chance, if we follow Reith in defining a chance event as one with *no identifiable cause and no particular meaning*. Although the elaboration of causality does not necessarily imply determinism, neither does it preclude it. Indeed, a deterministic universe is one where cause and effect work like clockwork: no effect ever becomes detached from its cause, and no cause ever fails to bring its twin effect into being. If we can show why things happened, then they happened for a reason, however obscure. Once you have a reason, of course, it is not a huge leap to assuming that the event, given that its motivating reason pre-existed it, was more or less inexorable. A concentration on causality for any explanatory framework in the nineteenth-century narrative novel was therefore able to co-exist happily with a deterministic universe, and so was less threatening, for reasons we shall see, to the status quo.

Chance in the twentieth and early twenty-first centuries has become so entrenched in the way we live that it has become, as Reith points out, a mode of perceiving – a specifically modern phenomenon that is reflected in the development of the novel. This chapter will try and trace how this happened, and in doing so, provide a background for some of the cultural assumptions that twentieth-century novelists will bring to bear on the subject. Ian Hacking has noted that the intrusion of chance into every aspect of our consciousness began in the Enlightenment with the 'avalanche of numbers' that fomented the discovery of probability theory (Hacking, 1990, p. 2). The importation of the contingent into narrative and art, the very vehicles of its suppression, has been traced to various cultural moments by a range of critics whose illuminating work has helped to open up this field of research. Thomas Kavanagh argues that Voltaire's *Candide* (1759), as a direct product of the Enlightenment and as a direct response to a chance event (the Lisbon earthquake of 1755) is similarly radical in its response to chance's unruly power (Kavanagh, 1993). David Trotter uses Turner as a prominent example to suggest that a nineteenth-century increase in crowd painting was a further possible vehicle for the contingent, arguing that the representation of the unpindownable hustle and bustle of life itself imports a sense of the random into painting (Trotter, 2000).[5] Ross Hamilton notes that the birth of photography was one of the key developments that affected our perception of the accidental and random (Hamilton, 2007, p. 248). Photographs capture fleeting moments, and therefore assign meaning to the essentially meaningless, foregrounding the normal sleight of hand that goes on with selection. I would argue for the importance of Laurence Sterne's *Tristram Shandy* (1759–67), in which the exposure of the mechanics of cause and effect, through the narrative's constant digressive meanderings, eventually makes its inadequacy as an explanatory device self-evident. So although I read the irruption of chance into the novel as a distinctively modern (if we still view the mid-twentieth century as modernity) phenomenon, I am aware that it is a phenomenon with long and complex roots. This chapter will therefore take the long view of chance, trying to give a sense (although one that will be necessarily fitful and partial) of chance's literary, scientific, philosophical and religious contexts, so that we can better see the radical nature of the change that took place in the mid-twentieth century.

The Origins of Chance and the Manifestations of *Fortuna*

Most scholars of chance agree on one thing: chance was not chance as we understand it until the seventeenth century. As Gerda Reith says, until the seventeenth century chance had yet to become autonomous; it could not be considered as 'an ontological category in its own right' (Reith, 1999, p. 14). The word itself therefore had a fundamentally different meaning to the one it has for us. Throughout most of human history, chance existed mainly as a sacred channel for divine knowledge, and events were interpreted for what advice or judgement they may hold for humans. So the unexpected occurrence, the event that happened out of the blue, would not be understood as an event without a cause or a purpose. Both were there, but were occluded by the mysterious workings of Providence. The idea that an event could be causeless was largely unimaginable, and people who avowed a belief in 'blind' chance were thought to be somehow blasphemous: by believing in a causeless event, they denied the reality of the ultimate cause, the Providential scheme that lies behind all things.

The word chance was instead a euphemism for ignorance. To explain something away by chance meant you either didn't know the reason, and were dissembling, or you had a reason for obscuring the cause. Chance as we would understand it, then, was distorted to the point of being unrecognizable, and it occupied this awkward, liminal space for centuries. If, on the one hand, it was denied existence by the pious, and subsumed entirely by the concept of Providence (*Fortuna*), it still hovered in the ontological background, real enough to threaten those who sought to deny it.

For large portions of history the word has been inseparable from *fortuna* (*Tyche* in ancient Greek), which is an obvious linguistic antecedent of fortune in English. The basic meaning of this has remained the same; fortune is in rough accordance with luck, both as chance and as a piece of the universe's good will that has been apportioned out, presumably by some intelligent and decisive being. All events, in early Christian culture, and certainly for the Ancient Greeks and Romans, were underpinned by a rigorous and totalizing determinism – God's, or the gods', omnipotence. This fact is apparent in the earliest recordings of the concept of chance: in Greek, the figure of Tyche represents destiny as well as chance, and chance, in this alliance, is barely allocated any epistemological space at all: the determinism of the Greek theological system tells us that every aspect of an individual's life has been mapped out before their birth. Everything happened for a reason, albeit one that was usually undisclosed, so any unlikely event could hardly be a 'mere' coincidence; how a die falls may reveal something about the gods' wishes, or fate's as yet unrevealed direction. Oedipus, for example, makes this same category mistake: in thinking of himself as the object of a series of coincidences, he is ignorant of the truth, which is uncovered when each coincidence, in turn, is revealed as a necessary staging post along the way towards the predetermined outcome. The Greek belief in destiny therefore underpins all questions of causality and aetiology, and highlights an instability in the meaning of *fortuna* that leaves as its legacy an intertwining of chance and destiny, the traces of which still exist.

The word chance itself is derived from *cadere*, the Latin for 'to fall', so chance is what 'befalls' us; how the dice fall for us; what falls to us (or on us, or what we fall into); the unforeseen, the random occurrence with no obvious cause or design.[6] 'The fall', of course, as distinct from *a* fall, is the fall of man into sin in Judeo-Christian mythology, and this sense remains in other words derived from the same root: 'cadence', for instance. Jacques Derrida, in his seminal essay on chance, exploits this point: 'Is not what befalls us or descends upon us – coming from above, like destiny or lightning, taking our faces and our hands by surprise – exactly what thwarts or undoes our *anticipation?*' (Derrida, 2007, p. 348). In German, the link is more explicit: *Zufall*, or *Zufälligkeit*, means chance; *Zufallen*, to 'fall due'. *Hasard* in French has also bequeathed us an echo of its meaning, which has leaked into the modern understanding of hazardous. Shakespeare's Richard III was able to say: 'I have set my life upon a cast, / And I will stand the hazard of the die' (Shakespeare, 1988, pp. 9–10) which carries the full weight of the French, implying as it does both risk and danger; anything, indeed, beyond our control, which of course uncertainty and chance always are. However, the unpredictable outcome of the dice, or of the casting of lots, is not subject to chance as we understand it, but to a version of 'chance' at best subordinate to discussions of the limits of fate and free will.

Chance originated in the Greek idea of the primeval disorder, or chaos, which existed before the world, and therefore order, were brought into being. Chaos was not mere nothingness, but had dark powers of destruction of its own, as Plato tells us that God feared 'all might be dissolved in the storm and disappear in an infinite chaos' (Plato, 1987, p. 588). As Brenner points out, in fact, chaos was brought to order through an engagement with chance, as Poseidon, Zeus and Hades divided the world between them in a dice game: Zeus got the sky, Poseidon the sea and the loser, Hades, the underworld (Brenner, 1990, p. 4). The origins of chance are thus inextricable from those of gambling, and also, initially, strike us as oddly modern: chance, as for us, is a useable aspect of the rational world, and randomness is presented as a fair and just method of distribution, completely without agency. This is perhaps explicable by the oddly unique circumstances of that first completely random gamble: since these three were the supreme beings of the world, there was no higher god to whom they could appeal. Oddly, chance therefore existed for the Greeks before existence itself, as its midwife and arbiter, but once being had been brought into existence, and the pre-being chaos had been quieted into abeyance, it becomes the distorted synonym for ignorance that a totalizing determinism insists it must be.

Similarly, gambling, as the most characteristic and pure engagement with chance, was seen primarily in Greek society as a means to determine what the gods willed a man's fate to be. Aristotle identifies two different kinds of chance, *tyche* and *automaton* (which would later form the basis of an influential discussion of the narrative uses of chance by Jacques Lacan[7]) which are both part of natural chains of causation. *Tyche* is chance as experienced by the mind, and *automaton* is chance as incorporated into the natural world.[8] In a discussion of chance in his examination of final causes in the *Physics*, Aristotle makes clear that his idea of chance is fully subordinate to his teleological explanation, rigorously delimiting chance's operation by using it as a synonym for 'coincidence', or the impetus for a 'coincidental cause' (which, as the intersection of two separate causes, is not incompatible with determinism). The intermingling of the ideas of chance and coincidence is another, perhaps more rational, way to infect the subversive idea of chance with the religiously coded obsession with meaning and purpose: coincidence is, in one sense after all, just randomness that has been brought to our attention.[9]

Further evidence for the elision of the sometimes contradictory concepts surrounding chance comes from Huizinger, whose *Homo Ludens* (1938) is a seminal analysis of the psychology of play. He notes that on Greek coins the figure of Dike, the goddess of justice, blends with the figure of Nemesis (vengeance) and with that of Tyche (Huizinger, 1998, p. 94). Huizinger remarks that for the Ancients the concept of 'how the dice falls for us' can mean not only 'how the gods want the dice to fall for us', but also, 'how the dice should fall for us, if our enemies have their way'. This domination of aetiology by determinism is borne out by literary treatments of teleology, with Sophocles' *Oedipus Tyrannos* emblematic of the Greek attitude towards man's fate. Oedipus is an examination of how closely our actions, which we believe are performed under our own volition, are intertwined with our destiny, even when we vainly try to act in opposition to that fate. The crushing wheel of destiny, as it was so often limned, was inescapable.

The clash between the creation myth of Greek society, which relied on chance for its very existence, and the utter impossibility of chance's co-existing with a culture where free will was a hotly contested concept, subject at the very least to strict limitations, is mirrored in other early societies. An early fascination with games of chance in the Bible seemed to sit happily with the early Christian belief in predestination. The history of lotteries suggests a similar ability to elide the divine will with chance events. The word 'lot' comes from the Teutonic hleut, which was the pebble cast to settle property disagreements and other legal squabbles.[10] From this root we also get the French terms *lotterie*, and the Italian *lotteria*, but in both English and Dutch the word 'lot' carries with it a suggestion of destiny: one's lot in life is equivalent to one's fate. 'How the dice fell' for people was therefore not only indistinguishable from their destiny; it could also be used as a supposedly accurate instrument of augury, a practice employed to determine God's position on any number of subjects, and was so widespread in Western culture that traces of this practice, and the resulting systematic suppression of chance, survived in Britain into the nineteenth century.

The divine sanction for the casting of lots in early Christian society is Biblical. Exodus 28:30, for instance, relates how high priest Aaron was ordered to wear lots 'Urim and Thummim', thought to be two dice, one for a positive answer one for the negative, when going before the Lord. In such a wholly theocratic culture, gambling was not blasphemous, but was used purely as an instrument of knowledge, or in Reith's terms, it was not yet an epistemological category, but merely an epistemological tool.[11] In contrast, gambling was also widespread in pre-Islamic Arabia, but in this case it was seen as running contrary to the proper worship of God in Islam. Reuven and Gabrielle Brenner, who have written extensively on gamblers and the history of gambling, have suggested that the Qur'anic condemnation of gambling (in the form of the pre-Islamic game of chance *maysir*) can be read as an indication of its prevalence (Brenner, 1990, p. 4).

Similarly, Clement of Alexandria, Tertullian and others, condemned gambling on the grounds that it reflected an interest in material things, in being a 'partner with the world' (ibid., p. 52). This suggests an interesting awareness of the rational aspect of chance, a perception of it as dealing not merely with divine wishes, but as actually being in opposition to them. It might even be argued that this implies a conflict between the world of humanity and the world of the gods, with chance firmly on the side of man, although the materiality of the objections suggest that it may have been the fiscal side-benefits of an engagement with chance that were actually meeting with disapproval. In fact, a shift had occurred in Greece when pious belief in the Olympian system started to dissolve; a parallel shift occurred in the perception of *fortuna*, and the active worship of fortune and fate began. Although *fortuna* was still a confused concept – sometimes interchangeable with chance, and sometimes, as destiny or fate, starkly contrasted with it – this represented a significant evolution. Brenner cites an observation made by Pliny the Elder, which contains characterizations of chance that are strongly evocative today – chance is 'blind', 'fickle' and most gallingly, as always, 'friend of the unworthy':

Throughout the whole world, at every place and hour, by every voice, Fortune alone is invoked and her name is spoken: she is the one dependent, the one culprit, the one thought in men's minds, the one object of praise, the one cause. She is worshipped with insults, counted as fickle and often as blind, wandering, inconsistent, elusive, changeful, and friend of the unworthy. . . . We are so much at the mercy of chance that Chance is our god. (ibid.)

'The Rabbit of Our Ignorance': The Birth of Probability Theory

Probability theory has in fact carried off an enormously seductive sleight of hand, making the embarrassingly visible rabbit of our ignorance vanish into the decidedly thick air of complex equations . . . the calculus of probabilities offers a demanding and rigorously mathematized discourse bristling with apparent proofs of our mastery over a situation that in fact escapes us completely (Kavanagh, 1993, p. 16).

Blaise Pascal, it can be argued, gave us the modern concept of chance in a 1654 bar-room debate that changed our understanding of the world.[12] Along with the writers Cardano and Pacioli, he was involved in a card game that was brought to an abrupt end. The question arose: how should the players divide the winnings? The others argued that the spoils should be divided according to whichever of them was winning at the time the game ended. How the game had gone so far, they reasoned, was the best basis from which to predict how it would continue. They had no reason to believe that what was currently happening would stop happening in the future – in other words, they contended that life is essentially consistent from one moment to the next. Pascal, however, disagreed, and argued that past events, no matter how consistent they had been up until the present moment, had *no bearing whatever* on predicting future events.

This was radical. From this initial observation, Pascal was able to deduce that questions about uncertain phenomena in general could be treated rationally, and that there existed indices of probabilities of how a thing would behave. Each event happened in isolation, with no knowledge of anything, and beholden to nothing. Only the laws of probability could, on a very large scale, tell us anything. As Thomas Kavanagh shows, the study of probability and the explosion of statistics in the late seventeenth and eighteenth centuries, rather than conquering chance, merely revealed a whole new range of possibilities for computing our ignorance. Before the sudden growth of this new mathematical field, our ignorance of why things happened merely masked an intelligent, divinely run world order that not only understood why things happened but controlled and determined everything that did; probability theory, on the other hand, allowed for the possibility that the universe was reasonless. That chance is an ontological lack or deficit is, as we've seen, an idea that crops up frequently in the history of chance, both before and after the Enlightenment. Probability theory represented a significant evolution from this: our ignorance was now a fig leaf over an abyss, or a growing awareness that ignorance or uncertainty may be the defining mode of the universe. The recognition of this was a fact only made palatable, or even possible, by the growing and parallel sense in the mathematical community that we may be able to predict what very large groups of people or numbers are likely to do. The realization that the world may not, in fact, be knowable, was an awareness that could stand as a definition for scepticism – a vital epistemological premise for the Enlightenment. Descartes had suggested that doubt could be the basis and the instrument for philosophical enquiry, and Reith argues persuasively that this new weight and validity accorded to the principle of uncertainty, coupled with the gradual expansion of speculative mercantile capitalism, effectively gave us the birth of modern society.

The shift that occurred at some point in the eighteenth century was catalyzed by the fact that the birth of probability theory effected a change in human consciousness. A space for the secular comprehension of the aleatory, they argue, opened up where previously there had been nothing; it was, in fact, that rare occurrence, a wholly new idea. This emergence and growth of the nascent probability theory in the Enlightenment period achieved the taming of chance, a rationalizing and normalizing of it. For Kavanagh it made possible the birth of the modern novel, and for Reith it initiated what she describes as 'the age of chance', which runs from the mid-seventeenth century to the nineteenth century. Hacking states:

> Throughout the Age of Reason, chance has been called the superstition of the vulgar. Chance, superstition, vulgarity, unreason were of one piece. The rational man, averting his eyes from such things, could cover chaos with a veil of inexorable laws. (Hacking, 1990, p. 1)

The rational man, then, defers or postpones any acknowledgement of the existence of chaos: like the rabbit of our ignorance that has been magicked out of sight, he takes refuge in the reassuringly large-scale 'inexorable laws' of probability theory. Pierre Simon Laplace was perhaps the most instrumental of the theorists in bringing the new science to the wider world. Frequently working in conjunction with Cardano, Huygens, Bernoulli, Pascal, Fermat and others, a group known as the 'classical' European probabilists, Laplace wrote his authoritative examination of what he came to call the 'calculus of probabilities' in his classic work *A Philosophical Essay on Probabilities* (1814). Here, through scrutiny of gambling, or what Reith calls 'the paradigmatic aleatory contract' (Reith, 1999, p. 29), Laplace established the mathematical bases of probability. That they used gambling as the premise of their calculations is instructive: it represented not merely a forum for uncertainty, but an action actually *regulated* by chance. As Reith comments: 'In this development, probability theory, which began as a pure "geometry of chance" (Pascal), became increasingly remote from the direct experience of the wager. It emerged, indeed, as the antithesis of the gambler's "plunge" into the unknown' (ibid., p. 15). Science, by means of calculable ratios rather than the divine, was now the voice that spoke to us through gambling. This is crucial, as it represents the shift from the study of uncertainty to the calculation of probability or, potentially, *predictability*. These scientific developments were paralleled by a society increasingly inured to the perceived dangers of gambling; risk was becoming an element of life in a sense in which we would understand it.

Pascal's famous wager about the divine demonstrates, and was made possible by, this new, rational approach to the prediction of outcomes, and reflects an unspoken acceptance of an encroaching atheistic atmosphere that sustained and paralleled the rise of rational perspectives in the new science of probability.[13] The foundations of belief in a deity, Pascal proclaimed, could be reduced to two possible premises: either God exists or he does not. From this, he determined that belief was preferable to unbelief, given the uncertain situation in which man finds himself, and taking into account an appraisal of the possible benefits and / or punishments given either of the two possible outcomes. If there is no God, neither belief nor unbelief will have any effect on us; but if there is a God, then the consequences are infinite. These consequences are either eternal damnation, if God exists and we have chosen not to believe, or salvation, the best possible outcome, if we are right. The possible benefits of being right about God's non-existence, then, are negligible compared to the catastrophic consequences if we are wrong about his non-existence. Similarly, the potential benefits if we are right that God does exist are so great that they would outweigh the potential consequences of being wrong, *even if* the chances of God's existence are microscopically small.

The significance of this was two-fold: not only was Pascal blithely reducing the question of whether or not to believe to a logistical tactic, which itself was an ironically atheistic manoeuvre, but his decision-making process also accords a radically new status to probability and chance. Before the eighteenth century chance had amounted to an index of wickedness, occasionally and of ignorance – a stance that could be summarized thus: we do not understand why a particular thing has happened, but, since everything is determined by God, that which we don't understand must result from our ignorance of his purposes. With Pascal's wager, belief, for the first time, was made to adapt to an understanding of the world based on contingency. We are prepared to believe, but only if an analysis of the possible outcomes, based on chance, dictates that it is the right course of action. This, for us, is a recognizable response. In the early twenty-first century chance is understood as an integral and codified part of the world; it is inscribed in our understanding of the universe, as demonstrated by the widespread cultural dissemination of the distinctively modern scientific fields of probability theory, Quantum Mechanics and Chaos Theory.

Laplace originally believed that 'All events, even those which on account of their significance do not seem to follow the great laws of nature, are a result of it just as necessarily as the revolutions of the sun' (Laplace, 1951, p. 3). Most of the European probabilists had a similarly determinist, and usually religious, worldview. The implied problematization of their conception of chance, therefore, meant a rigorous and subjective limiting of the parameters of their investigation. They held that 'all events were in principle predictable and that probabilities were therefore relative to our knowledge' (Gigerenzer et al., 1989, p. 11). The very radicalism of probability as an idea seems to have encouraged a sort of self-censorship; the familiar concept of chance as having a negative status, of existing as a sort of ontological lack, still pervaded Enlightenment discussions on the subject. Spinoza, writing in the mid-seventeenth century, was a determinist, as was Leibniz, and de Montmort, writing in the early eighteenth century, defined chance as an index of human ignorance. Alexander Pope's *Essay on Man* (1732–34) includes the lines 'All Nature is but Art, unknown to thee;/ All Chance, Direction which thou canst not see;/ All Discord, Harmony not understood' (Pope, 1950, p. 50).

However, this uncomfortable liaison between religious determinism and the rationally figured calculus of probability that was gaining influence could survive only fitfully. De Montmort wrote in 1731:

> It is especially in games of chance that the weakness of the human mind and its tendency towards superstition manifest themselves. . . . And it is much the same for people's behaviour in all those areas of life where chance plays a role. The same prejudices govern them, and imagination dictates their conduct, blindly giving birth to fears and hopes. (Cited in Kavanagh, 1993, pp. 12–13)

This seems to represent a shift in eighteenth-century thinking. The weakness of the human mind is not, here, demonstrated by its attraction to chance, as in the medieval formulation, but is present in those who would *deny* chance. Prejudices, imagination, hopes, fears – none should play a role in determining what will happen, as it is purely, now, a matter for chance. Superstition, or the attachment of meaning to what will happen, has adopted the appearance that it retains to this day – that of a primitive prejudice, coloured by ignorance:

> I thus thought it would be useful, not only for gamblers, but for mankind in general, to show that chance does obey knowable rules and that, for not knowing those rules, we make mistakes every day whose unhappy consequences should far more reasonably be attributed to us than to the destiny we lament. (Ibid.)

Chance does not yet have the air of blank neutrality that it acquires in the twentieth century, and yet it is quiescent enough to 'obey knowable rules'. It is this sudden association of the aleatory with knowledge that is striking: as I have shown, chance and ignorance have previously been aligned together where chance existed at all. Fate may still exist, but it is now an internalized force, coming, humanistically enough, from our selves, rather than from God. Kavanagh comments on this:

> De Montmort's analysis of card games, his contribution to the development of probability theory, is philosophically conceived as a demonstration that there exists no capricious superior power, no Fortuna or *hasard*, determining the fall of the cards. The only divinities at work in what the superstitious mistakenly persist in seeing as a brush with fortune are the mathematically calculable ratios between the chances for the card we want and the chances for other possible outcomes. (ibid., p. 13)

Hacking describes what happened between 1730 and the mid-nineteenth century as an 'avalanche of . . . numbers' (Hacking, 1990, p. 2) and certainly, the battle between the coldly calculable and the mysterious and unknowable was, at least in the scientific realm, being won, if not yet decisively, by the former. The development of scientific/mathematical probability is, however, a philosophical evolution as well as a mathematical one, and this is a crucial point if we are to accept that the onset of probability theory represents 'the most important mutation in human thought since Aristotle' (Kavanagh, 1993, p. 21). That this is so is not only related to the creation of rational man and the image-making of the Enlightenment's sense of itself,[14] but also for the proto-humanistic impulses that will still be traceable in the development of the study of chance three centuries later (for instance in the Existentialism of the mid-twentieth century). Even if the reverberations would not be felt for some time, the philosophical encroachment of chance crucially delivered the form, if not the content, of atheism.

An important tenet of probability theory was the idea that has come to be known as the 'Monte Carlo fallacy', which was first articulated by Poisson in 1835. This stated that probability, when limited to specific occurrences, had limited power, but that its accuracy was greater the larger the number. Therefore, if a coin flip comes out heads fifty times in a row, the instinctive position is that it is more likely to come out tails on the fifty-first flip. The chances, though, remain exactly the same: 50/50. Each independent event, in other words, has no knowledge of the previous events. However, probability theory states that given infinite (or very large) numbers of coin flips, the ratio would come out as exactly 50/50. This made probability theory seem a peculiarly distant science, mute on the specifics of actual events, but able to predict how large numbers of people, or things, would behave with alarming accuracy. In this way the new science represented a philosophical reverse to humanism; where humanism described how a growth in emphasis on will and rationality formed the basis of human freedom, probability theory suggested that the actions of mankind could be considered *en-masse*, and that the individual was much less significant – and perhaps less free – than had previously been possible.

These twinned and yet contrasting attitudes co-existed perfectly happily, as did the probabilists' growing distaste for determinism, which contrasted with their (in the main) pious religious belief. As we saw earlier, de Moivre, in his *Doctrine of Chances*, had dismissed chance as a 'mere word'. Around the same time appeared David Hume's *Treatise of Human Nature* (1739), which shows that the strain of thought that dismissed chance as either blasphemous or as that which we happen not to know was still virulent. Hume wrote: ''tis commonly allowed by philosophers that what the vulgar call chance is nothing but a secret and conceal'd cause' (Hume, 1888, p. 130): the difference was that the 'vulgar', now, were in the ascendant.

Laurence Sterne's *Tristram Shandy*: The Novel and Aleatory Oppositions

Kavanagh argues that the emergence of probability theory 'paralleled and in a very real sense sustained' (Kavanagh, 1993, p. ix) the hegemony of the modern novel. Together, he claims, they formed a single shift in how we saw and understood the world and how we represent our place in it. Monk too emphasizes the link: 'The discovery of probability theory in the sciences . . .

[is] here aligned with the newly devised aesthetic practices of the novel, most notably its redefinition of existing theories of verisimilitude' (Monk, 1993, p. 31). While Kavanagh rightly emphasizes the achievement of, and the continuing reverberations from, probability theory, it is equally vital to note that this did not happen in a single, swift, paradigm shift. The contradictory thread of culture, the one that denied chance, and indeed, human agency, was still palpable. One possible rebuttal to this came from Voltaire's *Candide* (1759), perhaps the first novel to consist almost entirely of chance happenings and acts of random violence, exaggerated to a comic degree to better display chance's cruelty. Voltaire sought to evoke the power of the aleatory as it turns upon the individual at random, and, indeed, to celebrate its power to make a mockery of the distinction between 'good' and 'evil' by emphasizing chance's neutrality, but he also set out to satirize and to attack it for this. The meaning and purpose of life, the novel suggests, may only exist retrospectively: that is, fate will turn out to be what happened, rather than what had to happen. The narrative significance of this, in *Candide*, is revealed through the bankruptcy of language, and the inadequacy of the Panglossian vision of the world when confronted with the messy reality of a world ruled by chance.

Laurence Sterne, in England, was perhaps reacting to some of the same wider intellectual concerns when he wrote his famously haphazard and disordered masterpiece *The Life and Opinions of Tristram Shandy, Gentleman*. I will here offer a brief reading of the novel as a case study, as its importance in the history of the novel and chance is profound. It is a novel in which chance informs the lack of a linear, sequential narrative, the digressive obsession with causes, and the seeming disorder that is both an organizing principle and a totem spirit of the novel. Tristram's task as narrator is essentially one that pivots on chance: as he declares early on in the novel, his dilemma rests upon how to plot a 'tolerable straight line' through the vast swell of information he would like to share with us (Sterne, 1997, p. 425). This information seems to consist of comically improbable chance events, and the novel comments ironically on how one seems to lead to another in a tissue of contingency that starts to look a lot like fate. The maid's chance misremembrance of Tristram's father Walter's chosen name for his son, Trismegistus, collapses it into the hated and unlucky 'Tristram'. Tristram's 'circumcision' is performed by a sash window which had been fatally weakened by the removal of some of its lead for his Uncle Toby's obsessive fortifications of his model army. Because of Walter Shandy's obscure theories Tristram ends up being pulled out of the womb with forceps 'so that I was doom'd, by marriage articles, to have my nose squeez'd as flat to my face, as if the destinies had actually spun me without one' (ibid., p. 38). Inevitably enough, it turns out that Tristram's father is a great believer in the power and significance of noses in general, and that Tristram's lack of a decent one is likely, it seems, to condemn him to a life of misery. In the face of this, the reader is implored to pity Walter, whose attempts to impose rationality on the world of chaos around him are continually vexed by chance.

This thematic engagement with contingency is framed by a myriad of devices to divert the reader from that 'tolerable straight line'. *Tristram Shandy* contains missing chapters that turn up at the end of the book, pagination that at one point starts going backwards, missing or blank pages, an entirely black page, squiggly lines to represent the narrative haphazardness of the novel, and one page that has been beautifully marbled – a page, I suggest, with profound ramifications for Sterne's attempt to represent chance. The marbled page (or rather pages, as each side of one leaf has been marbled) seems to exist for no fictionally relevant narrative reason. The narrator refers to the leaf as 'the motly emblem of my work!' (ibid., p. 204). The word 'motly' evidently refers to the visually striking mixture of colour, pattern and shape, and 'emblem' makes clear that this is a visual page, an abstract counterpoint to the text, not to be read at all. The very messiness of the word, and the variegated colour of the emblem, therefore reinforces the page as an icon of disorder – both in contrast to the writing that surrounds it, and as the purest symbol of that writing.

Each marbled page was individually made, and entirely unique. The process is long and tricky, and the extent to which the marbler exercises his artistic choice on the final product is disputed – the marbling liquid is constantly moving, and though he chooses when to dip the paper into it, the outcome is still largely unpredictable. In fact the process of marbling in itself is a metaphor for chance, and offers a potent analogue for *Tristram Shandy* itself. It suggests the capturing of something mobile, and, as it is a picture of its own process, the mobility in this case is literally what you see, rather than a thing that is moving. It is the representation in an inanimate object of something in flux, but that also contains the knowledge that capturing the movement has killed that very kineticism: an image of unpredictability, of contingency itself, condemned to stillness on the page. That the marbled page should speak so eloquently of uncertainty itself suggests an implicit criticism of the book's ability to demonstrate randomness adequately, and its elusive meaning therefore contributes to the novel's commentary on indeterminacy.

The novel's blank page, at the end of chapter xxv, Volume I, is also significant in terms of the novel's engagement with chance, and furthermore, it can be read as a specific response to an anxiety about chance. The narrator tells us, with a swelling sense of righteousness, that

. . . what these perplexities of my uncle Toby were, – 'tis impossible for you to guess; – if you could, – I should blush; not as a relation, – not a man, – nor even as a woman, – but I should blush as an author; inasmuch as I set no small store by myself upon this very account, that my reader has never yet been able to guess at any thing. And in this, Sir, I am of so nice and singular a humour, that if I thought you was able to form the least judgment or probable conjecture to yourself, of what was to come in the next page, – I would tear it out of my book. (ibid., p. 70)

In the original edition, the next page is a blank. J. Paul Hunter calls this blank page 'easily guessable' (Hunter, 1994, p. 55) thereby suggesting that since the contents of a blank page are the most predictable he could come up with, Sterne is humorously undermining the pompous assertion of his authorial power that has preceded it. This explanation seems inadequate to me, and I would like to offer an alternative interpretation that links the blank page to the novel's preoccupation with chance. The blank page, I suspect, was in fact supposed to suggest that the narrator had torn a page out. If this is so, the clear message is that the reader had already guessed what was on it, and Sterne had responded with his promised protest against the predictability of narrative. That the reader had therefore successfully predicted what would happen next is a clear condemnation of the novel's inability to represent the unexpected adequately, and Sterne's uncompromising response presents us with an equally clear denunciation of the same. Sterne would rather tear his book in two, it seems, than accept with quietude the determinism of narrative and its corollary, narrative's suppression of chance.

This reading of the blank page complicates the novel's approach to causality in general. As one of *Tristram Shandy*'s first critics, Horace Walpole, pointed out, the novel's 'great humour . . . consists in the whole narration always going backwards' (Walpole, 1857, p. 298). The narrator famously must explain in a continual backwards loop the cause of one thing, then the cause of that cause and so on, which is why the book barely features Tristram at all. The whole book, you could say, is a parody of the normal narrative workings of cause and effect. The narrator describes this impulse early on as a desire to: 'come at the first springs of the events I tell' (Sterne, 1997, p. 59). This impulse is, however, constantly and comically thwarted as we realize that every event is connected to another, and that it would take an infinitely long narrative to explain the intimately connected causes of each happening, until the book should rightly explain the whole universe before it had a hope of reaching the 'first springs' of even the smallest event.

In fact, the obsessive preoccupation with causal explanations for events in *Tristram Shandy*, rather than confirming the necessity of these events in a series of small determinisms, actually highlights their arbitrariness. The backwards, digressive, explanatory impulse builds and builds until the tissue of explanation becomes a satire on the possibility of any event's explicability. A complex web of chance, circumstance and improbable contingency spreads out and threatens to overwhelm the rational meaning of the explanations. Cause and effect is thus simultaneously reinforced by Sterne's fealty to the need for causal explanations, and evacuated of power by their ridiculousness: now a narrative fatalism takes hold; now we are shown its absurdity. As Tristram comments balefully in Volume III, in one of his frequent ejaculations against chance: 'but there is a fatality which attends the actions of some men: Order them as they will, they pass thro' a certain medium which so twists and refracts them from their true directions——' (ibid., p. 22).

This undermines the randomness of events by implying that there is a supposed course along which they should run, that they have, no matter how thwarted, a 'true direction'. And yet in each case we are shown, in Tristram's words, the medium which they pass through and which twists them, or rather, a specific and intricate set of circumstances that have come about randomly to cause each unlucky mishap. It is inevitable that things will turn out badly, and yet for each misfiring of events, the Shandy family can call up an intricate explanation of contingency: there is a surface cause for each happening awaiting its own narrative digressive explanation. So the opposition of fate and freedom becomes blurred, and eventually meaningless, as both in turn are eroded and undermined. There is, eventually, in *Tristram Shandy*, no real opposition between chance and inevitability, as contingency is everywhere and yet meaningless: every decision the characters make is freely taken, and yet shown to be comically complicit in their unlikely, and yet somehow inevitable, fate.

Tristram Shandy celebrates chance while bemoaning its impossibility in the novel, just as its typographic experiments tell us of the artificiality of fiction, and parody its limitations, while re-creating the randomness of reality in a way that a more straightforward novel cannot do. The wandering that a writer like Sterne encourages us to do, away from sequentiality and towards the unpredictable or improbable in the reading experience, shocks us, and both diminishes and highlights the staid artificiality to which we are accustomed. Sterne therefore, I contend, associates chance with authentic lived experience, and so the points at which he tries hardest to get away from the artifice and predictability of the book are the points where randomness and chance are invoked. Chance is, in short, the demonic spirit of the book, stymieing the narrative order and frustrating the characters at every turn. As Sterne shows that to represent the chaotic randomness of experience is at odds with the physical fact of the book, chance is allied with the digressive, the dynamic, and the experimental; Sterne's attempts to slip out of the clutches of predictability start to look less playful and more like the serious obeisance to life as it is lived that makes *Tristram Shandy*, in Virginia Woolf's description in *The Common Reader* (1932), 'as close to life as we can be' (Woolf, 1932, p. 69).

The argument commonly invoked by Sternean critics runs somewhat counter to this. As Dorothy Van Ghent concludes, *Tristram Shandy*, in the last reckoning, is 'anything but haphazard or formless' rather; '[it obeys] formal laws of its own' (Van Ghent, 1987, p. 8). Peter de Voogd similarly detects a well-hidden order at the heart of the novel, which he deems operates on 'the paradoxical principle of accidental design, of carefully planned seeming chaos' (de Voogd, 1985, p. 281). This is no doubt true; of course there do exist design and order in the novel. Nevertheless, I would like to add the caveat that this approach perhaps gives less emphasis to the accidental or the chaotic as an ordering principle than Sterne would intend, and in the main, I think this impulse to deny the randomness of *Tristram Shandy* does the novel a disservice. Moreover, Sterne himself explicitly contradicts it when he says, in Volume VIII: 'I begin with writing the first sentence – and trusting to Almighty God for the second' (Sterne, 1997, p. 490). He thus claims a compository method that entirely subverts the customary determinism that would seek to smother chance: he has no idea what is going to come next. *Tristram Shandy*'s backwards narrative, eccentric pagination, the missing chapters, the marbled page, the blank pages, could all be described as devices to postpone, disguise or perhaps even to avoid determining what will happen. Sterne refuses to 'write' the future, and thus make certain what he knows is not, and his repudiation of this responsibility makes *Tristram Shandy* unusually capable, in any period, of a sophisticated rebuttal of narrative determinism.

Statistical Fatalism and Radical Chance – the Nineteenth and Twentieth Centuries

A cluster of writers and thinkers that emerged in the nineteenth century enthusiastically accepted new opportunities for the increasingly secular appreciation of chance to flourish. I will look at just a few of those whose understanding of chance is freighted with particular significance, or whose writing reverberates beyond their particular discipline. One such thinker was Darwin, whose consolidation and extension of chance's domain originates in a small adjustment in his theory of variation in natural selection. The prevailing theory of the origins of variation at the time was called 'use and disuse', which invoked the idea of adaptive necessity. In contrast to the dominant scientific mood of the time, Darwin used the idea of random selection for his explanation of how variation came about. It was, he posited, a matter of randomness whether or not variation occurs, but, once it has, its survival and repetition conforms to the normal dynamics of natural selection. Chance and the origins of life thus became inextricable in the post-Darwinian nineteenth-century scientific understanding of the world, an association that instilled in us a knowledge of the intimidating one-in-a-million shot that we all miraculously achieve in being born at all.

Philosophically, too, chance was securing its dominion. Nietzsche declares the role of chance through his Zarathustra: 'I have found this happy certainty in all things: that they prefer to dance on the feet of chance' (Nietzsche, 1982, p. 186). Nietzsche takes pleasure in reviving the old idea of chance as rebellion against responsibility, consensus and logic, and simultaneously foreshadowing the existential twentieth-century sense of chance as something to be plunged into, with abandon. As Zarathustra instructs us: 'Live dangerously! Build your cities on the slopes of Vesuvius!' (ibid., p. 18). Nietzsche consistently espoused a belief in pure chance. In *Thus Spake Zarathustra* (1883–85) he says: 'Over all things stand the heaven accident, the heaven innocence, the heaven chance, the heaven prankishness.' He goes on to explain: 'By "chance" – that is, the most ancient nobility of the world, and this I restored to all things: I delivered them from their bondage under purpose' (ibid., p. 14). Purpose is the thing to be feared, and if man could liberate himself from it, then he could be free. Nietzsche was not immune to the idea of necessity as a controlling force, however:

> Those iron hands of necessity which shake the dice box of chance play their game for an infinite length of time: so that there *have* to be throws which exactly resemble purposiveness and rationality of every degree. *Perhaps* our acts of will and our purposes are nothing but such throws. (Nietzsche, 1982, p. 130)

This intertwining of the concepts surrounding chance is explained by Gilles Deleuze: 'The dice of creation thrown once are the affirmation of chance,

the combination which they form on falling is the affirmation of necessity.
. . . What Nietzsche calls necessity (destiny) is thus never the abolition but
rather the combination of chance itself' (Deleuze, 1983, sec. 11). Hacking
explains this passage by the elision of chance and necessity: 'Chance,
Nietzsche asserted, makes sense only when we have a concept of purpose.
But we get this idea of purpose and reason in part from being in what looks
like an orderly world. . . . Necessity and chance are twinned, and neither
can exist without the other' (Hacking, 1990, p. 148). William Beatty
Warner, whose *Chance and the Text of Experience* (1986) examines Nietzsche,
Freud and Shakespeare's *Hamlet*, has argued cogently that Nietzsche's
concentration on chance as an affirmation of life was in fact a pragmatic
elision of chance as pure coincidence, and chance as willed result of unconscious desires, or a retrospective assimilation of the contingent event into
necessity (Warner, 1986).

In continental Europe, both Dostoevsky and Mallarmé extended and
explored some of the issues raised by Nietzsche's philosophy. Dostoevsky
examines the psychological and social effects of an obsession with chance
in *The Gambler* (1866). Alex, the gambler of the title, expresses the adrena-
lin-soaked thrill of experiential risk: 'I ought to have left at that point, but
a strange sort of a feeling came over me, a kind of desire to challenge fate,
a longing to give it a fillip on the nose or stick out my tongue at it'
(Dostoevsky, 1992, p. 39). A reliance on chance then is not a rejection of
destiny, entirely, or a belief in it wholeheartedly either: it is a metaphorical
rebellion, an existential challenge to destiny, daring it to prove its authen-
ticity. The curious doubleness of the gambler's approach to chance is
explored here too: the sense, common among gamblers, that 'it was so very
necessary for you to win. It's exactly like a drowning man clutching at a
straw. You must admit that if he wasn't drowning he wouldn't take the straw
for a tree-trunk' (ibid., p. 44). The gambler experiences life as random,
but retrospectively reorders it as fate. What did happen in fact becomes
what had to happen. The significance of *The Gambler* lies not, then, in its
psychologizing portrait of the gambling mind, but in its extraordinary
condemnation of the deterministic worldview, existential in its vehemence.
As Alex says about women: 'The very proudest of them turn out to be the
most abject slaves! . . . there is something predestined, condemned, fated
there!' (ibid., p. 72). The easy association between fatedness and abject
slavery foreshadows Sartre and Camus, and develops the familiar twentieth-century dialectic of freedom and fate, liberated from its religious
origins.

Thirty-one years later, Mallarmé's 1897 poem *Un Coup De Dés* was a formal departure not just for the poet, but also for the history of chance in literature. As Peter Nicholls describes, it is a 'protracted meditation on language and chance: here a shipmaster has to decide whether to throw the dice which, in yielding a definite number, will overcome chance and the chaos of the raging sea. But the act of throwing the dice depends on chance' (Nicholls, 1995, p. 41). The poem as a physical artefact is striking. It is laid out in irregular, sloping lines – some of which consist of nothing, others of a single word. The ideogrammatic text grows larger then shrinks, apparently at random. The motifs and themes are also differentiated typographically, as Henry Weinfield notes: 'the poem incorporates contingency at the same time it attempts to come to terms with it philosophically . . . the old problem for Mallarmé of how to establish meaning in an essentially meaningless universe – that is, a universe from which the gods have disappeared' (Mallarmé, 1966, p. 266). Contingency and chance thus function as a nexus of atheistic daring, whereupon one makes a wager with the universe, echoing Nietzsche, and, remarkably Pascal – the dice throw resonating with his wager of more than two hundred years before.

The turn of the twentieth century saw one of the most significant anti-determinist philosophers, the unconventional American C. S. Peirce, decide to 'examine the common belief that every single fact in the universe is determined by law'. He comes to the striking conclusion that:

> The proposition in question is that the state of things existing at any time, together with certain immutable laws, completely determines the state of things at every other time . . . I believe I have thus subjected to fair examination all the important reasons for adhering to the theory of universal necessity, and shown their nullity. (Peirce, 1932, p. 28)

Hacking describes him as 'riding the crest of an anti-determinist wave'; nevertheless, this would have been a controversial piece of work (Hacking, 1990, p. 11). His significance partly stems from the absoluteness, as well as the radical nature, of his views. In early 1893 he wrote in 'A Reply to the Necessitarians': 'Chance pours itself in at every avenue of sense: it is of all things the most obtrusive' and that 'it is absolute is the most manifest of all intellectual perceptions.' In utter certainty, he continues: 'That it is a being, living and conscious, is what all the dullness that belongs to ratiocination's self can scarce muster the hardihood to deny' (Peirce, 1932, p. 425). Peirce, then, is instrumental in the increasing sense, at the turn of the century, of chance's dominance. In a neat counterpoint to the centuries where chance's very ontological status was denied, Peirce concentrates on figuring the idea of chance as a substantial, almost tangible 'thing', 'a being, living and conscious'.

Gambling, as chance's dominant cultural manifestation however, is still in the early twentieth century described as a self-destructive madness. In his essay 'Dostoevsky and Parricide' (1928), Freud examines *The Gambler* and Stefan Zweig's *Twenty-Four Hours in a Woman's Life* (1927), and comes to the conclusion that the gambler's hand movements, in which he detects a mirroring of masturbatory gestures, prove that the thrill of gambling are rooted in the gamblers' wish to punish himself for his Oedipal fantasies, by *deliberately losing* (Freud, 1928).[15] One significance of this, I think, is in the insight that gambling and punishment, chance and sin, are still so entwined: we can clearly see the moralistic gloss still apportioned to condemnations of gambling in the early twentieth century. We are reminded of Bergler's description of it, cited earlier, as a 'latent rebellion against logic, intelligence, moderation, morality, and renunciation . . . the one exceptional situation in life where the reality principle has no advantage over the pleasure principle. There blind chance rules' (Bergler, 1957, p. 2). The pleasurable physical effects of gambling were demonstrated more than a century earlier by Rousseau, whose stone-throwing assumed a magnitude common in the deliberate tempting of chance: 'I am going to throw this stone,' he decided, 'at the tree facing me. If I hit it, it is a sign that I am saved; if I miss it I am damned' (Rousseau, 1953, p. 18). Rousseau felt all that a gambler feels: 'a terrible throbbing of the heart' until he hit the tree and stopped worrying about it.

Chance, as we have seen, has throughout the ages proved inextricable from gambling, and from games in a more general sphere. Play has always existed as a space outside of normal life, where different rules are invoked, and different systems of reward and punishment operate. In *Homo Ludens*, Huizinger argues that play 'creates order, *is* order. Into an imperfect world and into the confusion of life it brings a temporary, a limited, perfection' (Huizinger, 1998, p. 10). In this sense, chance is the opposite of its earlier incarnation, a sign that one was too much 'a partner with the world' or interested in the material, quantifiable and randomized reality of life. Indeed, part of the disapprobation accorded to gamblers is that they are seen as not partners *enough* with the world. This dislocation between chance and real life seems to be a fairly recent development. As we have seen, chance used to exist only in relation to the divine, and indeed Huizinger, heavily influenced by the Platonic notion of sacred play, argued that civilization 'arises *in* and *as* play, and never leaves it' (ibid., p. 3). In this sense it represents an almost spiritual mode of existing, as it helps to impose order and meaning on the world and thus communicates our deepest thoughts and hopes for society.

As we have seen, the birth of probability theory and that of the modern novel have run a parallel course since the Enlightenment, each sustaining and informing the other. As Thomas Kavanagh says: 'The novel shares with probability theory the assumption that individuals act within a world of pre-existing causal sequences, of multiple determinisms compelling their reactions' (Kavanagh, 1993, p. 118). The fundamental and intractable problem with the narrative representation of chance which I have outlined is at least in part resolved by the useful comparisons that can be made with probability theory. As Richardson suggests, however, this interpretation of the causal function of the novel is a historically specific one. It's clear that probability theory has a complex relation to chance: it increases predictability in the long term, but has little bearing on actual events, or on the randomness of life as it is experienced. The causal theory of the novel, as we might call it, espoused by Kavanagh, perhaps emphasizes the former over the latter, by pointing out that the explosion of statistics meant a shifting of consciousness from the Enlightenment's ideal of 'a single rational consciousness' to a measuring of the self against 'a potentially infinite series of averages and means' (Hacking, 1990, p. 2). This mutation in the novelistic and cultural understanding of chance was an important weapon in the increasing corrosion of determinism.

But if, as Poisson had suggested a century earlier, statistics stripped people of their individuality, then Kavanagh's point is pressing. Chance, in both the novel and in probability theory, is threatening to slip between the floorboards. Dostoevsky's Underground Man jeered at the utilitarians who 'deduce the whole range of human satisfactions as averages from statistical figures' (Dostoevsky, 1992, p. 30). As noted before, the paucity of what probability had to say about the predictability of individuals or individual acts, meant that there was a possibility, or even a likelihood of human existential freedom. In other words, only the behaviour of huge numbers and groups was predictable, so individuals who existed within a larger society were free to act as they pleased. Hacking argues that this is the obverse of statistical fatality, whereby individuals feel, or are seen as being, compelled to act in a certain way because that is how it has been predicted that their demographic will behave. The implications of this for the individual are perhaps most famously depicted by Charles Dickens, whose *Hard Times* (1854) expresses a forcefully anti-statistical rhetoric. Gradgrind declaims the integrity and perfection of statistical laws, while ignoring the individual repercussions of such assumptions. When his son is revealed as a thief, Gradgrind claims:

> 'If a thunderbolt had fallen on me, it would have shocked me less than this.'
> 'I don't see why,' says the son, with perfect and infuriating logic. 'So many people are employed in situations of trust; so many people, out of so many, will be dishonest. I have heard you talk, a hundred times, of its being a law. How can *I* help laws? You have condemned others to such things, Father. Comfort yourself'. (Dickens, 1978, p. 378)

Dickens's anxiety about the undercutting of human will and individual responsibility here is palpable, and shows that in the wider, non-scientific culture it had become a real concern. Anxieties about freedom and determinism were played out in the public debates about the related pseudo-sciences of phrenology, criminology and degeneration in the late nineteenth century and in the early part of the twentieth. If traits are determined by certain physical characteristics, could then a person help being vicious, or perverted? Was he free? Could he be punished for his criminal actions? This idea, after phrenology was widely discredited, would be revived by Karl Popper, who invented a 'propensity' theory of probability in the 1950s. The idea of propensity towards a particular type of behaviour or *penchant au crime*, was clearly related to statistical fatality: if a man was part of a group who were probabilistically more likely to commit a certain crime, that man would not necessarily be more inclined to do so, but statistically, he would have a propensity for it. His individual conscience, freely applied, could overcome it, and as such the *penchant au crime*'s ontological status is external to the individual; sociological rather than psychological, and therefore has little to say on the subject of free will.

The Early Twentieth Century and Chance – the Birth of 'Pure' Chance, Quantum Mechanics and Dada

> *First learn to be spasmodic*
> *A very simple rule*
> *For first you write a sentence*
> *And then you chop it small:*
> *Then mix the bits, and sort them out*
> *Just as they chance to fall;*
> *The order of the phrases makes*
> *No difference at all.*
>
> Lewis Carroll

Lewis Carroll's 1860 poem advocating the introduction of chance into the creative process of poetic composition was published as 'nonsense verse'. Humorously advocated by Carroll, the method, whereby chance could be allowed to determine a work of art, was undertaken as a serious literary project in the early twentieth century by the Dadaists. This idea, which I delineate throughout this book as finding its purest expression in aleatorical art or compositional chance, elaborates the concept of chance as 'pure' chance – that is, not mediated and undermined by the demands of narrative. As such it is radical; it addresses and seeks to 'solve' the problem of chance, an acknowledgement of which lies at the heart of my project. The construction of narrative recreates our search for meaning and purpose through the modifying refraction of art, and novels that deny chance to represent a totalizing and meaningful teleology are therefore incompatible with a version of life that contains the randomness that composes our day-to-day perceptions. The Dadaist contribution to the history of its representation is that they recognized this, and responded to the tension between chance and narrative by letting the former disrupt the latter. In some ways, aleatorical composition remained, and continues to remain, nonsensical – in that 'nonsense' implies a subversive refusal to play by the conventional literary assumptions about order, meaning and sense. Chance has always been allied to 'non-sense'. The Dadaists elevated this same understanding of 'nonsense' to the status of art, and in doing so, disrupted art's very definition. In this challenge to convention, chance was both the Dadaists' favoured mode of operation and their best subject. The decline of determinism was thus rapid in the first part of the twentieth century: indeed, by the 1940s the modern sense of uncertainty as a mode of existence had been established: this is what Reith describes as 'an "orientation" to reality or, rather, as the fundamental category of reality to which we must orientate ourselves . . . social life has become increasingly and openly randomized' (Reith, 1999, p. xvi).

The 'fundamental category of reality' to which the twentieth century needed to adapt was brought about by a variety of cultural factors: the inexorable decline of deterministic thinking brought about by the avalanche of statistics in the late nineteenth and early twentieth century; the cultural movement and attraction to uncertainty, especially as expressed by the avant-garde represented by Dada; and the new scientific developments of the first third of the century. Quantum Mechanics, which took hold as the dominant mode of explanation in physics in the 1930s, in one fell swoop invalidated whole swathes of the previously predominant deterministic worldview. In fact, the period after the 1940s, on which the bulk of this book concentrates, is, I suggest, one of perhaps unique susceptibility to the aleatorical, and its artistic culture ran parallel to a scientific culture in which the doctrine of uncertainty was in the ascendant. Moreover, this period has since been proven finite. From the establishment of Quantum Mechanics in the 1930s, uncertainty as a scientific principle was dominant. However, Chaos Theory, which emerged in the 1970s and 1980s, and which filtered through to the cultural sphere with surprising rapidity, can be said to have undermined and problematized the concept of pure chance: the central, easily communicated idea was that pattern and order lie, deep down, in even the most chaotic-seeming system. James Gleick describes Mitchell Feigenbaum's experiments on cloud formations in 1974 as the paradigmatic beginning of chaos (Gleick, 1988); from this point, non-linear dynamics were in the ascendant. Chaos Theory compromises our conception of chance because it allows for irregular actions, including those that would have previously looked random, as part of a system susceptible to regulation; indeed, its first principle is that chaos gives birth to order, and that deep, previously unthought-of patterns exist at the heart of what we perceive as stochastic anarchy. There is, in fact, a predisposition to those very events which would previously have been thought of as unpredictable, as Stewart has it: 'Deterministic laws can produce behaviour that appears random. Order can breed its own kind of chaos' (Stewart, 1989, p. xii). In as much as science has always informed our understanding of chance, the advent of Chaos is an unmistakeable shift in its very definition.[16] Wherever Chaos Theory takes us in the future, it is possible that our conception of randomness has been compromised for good.

The advent of Quantum Theory in the early twentieth century happened in tandem with the cultural encroachment of indeterminacy that was fomented by the Dadaists and the surrealists. As Brian Richardson points out, 'the surrealists' *hasard objectif* is an essential item in the intellectual history of chance' (Richardson, 1997, p. 36). Automatism, for the surrealists, was a way of circumventing agency, to access the uncertain and unwilled shifting desires and unfocused drives 'below'. The surrealists believed in something they called 'objective chance'. This idea, as elaborated by André Breton, was similarly a way around will and agency: a belief in coincidence, he believed, was a way around causality: if coincidences can be made to stand in for will and for cause then experience could perhaps be reconnected to the random. And yet this necessarily re-invites control into the picture: just as the Oulipo group would later use chance as a small element of an overdetermined aleatorical system, the surrealists theory of objective chance was deeply compromised by notions of control. As J. H. Matthews states '. . . a belief shared by all surrealists that chance had nothing to do with the haphazard . . . the invocation of chance, when the surrealist artist invited its intervention, signified confidence in its power to reveal something he could never have known without its cooperation' (Matthews, 1991, p. 103). Chance, in other words, is being used in the ancient Greek sense of augury, an epistemological category that is revelatory of a truth just beyond our knowledge. Surrealism's engagement with chance is therefore complicated by shades of determinism, and by the sort of assumptions that converge upon a coincidence or a chance happening as an over-determined event, eventually undermining any claims to randomness. 'Objective chance' stops just short of 'pure chance'.

Dada perhaps offers us a clearer artistic use of pure chance. Harriet Watts explicitly links Dada to the revolution in scientific thought that led to the theory of indeterminacy (Watts, 1975, p. 104). According to her argument, the arts work as a barometer in the revolt against determinism: they are joint participants in the cultural redefinition of the concept of uncertainty, and therefore of chance. She goes on to suggest that the cross-fertilization that takes place between the arts and sciences in fact works mutually. There are instances of philosophy in some case inspiring scientific innovations: Niels Bohr's greatest influence was not one of his fellow scientists but Kierkegaard. He associated the Kierkegaardian irrational leap, with its exaltation of discontinuity and irrelevance, with the liberation from causality evident in the new particle physics. Dada, then was the artistic manifestation of ideas fomenting in different disciplines. In fact, as Watts notes, chance, and compositional chance specifically, is the paradigmatic Dadaist contribution to the twentieth century:

> The Dada artist freed himself from the rule of reason and causality by welcoming chance into the creative act itself. Chance is the new factor in Dada productions. Through chance, the artist can destroy old aesthetic habits as well as create new patterns of perception. Dada's unique contribution to the modernist movement was its receptive attitude to the phenomena of chance. (ibid., p. 1)

Dada's iconoclastic attitude to its artistic and literary heritage relied heavily on the power of shock, surprise and a playful resistance to meeting the viewer or reader's expectations. And yet this playful pose also served to obscure Dada's undoubtedly substantial philosophical and intellectual contribution to the history of ideas.

At the forefront of this new artistic movement was Marcel Duchamp, one of the major figures of Dada and one of the instigators of this association – sustained throughout the first half of the twentieth century – of Dadaism with the notion of 'pure' chance. Duchamp's goals were, according to Watts, 'the negation of causality, the questioning of iron-clad notions of meaning, the revelation of an underlying ambiguity in all experience that belies the pretensions of any one system, or any number of systems, to contain it' (ibid., pp. 45–6). Duchamp's major works include *Erratum Musical*, which allowed the vicissitudes of chance to dictate his compositional method; he wrote the names of notes on slips of paper, mixed them in a hat and then randomly selected the order in which they were to be played. Similarly, *Three Standard Stoppages* consisted of three dropped pieces of string, whose accidental shape as they landed was re-created in wood. This Duchamp then kept in a croquet case and referred to as 'Canned Chance', creating, like Sterne's marbled page, an image of movement in fixity, or fluidity stilled.

For Duchamp, chance was a mode of perceiving opposed to logic and taste: a means of effacing individuality. The role of chance was to help the artist 'forget his hand': 'L'intention constituit surtout à oublier la main, puis qu'au fond même votre main c'est du hazard' (Cabanne, 1967, p. 81). As Watts points out, the 'hand' here stands for a symbol of taste as well as of artistry: after all, 'what better assurance of aesthetic indifference than random selection?' (Watts, 1975, p. 36). Interestingly, the association of chance with the undermining of individual physical determinants is echoed in the phrase 'blind chance', commonly used then as now. Chance becomes a mode of epistemological perception that short-circuits our physical selves. The relation between accident and the self de-emphasizes our conscious intentions while perhaps concentrating more on our unconscious ones – which of course contradicts the avowed belief in the importance of the accident. Dada's recourse to mystery as an explanation for chance, whether to reveal subconscious intention or a belief that external randomness is actually a staging of a higher meaning or purpose, played out for our sublunary bafflement, is a tendency that any examination of randomness in art must confront. It is tempting to read it as a shying away from the conclusions of one's own experiment, a fearfulness of the truly random and a desire for that which the artist avows to escape – the constant search for meaning and order, and the resulting, inevitable, effacement of chance.

Other Dadaists whose work revolved around chance included Hans Richter, Tristan Tzara (who was experimenting with randomly ordered poetry in the first decade of the twentieth century), and Hans Arp. In his seminal work *Entropy and Art* (1971), Rudolph Arnheim examines Arp's attraction to randomness in his work in relation to the concept of entropy:

The vision of . . . harmonious striving for order throughout nature is disturbingly contradicted by one of the most influential statements on

the behaviour of physical forces, namely, the Second Law of Thermodynamics. The most general account physicists are willing to give of changes
in time is often formulated to mean that the material world moves from
orderly states to an ever-increasing disorder and that the final situation of
the universe will be one of maximal disorder. (Arnheim, 1971, p. 7)

Watts similarly links Arp's approach to chance to entropic figures of
decline and fragmentation: 'Much of Arp's aesthetic preoccupation with
chance is expressed in his oscillation from one extreme to the other in
reaction to the fact that the human hand imposing order on the face of
disintegration and primal chaos is in fact a participant in the inevitable
process of disintegration' (Watts, 1975, p. 34). Entropy is a scientific idea
concerning disorder and randomness that lends itself particularly well to
use as artistic metaphor. Stated simply, entropy is the amount of disorder
in a physical system. The second law of thermodynamics states that in a
closed system, there is a natural and immutable predisposition towards
disorder, or higher levels of entropy. An understanding of the second law
as integral to existence therefore inculcates a vision of the universe lean-
ing irrevocably towards disorder, like a heliotropic flower permanently
inclined towards the sun. It envisages our environment, and therefore to
a degree ourselves, as permanently having one foot in the camp of the
messy, the chaotic and the random, 'righted' only by the intensive
application of human effort and a yearning for that which does not come
naturally to us: order.

The entropic or disordered aspects of the culture of the mid-period of
the twentieth century, and the fascination with the idea of chance as compositional in the 1950s and 1960s, was directly inherited from the Dadaists
of the early and mid-twentieth century. This interest in the creative potential of chance complemented an interest in its contradictory ability in the
destruction of order. This book therefore concentrates on depictions of
chance as it relates to and absorbs a specific culture: the period from the
1940s to the 1970s. As we have seen, the perception of chance as a meaningful concept begins in the late seventeenth century with the advent of probability theory, but as I have also shown, this brings with it numerous anxieties
about statistical fatalism, phrenological determinism and the superstition
and condemnation still accorded to any chance-related activities or thinking, and it is evident that even in the early twentieth century the shadows of
destiny and determinism still operate. It was during the long mid-period of
the twentieth century, from the end of modernism, through the post-war
period of the 1950s, and into the 1960s and 1970s, that indeterminism or
chance became a guiding explanatory force for the world, philosophically,

novelistically and scientifically. This chance is not only a feature of modern physics but of modern thought: it is reflected in culture, in the random noise symphonies of composers like John Cage, and in the apparently haphazard compositional methods of artists like Jackson Pollock and Robert Rauschenberg. This increasing presence of chance runs a parallel course with a growing scientific erosion of deterministic modes of thinking. Our conception of uncertainty had also been destabilized and complicated by the existentialists on the continent, who had formulated a mode of existence based on freedom and the operation of chance.

The effect of these wider cultural changes on the novel was, as Brian Richardson has argued, a twentieth-century aversion to the sort of nineteenth-century narrative novel that sought to explain the world through an examination of sociological, political or psychological cause and effect ('by contrast, many twentieth-century works assert the objectivity of chance and the arbitrariness of human destinies' (Richardson, 1997, p. 42)). The twentieth century increasingly developed a sense of the stuff of everyday life as the proper study of the novel: characters in works by writers such as Samuel Beckett and Henry Green are drifters, whose choices prove profoundly inconsequential; plot recedes, and the author's omniscience is continually questioned and undermined. In this way, *how things are* is culturally privileged over grand narratives of control. The move away from a constant denial of contingency to its assumption of a pleasurable, everyday aesthetic, is thus a movement shadowed by the retreat of various deterministic ways of interpreting the world, both scientific and religious, in the twentieth century (the conquest of religion representing a retreat which may yet prove to have been temporary). As I will go on to argue, all of these developments represent a way to try and deal – sometimes obliquely, as with Henry Green, and sometimes with a blunt literal force, as with B. S. Johnson – with the problem of chance. As such, causation in the novel was problematic for its ability to properly represent the twentieth-century experience, and writers from Samuel Beckett to Jean-Paul Sartre consistently attacked, minimized or ignored its previously integral role in their construction of narrative. This assumption, that the twentieth-century novel is necessarily preoccupied with, and disturbed by, a profusion of chance, and as such, refuses to fully engage with an entirely causal system of explanation, is one which I share, and is the background against which the authors whose works I will discuss throughout the rest of this book emerged. The tension between the new dominion of chance and the novel's inadequacy to the task is taken to be the primary motivation for much innovation that I will describe, and this changing understanding of chance informed and shaped their work in any number of different ways which I go on to discuss.

If we have become epistemologically attuned to chance, in as much as it became a mode of perception, and if our slow recognition of our contingency was the major shift that occurred somewhere between Dada and Quantum Physics and Chaos Theory, during which time scientific postulates largely agreed that determinism was being, or had been overturned, and that the universe on a molecular as well as an everyday level, operated on a random basis, then the novel, which is supposed to be the cultural form which is expansive enough to echo our experience most nearly, is left exposed and uncertain. Its inability, in its traditional form, to render chance suddenly begins to look fatal: a gaping hole opens up between our (chancy) lives with its hopeless reliance on cause it and effect, its continued provision of reasons and motivations, its vast psychological scope, and plotted deterministic structure. If we allow chance to become meaningful – as Adam Phillips has put it, if 'meaning is made out of accidents' (Phillips, 1994, p. 11) – then a fault line inevitably opens up when novels depicting this contingency, by their very nature, are curtailed from conveying their own deepest meaning: their meaninglessness.

Chance's existence, while consistently marginalized and frequently denied throughout history, has perhaps always had a foothold on the human imagination, if only as an idea that represented a seditious form of freedom – freedom from God, but also from all other sorts of authoritarian or economic hierarchy: as chance has the unique and radical ability to redistribute wealth and power other than through the normal, deterministic channels.. Chance's subversive powers remain, although perhaps somewhat dimmed: in the late twentieth century and the beginnings of the twenty-first there exists still an air of moral, rather than merely fiscal, unsavouriness around gambling, and those with a belief in superstition or coincidence (often referred to as 'synchronicity') are routinely castigated for their stupidity (as Derrida points out, it is eminently respectable to believe in the existence of chance, but not to believe 'in' it: 'one believes in the existence of chance, but just as well that one does *not*, above all, believe in chance, since one looks for and finds a hidden meaning there at all cost' (Derrida, 2007, p. 347)). Aleatorical art, meanwhile, has become established since the 1960s as a shortcut to rebellion from prescribed ideas of artistic authority. Perhaps in the twentieth century we have not yet entirely moved on from the routine denial and vitriolic condemnation of chance

that was common in the past, as this characteristic eighteenth-century view
by the determinist scientist Abraham de Moivre typifies:

> *Chance*, in atheistical writings or discourse, is a sound utterly insignificant
> . . . it can neither be defined nor understood: nor can any Proposition
> concerning it be either affirmed or denied, excepting this one, 'That it is
> a mere word'. (de Moivre, 1756, p. 253)

Chapter Two

'Swear to tell me everything that goes wrong': Henry Green and Free Will in the Novel

Chance has, throughout the history of its representation in literature, spo-radically threatened to undermine the god-like creative omnipotence of the author. This reduction of the author's role appears to become more pressing in the middle decades of the twentieth century, as writers responded to the destabilizing effects of modernism. Samuel Beckett articulated this distinction usefully as he spoke about the difficulties of trying to individu-ate himself from Joyce, and, to a lesser extent, the legacy of modernism in general.[1] In an interview with Israel Shenker that was published in 1956 Beckett insists on Joyce's minute attention to, and weighing of, every word, and calls attention to his obeisance to ideas of order and control:

> The difference is that Joyce was a superb manipulator of material –
> perhaps the greatest. He was making words do the absolute maximum of
> work. There isn't a syllable that's superfluous. The kind of work I do is
> one in which I'm not master of my material. The more Joyce knew the
> more he could. He's tending toward omniscience and omnipotence as an
> artist. I'm working with impotence, ignorance. . . . My little exploration is
> that whole zone of being that has always been set aside by artists as some-
> thing unusable – as something by definition incompatible with art.
> (Shenker, 1956, p. 3)

The 'zone of being' that is 'by definition incompatible with art' is a familiar rendering of the contingency and randomness of the universe. Beckett's movement away from absolute authorial control and his attraction to the dramatization of doubt, ignorance and randomness, is characteristic of the period, as the desire to move away from omniscience had become more pressing in the literary culture of England in the 1940s and 1950s, and con-tributes significantly to the prevailing literary mood of the immediately post-war period.

In *Mimesis* (1946), Erich Auerbach argues that modern writers display a preoccupation with the random and accidental in their work:

> These are the characteristic and distinctively new features of the technique: a chance occasion releases processes; a natural and even, if you will, a naturalistic rendering of those processes in their peculiar freedom . . . [the modern author] submits, much more than was done in earlier realistic works, to the random contingency of real phenomena; and even though he winnows and stylizes the material of the real world – as of course he cannot help doing – he does not proceed rationalistically, not with a view to bringing a continuity of exterior events to a planned conclusion. (Auerbach, 1953, p. 538)

Taking Virginia Woolf as a representative figure, Auerbach suggests that this 'modern author' is, rather, keen to render naturalistically the inconsequential, or events in their peculiar freedom; in other words, chance. The focus on the random, the everyday, and the inconsequential is thus a result of an authorial reluctance to engage in what we might term 'selection': the desire to choose and represent events and reality that further a plot. As Auerbach concedes, every author 'winnows and stylizes' his material during the process of its transubstantiation into literature, but the modern author, importantly, 'does not proceed rationalistically, not with a view to bringing a continuity of exterior events to a planned conclusion'; in other words, the author tries not to predetermine the outcome of his own work. In this way, the impulse to plot is subdued as much as possible. Auerbach goes on to clarify the reluctance of the modern novelist to 'impose' an external structure on to his work in the form of a story arc with a clear chronological and temporal structure: a beginning, a middle and an end. The fear that this imposition might overwhelm the 'natural processes' that he wishes to depict, and prevent the novel from fulfilling its task of mimesis:

> Then too [the modern novelists] hesitate to impose upon life, which is their subject, an order which it does not possess in itself. He who represents the course of a human life, or a sequence of events extending over a prolonged period of time, and represents it from beginning to end, must prune and isolate arbitrarily. Life has always long since begun, and it is always still going on. (ibid., pp. 548–9)

The determinism inherent in the novelist's task is intensified by selection; the greater the author's role, the more unlifelike the text becomes. Writers who do 'hesitate' over this aspect of their task, who flinch at the sleight of hand that would seek to conceal the disjunction between their arbitrary pruning and real life, which is 'always still going on', are displaying a sensitivity to the unrepresentability of the randomness of life within the novel; a sensitivity to which, if we can detect its presence accurately, we can use to determine those authors and those works which most show the effort to depict chance's operations realistically. That 'life has always long since begun' is an admission of the author's inadequacy in the face of the 'random contingency of real phenomena' that he or she must attempt to represent in fiction. When incorporated into the process of literary creation, where chance determines the arrangement of words or sentences and thus in a sense 'creates' the work, this can in fact threaten the very idea of authorship entirely.

One inheritor of this tendency against plot and selection noted by Auerbach was Henry Green. As Jeremy Treglown points out, 'not since Laurence Sterne was a novelist more willing than Green to take his readers up false paths and leave them in confusion' (Treglown, 2000, p. 109). Green published his first novel, *Blindness* (1926) when he was still a teenager, and his last, *Doting* (1952), while still a comparatively young man. Green, whose best novels were stylistically experimental responses to, in Rod Mengham's phrase, 'the idiom of the time' (Mengham, 1982) is a writer who is somewhat awkwardly placed in literary history. Much influenced by Woolf and Joyce, but contemporary with Isherwood, Waugh and Powell, he is often thought of as primarily a writer of the 1930s, though in fact his best work was done for the most part in the 1940s. Born Henry Yorke, Green was prolific for a relatively short space of time; by 1952, although he was still a comparatively young man of 47, his fictional output had all but stopped, and although he had intentions to do so, he was in fact never to write a novel again. Throughout the 1950s, Green suffered a slow descent into alcoholism, peppered with bursts of critical activity. He gave two lectures on the mechanics of his style to the BBC, entitled 'An Author to His Readers', wrote a few book reviews and published one or two other short pieces. His fascination with the accidental, the inconsequential and the unruly remained undimmed, however: Treglown reports that by the end of the 1940s Green frequently turned maudlin, crying 'One can't do right', and 'There's no hope, there's no hope', and gloomily observing that 'life consisted entirely of mistakes – not disasters, just mistakes' (Treglown, 2000, p. 190). Treglown also tells us that V. S. Pritchett, in giving a speech at Green's memorial service, spoke of how Henry had once begged him gleefully as Pritchett was going to a wedding to 'swear to tell me everything that goes wrong' (ibid., p. 257).

As Angus Wilson has noted, the revival of traditional novel forms that took place in the 1950s seemed to Green 'a betrayal of what the twentieth-century masters had done' (Wilson, 1983, p. 386), and it is in this resistance to neo-realist forms that Green deserves to be considered as 'the most prominent novelist of the forties and fifties with experimental leanings' (Weatherhead, 1959, p. 112). His attraction to the experimental grew from his desire to find ways of exploring how better to capture the experiences he wished to represent: to this end he quoted approvingly Henry James's famous words about 'the effort really to see and really to represent', which had been published in the Preface to the New York edition of *What Maisie Knew* in 1909 (Green, 1992, pp. 93–4). In a late interview with Terry Southern, and with a sentiment that foreshadows the novelist B. S. Johnson's most fervent beliefs, which I will discuss in more detail in Chapter Four, Green described the innovatory impulse as a simple necessity caused by the tectonic shift effected by modernism: Joyce and Kafka, he complained, are 'like cats who have licked the plate clean. You've got to dream up another dish if you're to be a writer' (Green, 1992, pp. 93–4).[2] Similarly, his refusal to limit his prose to the 'correctness' of English was deliberate, and reflected his love of Joyce: 'In "good English"', he observed, 'the brain is dulled by clichés' (Green, 1950, p. 20). My analysis of Green's engagement with chance in this chapter will concentrate on *Back* (1946), after a brief discussion of its precursor, *Caught* (1943), and will concentrate on Green's resistance to certain aspects of his authorial task, those that would, in Auerbach's formulation, ally him with those authors who hesitate to impose on life an order which it does not possess of itself, and on his resulting reconfiguration of the relationship between character and author, and its relation to the perception of chance.

Reconfiguring Concepts of Character

As Donald S. Taylor has observed, 'this final abdication of the determining, evaluating authorial role, however concealed, is Green's major break with the traditions of the English novel' (Taylor, 1965, p. 82). Green's distrust of plot, and of selection, emerged from his essential contrariness in respect to the tradition and idiom in which he was working, which was largely the neo-realist strand of English fiction dominated by writers such as Evelyn Waugh and Anthony Powell. Each of Green's novels reveals an attention to verisimilitude that consistently threatens to undermine the novel's traditional alliance with form and structure. Green's construction of his novels gives just as much weight to the inconsequential as it does to the supposedly 'significant', leaving the reader to doubt which aspects of the story are meaningful. As John Russell notes, 'Green will not falsify experience when he formulates it' (Russell, 1960, p. 27). This consistent refusal to play by the rules of authorship (the principle of 'falsification', or the author's imaginative powers and art), and Green's authorial reluctance to 'impose' himself upon his creation, come to embody an almost existential idea about freedom in the novel.

Green's reluctance to meddle in the lives of his characters, an impulse that Southern describes as Green's 'non-existence of author principle', aimed 'to leave characters alive enough to go on living the life they have led in the book'. Together these aspirations amount to no less than a desire for his story to 'be alive. To have a real life of its own' (Green, 1992, p. 234). Green shows this desire to shift the emphasis from creator to created again and again. In the interview with Terry Southern, Green speaks of his characters as if they were real people that he needed to persuade into a state where they could act for our enjoyment: 'Laughter relaxes the characters in a novel' (Green, 1992, p. 234). As he told David Lambourne in an interview published in *Shenandoah* in 1975, he wanted to remind his readers in every novel that, after his story ended, the characters 'arose the next day and life went on as before' (Sinfield, 1983, p. 326). These ideas dominate his off-stage pronouncements, and the desire to introduce an element of freedom into his novels could be described as Green's most clearly defined literary philosophy.

John Updike describes this desire of Green's to produce something approximating life in his novels as 'almost hierophantic' in his introduction to Green's uncollected writings (Green, 1992, p. xvi). It is undoubtedly an odd idea, and one that is easily demolished with logic: of course, no character in a novel is ever free to act. No character can rebel against the author, and chance cannot operate. The novel is always unfree because narrative by definition contains its own determination. Certainly, the feeling that Green's monomania in his fealty to the re-creation of freedom for his characters represents a sort of oddity pervades the growing body of Green criticism. The general consensus among his critics is that Green's desire to grant his characters autonomy is a peculiarly romantic idea, one that need not be paid too much mind. Indeed, in criticism in general, there is the sense that authorial pronouncements about the freedom of characters, the aim to give them 'a life of their own', ought not to be taken entirely seriously a sense that these writerly indulgences are fantasy and as such not the proper study of the critic. As a result, they have been given little, if any, attention.

However, I would argue that these statements deserve to be treated with a critical seriousness equal to the seriousness with which Green proposed – and consistently reiterated – them, and that notes the idea's relation to other aspects of the novel, namely the difficulty of the representation of chance. When approached as an essential facet of the retreat from authorial omniscience that he so desired to achieve in his work, this reconfiguration of the place of character contributes significantly to the representation of chance in the novel. In fact, Green's attachment to the creation of freedom in the novel complicates the representation of the free operation of chance in narrative in interesting ways, and although his attempts to loosen the bounds around his characters may not literally introduce free will into the novel, Green's confrontation of the problem is significant for various reasons. It seems to me that the idea of the possibility of free will for the characters in a novel also has relevance to the Auerbachian insight about selection, undermining as it does the author, and the author's functions, for it admits the cultural and philosophical questions of the time, and welcomes the introduction of chance into the narrative by attaching importance to seemingly unimportant things. When read as part of a composite, coherent literary philosophy and critical diagnosis, Green's desire and attempt to create a real, free life in his characters amounts to a reordering of the dynamics of fate, free will and chance in the novel of the mid-twentieth century.

In his first lecture for the BBC, 'A Novelist to his Readers: I' recorded and broadcast in 1950 and subsequently published by *The Listener*, Green expounds upon his theory of what he calls 'non-representational' art 'meaning to create a life which is not':

> That is to say, a life which does not eat, procreate, or drink, but which can live in people who are alive . . . if it exists to create life, of a kind, in the reader – as far as words are concerned, what is the best way in which this can be done? Of course, by dialogue . . . because if you want to create life the one way *not* to go about it is by explanation. (Green, 1992, p. 136)

Explanation, he goes on to state, is an intrusion and an imposition on the life of the story: 'the writer, who has no business with the story he is writing, intrudes like a Greek chorus to underline his meaning' (ibid.). As I have already suggested, novelistic explanation is the central plank of narrative cause and effect: where reasons for happenings are given, anxieties about chance can be shushed into a kind of quietude and the reader is back in the deterministic world of literary reassurance. Green's emphasis on 'his meaning' – the author's – here suggests that he sees it as is a rude imposition, one that has no right to be privileged over any other, and which functions as a sort of monolithic entity which, in its certainty, would undermine the principles of misunderstanding that are so central to Green's aesthetic. Green's essential scepticism about the author's ability to 'know' extends to his plan for his readers, who should ideally be cast into a state of doubt and uncertainty: only then can they experience the narrative of the novel as they experience life.

This idea has obvious parallels with the representation of chance. Chance's characteristic marginalization in narrative, its smothering by textual determination, will, if Green's task succeeds, be reversed. Uncertainty will instead become the key mode of communication between author and reader, and the action will thus become more contingent and the characters more free. The centrality of our inability to know, finally, is also fundamental to a character's verisimilitude and existential freedom: 'and do we know, in life, what other people are really like? I very much doubt it. We certainly do not know what other people are thinking and feeling. How then can the novelist be so sure?' (ibid., p. 139). The ignorance of the creator has become an essential facet of the character's privacy and freedom. 'Mood', a very early piece of 1926 that was supposed to become a novel, but that remained unpublished in Green's lifetime, also shows an early preoccupation with the idea that there is an inescapable loneliness within each human being:

> Of everyone you met was only you you would be with always and she thought that's how it is, don't lets have any monkey business with other people, the issue ultimately is with ourselves. As my two eyes are coordinated so let me have myself as my friend, may I have that glory where I draw on no one, lean on nobody. May I learn to be alone. (Green, 1992, p. 47)

The language here, with three you's in the first eight words, alerts us to the speaker's underlying meaning – one which seems to stand in contrast to the one that he avows. 'You' here means 'one', but the effect of its repetition nevertheless serves to undercut the line's overt meaning by its preoccupation with the subject. You, you, you, it cries, expressing a longing to escape the confines of the solipsistic self, even while it asserts that very solipsism and indifference to the other.

Green's self-abasement in terms of his creative control was a direct reflection of this belief in human loneliness, and his fealty to recreating the essential unknowability and impregnability of each character. Since he believed an author's efforts to 'know' any character were acts of arrogance, it follows that the writer, as he said, 'has no business with the story he is writing' (ibid., p. 137). His palpable dislike of so much 'character', those unreal puppets who would dance for the reader, speaks of an awe he had in the face of his task. His subsequent efforts were always, therefore, to deal instead in the partial, the unknown and the unpredictable. As Valentine Cunningham has noted, Green's aversion to definite articles and other 'deictics' – *the, this, that* – which is especially evident in his second novel *Living*, could be read as a revealing contrast between this manner and the style of Auden, whose excess of demonstratives conveys 'an effort to assert authority, knowledge, command of experience' (Cunningham, 1988, p. 10). Not-knowing, then, is at the heart of Green's literary philosophy as surely as it is of Samuel Beckett's. The 'not-knowingness' of chance, where anything might happen, and we are in ignorance of the causes of what does happen, is in fact closely related to the 'not-knowingness' of Green's conception of character. He sees his characters as real people, and, like real people, they are essentially alone: incomprehensible from the outside, both to other characters and, crucially, to their creator. A refusal to 'know' what his characters will do next allows a chink of light, in the form of chance, to enter the dark, predictable world of the deterministic novel. In Green's work, the extent of his avowed ignorance of his characters' causal motivations and future actions is sometimes obscure, but his concentration on contingency and the distinctions between fate and free will serves to illuminate his approach for us. His characters are vulnerable to the machinations of happenstance; their volition is compromised, partial and their actions are distinctive for their lack of consequences. Exacerbating this existential loneliness, each is entirely isolated in a fog of misapprehensions and mishearings.

Misunderstanding, in fact, as a corollary to the essential impossibility of knowing another person, is central to Green's aesthetic, and interestingly, misunderstanding is also explicitly linked to the 'hierophantic' desire to create a 'life which is not'. In his interview with Southern, Green says, 'and if the novel *is* alive of course the reader will be irritated by discrepancies – life, after all, is one discrepancy after another' (Green, 1992, pp. 244–5). He makes a similar point in 'A Novelist To His Readers: I', saying that 'to create life in the reader, it will be necessary for the dialogue to mean different things to different readers at one and the same time' (ibid., p. 140). Terry Southern suggested that the bewilderingly confused aspect of *Back* in fact allowed readers to have a better grasp of the novel than Green, seeing 'more in the situation than the author does' (ibid., p. 144). As many critics have noted, Green's deafness formed a significant part of this aesthetic; he believed that deafness, whether pathological or willed (in other words a determined *refusal* to hear), was both a metaphor for, and a means of achieving, the misrepresentations and misunderstandings that constitute human intercourse. His dazzling skill at rendering his characters carrying on conversations at cross purposes is not merely stylistically exuberant but full of humour and pathos, and reminds us that his emphasis is always on the unbridgeable ontological gap between people that paradoxically confirms their freedom. Southern talks usefully about the disappearing author in Green's work, while simultaneously fending off accusations of sloppiness and lack of attention to detail, of which there were many:

> The reader does not simply forget there is an author behind the words, but because of some annoyance over a seeming 'discrepancy' in the story must, in fact, *remind* himself that there is one. This reminding is accompanied by an irritation with the author because of these apparent oversights on his part, and his 'failings' to see the particular *significance* of certain happenings. The irritation then gives way to a feeling of pleasure and superiority in that he, the reader, sees *more* in the situation than the author does – so that now all of this belongs to *him*. And the author is dismissed, even perhaps with a slight contempt – and only the *work* remains, alone now with this reader who has had to take over. Thus, in the spell of his own imagination the characters and story *come alive* in an almost incredible way, quite beyond anything achieved by conventional methods. (Green, 1992, p. 96)

Green was not alone in this period in showing an interest in ideas of narrative indeterminacy and free will, and this reordering of the traditional relationship between the narrative and character is reflected in a set of disparate, but contemporaneous, literary theories and practices. Ideas about the representation of randomness in narrative become increasingly prominent in the 1940s and 1950s in response to an emergent existential literature on the continent. In his groundbreaking study of novelistic polyphony, *Problems of Dostoevsky's Poetics* (1929, 1963), Mikhail Bakhtin describes the idea of a work that has somehow escaped the author's overweening control: 'as if the character were not an object of authorial discourse, but rather a fully valid, autonomous carrier of his own individual world' (Bakhtin, 1999, p. 5). He goes on to illustrate his argument with the example of Dostoevsky, his paradigm of an author who is able to achieve this: 'Dostoevsky, like Goethe's Prometheus, creates not voiceless slaves (as does Zeus), but *free* people, capable of standing alongside their creator,

capable of not agreeing with him and even rebelling against him.' For
Bakhtin, 'Dostoevsky's major heroes are, by the very nature of his creative
design, *not only objects of authorial discourse but also subjects of their own directly
signifying discourse.*' Indeed, each character '*freely* (without the author's
interference) reveals and substantiates the rightness of his own position'
(ibid., pp. 6–7, author's emphasis throughout).

Bakhtin's ideas would have been little known in England in the 1940s, if
at all. Nevertheless, it is apposite to note the idea of the possibility of novelistic free will emerging in apparently unrelated places during the period.
For Graham Greene, a writer normally grouped with the neo-realist set of
post-war writers, the creation of character was also a question of freedom,
though one where the metaphor of author as God has been imbued with an
intense, religious angst. In *The End of the Affair* (1951) Greene notes the
relation between novelistic 'selection' and the familiar metaphorical link
between God as creator and author: 'A story has no beginning or end:
arbitrarily one chooses that moment of experience from which to look back
or from which to look ahead.' He goes on, 'it is convenient, it is correct
according to the rules of my craft to begin just there, but if I had believed
then in a God, I could also have believed in a hand, plucking at my elbow,
a suggestion' (Greene, 1951, p. 51). Belief in God, for Greene, is thus
necessary for belief in creative determinism, or the idea that the writer is a
conduit for something beyond him; an indication that the engagement with
chance and freedom on its own terms was a largely secular undertaking.

Greene's religious imbuing of creative processes also, and more
importantly, extends to characterization, as he has his protagonist Maurice
Bendrix speak of an obstinate character, refusing to come to life:

> He never does the unexpected thing, he never surprises me, he never
> takes charge. Every other character helps, he only hinders. And yet one
> cannot do without him. I can imagine a God feeling in just that way about
> some of us. The saints, one would suppose, in a sense create themselves.
> They are capable of the surprising act or word. They stand outside the
> plot, unconditioned by it. But we have to be pushed around. We have the
> obstinacy of non-existence. We are inextricably bound to the plot, and
> wearily God forces us, here and there, according to his intention, charac-
> ters without poetry, without free will. (ibid., p. 154)

This attention to the representation of freedom in narrative is notable
for its recognition of the difficulty of chance or the unexpected being
made present in a predetermined plot, and in this Green foreshadows the

existentialist concern with freedom and the novel. In his famous essay 'M. François Mauriac et la liberté', Sartre declared that the amount of freedom which an author leaves to his characters is the true mark of art (Sartre, 1939). The 'obstinacy of non-existence' for Greene, which is also the obstinacy of the creation to the creator, establishes the essential truth that Henry Green was so concerned with – if his characters have no life or real existence then they cannot *choose*, and thus are no more than puppets. Greene, while diagnosing the problem usefully here, never seems to have attended to its narrative implications in his work, as Henry Green attempts with his rejection of omnipotence and omniscience. The concern noted by him is in fact tied closely to the impulse pondered by Auerbach in terms of the 'modern' novel's retreat from omniscience, and it is only through this that a greater representation of freedom in the novel can be attained. This realization represents one of Henry Green's key contributions to the various depictions of chance in the period, recast as an anxiety about representing freedom in the novel.

Henry Green's writing career was extraordinarily diverse, with a period of sustained brilliance from *Party Going* (1939), a novel about a group of frivolous rich young people stuck at a train station, to *Concluding* (1948), which is set in an imagined future in which schools have been replaced by state-controlled institutions with ambiguous *modus operandi*.[3] These two works bookend the period where my real interest lies,[4] which is in the three novels that were written and published during the war: *Caught, Loving* (1945) and *Back*. Of these three, *Caught* and *Back* deal directly with the war and its consequences; both rely on coincidence and are concerned with contingency as a fallout from the uncertainty of the war, and both brilliantly dissect the experience of the Blitz from the perspective of, respectively, a London fireman and a shell-shocked prisoner of war recently returned home. The burden of my analysis will be on *Back*, though I will briefly look at *Caught* as it foreshadows many of the same ideas that *Back* confronts.

Green's method varies wildly between books: his late adherence to a self-imposed restriction to pure dialogue (with a thin covering of stage-directions when needed) thwarted the ambition and range that we see displayed in his war novels. His subjects were similarly disparate, and his attention was divided between the social classes: *Living* (1929) is about factory workers; *Party Going* the idle rich; and he dissects the deceptions, social awkwardnesses and interior lives of each with an equally clear eye. His engagement with chance and freedom is also wide-ranging; both structurally and philosophically. His novels are a mixture of meandering, seemingly artless renderings of random timeframes (what Patrick Swinden describes as 'events occurring in almost plotless inconsequence' (Swinden, 1984, p. 66)) and action engendered by strings of improbable coincidences that start to look a lot like fate. The war novels, when read as a body of work, argue that contingency represents the reality of life, and in their very urgency this subtext becomes translated into a commentary on the chaos of the war:

> I was born a mouthbreather with a silver spoon in 1905, three years after one war and nine before another, too late for both. But not too late for the war which seems to be coming upon us now and that is a reason to put down what comes to mind before one is killed, and surely it would be asking much to pretend one had a chance to live. (Green, 1940, p. 1)

So opens *Pack My Bag*, written by Green in 1939, anxious to 'put down what comes to mind before one is killed'. This air of insouciance is belied by the determination with which he iterates this belief that he is about to die, and implies that it is no mere pose, but a conviction, as later when he states: 'This feeling my generation had in the war, of death all about us, may well be exaggerated in my recollection by the feeling I have now I shall be killed in the next' (ibid., p. 74). And later, 'it is impossible when saying goodbye to be certain that where one is going will be any better than what is being left. It is so much on the cards it may be worse' (ibid., p. 195). Rod Mengham, in *The Idiom of the Time*, describes this constant foreboding of what was to come as the book's 'premonitory quality' (Mengham, 1982, p. 53).

This tendency to adopt a fatalistic attitude towards death, to assume its proximity to the present at all times, is not, however, necessarily the dominant attitude of the war novels, which nevertheless dwell much on the chances for dying, and on the irony of luck. The opposition between fate and free will in *Caught*, published in 1943 and set during the 'Phoney War' (the period during which raids had not yet begun but were constantly expected) and at the beginning of the blitz, is certainly complex. Absolute freedom, allied with an awareness of the oppressive profusion of chance, is shown as potentially dangerous, while fatalism is consistently shown to be incompatible with happiness. *Caught* is primarily the story of Richard Roe, who becomes a fireman in London during the war. His wife has died some time before, and his son, Christopher, is living with Richard's wife's sister in the house Richard grew up in. Roe is alienated from his home, his job (before the war, he ran a factory, in an echo of Green's own industrial career) and his romantic life. He is haunted by images of his dead wife, and socially stymied by his ham-fisted attempts to fit in with the working men that make up the ranks of the fire unit. His young son, we are told at the start of the novel, has been abducted from a department store by a mad woman, an episode that we are privy to in the form of an extended flashback a third of the way through.

The plot consists of the firemen's day-to-day lives, as they fearfully antici-pate, and then finally become involved in, the war. The narrative draws increasing parallels between Roe and his superior, the working-class career fireman Pye, who has been promoted, it seems, before he is ready, and is self-consciously awkward in his wielding of the resultant power. Through a series of coincidences we see how constricted Pye's life has become, as his attempts to befriend and help his inferiors backfire through incomprehen-sion, conveyed by Green's characteristic resort to misunderstanding. Pye is haunted by an adolescent memory of losing his virginity, until one day the vagueness of the memory sharpens suddenly into relief, and he realizes that the girl he slept with – or perhaps, ambiguously, raped – in the dark of a garden shed was probably his own sister. The reader is aware that this sister, now in a mental institution, was also the woman who abducted Roe's son Christopher. This series of chance intersections between each of the two men's families has led critics to note that they are doubles of each other – Pye and Roe together make up Pyro, the Greek word for fire, and it is likely that Green consciously played with this idea. As Jeremy Treglown notes in the introductory essay to the 2001 Harvill edition of *Back*, 'there's no mis-taking the contrasts between the two men, claustrophobically entangled while utterly separated by the kinds of determinant not even war can change: luck, for example' (Green, 1943, pp. x–xi).

Indeed, the cruelty of luck, and how it can misdirect a good life, seems the conclusion to be drawn from Pye's tale. Free will is shown to be mean-ingless if one's volition is constantly thwarted by the equally meaningless, but seemingly cruelly inescapable, vacillations of chance. Roe, on the other hand, proclaims a belief in 'fate', but lives his life otherwise; his freedom is consistently shown to be real, if underestimated. Roe is clearly Green's alter ego, sharing his diffidence, his desire to be accepted by the working class and his recourse to that very 'easy determinism' of predicting one's own death – this is an echo of Green's own unshakable conviction, in *Pack My Bag*, of the proximity of his own death. Green describes this fatalism, which is here tinged with the opening up of possibility that usually is anathema to it: 'He has never felt war was possible, although in his mind he could not see how it could be avoided. . . . He was called up three days before the outbreak and, certain of death in the immediate raid he expected to raze London to the ground' (ibid., pp. 24–5). When the bombs finally start falling towards the end of the novel, and Richard is shown to confront death bravely, we can nevertheless see his agency consistently undercut by Green:

> Richard was number one, that is in charge of a pump, called during night blitz to an incident at which two heavy bombs had fallen within a hundred yards of each other. He found the driver had brought them to a statue, which still looked blindly on, in the centre of a London square. (ibid., pp. 94–5)

He is in charge, yet he 'finds' himself at the centre of the action. The statue, still looking 'blindly' on through the chaos, works as a literal figuration of his inactivity and passivity. Later, 'through shattering silence he heard two aircraft. Then machine gunning. He looked up. He expected a dog-fight he would not see. That flare, nearer, was still coldly, majestically descending with his fate' (ibid., p. 95). All that Richard can do, in the face of his 'fate', is look, blindly, searchingly. The repeated mention of his fate, which represents Richard's conviction of his own imminent death, does not, however, change his status as the one character whose fate is not actually sealed, the lucky one, as when he is injured and sent home: 'some months later, after nine weeks of air raids on London, Roe was unlucky one morning. A bomb came too close. It knocked him out' (ibid., p. 173). The 'unlucky' here, of course, is ironically imbued with the certain knowledge that Roe was, in fact, 'lucky' to have survived such a close shave.

Richard's odd and ambiguous occupation of a space between fate and freedom is further articulated in this exchange with Hilly, with whom he has a brief, unsatisfying affair:

> 'Isn't there something up between old man Piper and Mary?' he asked, to head her off.
> 'Don't be so silly.'
> 'There could be, you know.'
> 'Anything's possible, and all the more so now, but not between those two, please.'
> 'Then you do feel, as well, that anything is possible between people now?' said he, with purpose.
> 'But Richard, of course. This war's been a tremendous release for most'. (ibid., p. 98)

Here, the bounds of possibility that have been broken are primarily sexual. Roe, whose 'as well' and purposeful tone belie his eagerness for her assent in this matter, is invigorated by this lack of the old social determinants, and in his submission to a radical freedom he assents to a subsequent reduction in his agency: 'I never felt so alone in all my life. Our taxi was like a pink beetle drawing a peppercorn. We were specks. Everything is so different from what you expect, and this was fantastic' (ibid., pp. 179–80). His ally in this is Prudence, a girl he meets and is briefly attracted to, who in turn sleeps with and then discards Pye. Prudence, who believes that 'war is sex', uses the uncertainty and expectation of death as a means to freedom: 'It was danger Prudence sought in this lull of living' (ibid., p. 121). This exchange is later echoed ironically by Pye, who by this point is caught up in his web of deterministic contingency that will lead him to his inevitable fate: 'anything in this bloody country's possible, mate' (ibid., p. 168). Pye's words here assume a terrible force, as by this point the reader has begun to gather that although anything might be possible, only one outcome is possible for him. Nevertheless, in an inversion of the usual connotations of 'luck', it is emphasized throughout that Pye's fate is not synonymous with necessity, as here, where Pye's dismissal of the necessity of a government institution slips with disturbing ease into the greatest necessity of all – the existential necessity of existence: '"I don't hold with the necessity of the AFS," he would say, "because I don't hold with the necessity for war. But our parents didn't ask us if we wanted to be born, they couldn't ask me or any of you"' (ibid., p. 15). Green's identification of Pye with this rejection of determinism, however, remains on the surface level of character, while on a deeper, structural level of plot, he is hopelessly entangled in the very necessity he professes to abhor. He clings to a belief in chance, by not 'holding with' necessity, and yet, throughout the novel, Pye is the character that Green most ruthlessly allies with his fate. Pye is, in fact, in a further allusion to tropes of ancient Greek literature, a classically tragic figure – he represents the eternal image of helpless man, subject to the whim of a cruel and inevitable fate. He is 'caught'. He wasn't asked if he wanted to be born, nor was he really the agent of his own suicide, which becomes necessary because of the cruelty of events engendered by chance; he has long since ceased to be the subject and agent of his actions. This string of hellish mischances, as John Russell describes them, consists of 'so many terrible coincidences that Pye is led to distrust his own good will' (Russell, 1960, p. 20). Which is, of course, an observation that could be equally applied to Oedipus.

Coincidence here, then, is symbolic of the control that chance had over the lives of those living through the Blitz, and yet Green's employment of it holds it suspended in a complex interrelation with the characters' perception of fate and volition, and with the narrative determinism that Green himself so reluctantly wields. Pye, especially, is shown to be 'caught in the determinism of crisis' (Bardin, 1951, pp. 509–10):

> When he had finished with the electrician Pye went into his office, and picked up the telephone as though taking hold of a black handle of the box which held all his hopes imprisoned; delicately, so that he should not break his luck which had broken; fearful because he could not make the connection, he already knew. (Green, 1943, p. 151)

His hopes are imprisoned inside a telephone, figured as a box, which he doesn't want to 'open', because when he does it will confirm what he guesses will be bad news. This is, of course, reminiscent of Schrödinger's cat (the hypothesis which states that, if you put a cat in a box, with a theoretical 50/50 probability of ether being released and thus a 50/50 chance of the cat dying, then the cat can be said to exist in an indeterminate state, neither living nor dead, until the box is opened and we can observe the outcome). The image of Pye's hopes being similarly imprisoned inculcates the sense of a vulnerable indeterminacy surrounding his actions, and re-emphasizes the link between chance and ignorance mentioned earlier. Pye's absolute reliance on chance is a facet of his ignorance, but the state of not-knowing (here, before he opens the box) is also the blank slate on which chance can operate. The confusion of the tenses 'that he should not break his luck which had broken' makes clear this paradox: the outcome is unknown, yet his fatalism 'knows', simultaneously undermining that fatalism by showing it to be at odds with the indeterminacy, and underlining it; he is, after all, right. This adds an extra complexity to the idea of Pye trapped in a web of contingency: the contingency is the cause and effect of random phenomena, and yet it is self-fulfilling in a purposeful way that undercuts chance entirely. His fate will happen to him in part because he wills it to be so. Nevertheless, it is also clear that Green colludes, in a wilful undermining of his stated desire to lessen such authorial meddling, with his character's fatalistic instincts. Pye comes to an implausible conclusion about his own chances for ruin; the reader assumes this is a matter of his perception; then the universe of the novel proves him right. This ruthlessness on the part of Green, which underlines the author's power, imbues Pye's attempts at denying this fatalist position with cruel irony, as here, when Pye is discussing a stranger: '"You've never seen such filth lying about you in all your life. He simply would not fetch the water. He went on and on about his own brand of fatalism, making out that when your number was up, it was up, you can imagine the sort of thing"' (ibid., p. 185).

Caught ends with a delicate human sympathy for Pye that the narrative machinery of events and coincidences of the novel have belied throughout. Indeed, as we have consistently been made aware of the strength of solipsism and the subsequent impregnability of human existence, it is surprising to discover that sympathy, or fellow-feeling, is even possible. Pye is unreachable, Richard is unreachable; each exists in a heightened and entirely private hell. Nevertheless, the conclusion to the novel seems to suggest that sympathy, while its chances of affecting action remain slim, nevertheless remains the only human response that reflects the ultimate singularity at the heart of each human being. Richard, returned to his country house, is talking to his sister-in-law:

> She then said a very foolish thing, because it was true.
> 'I wonder what's the meaning of it all?' she asked.
> He felt a flash of anger. It spread.
> 'I know this,' he announced in what, to him, was direct answer, 'you've always been most unfair to Pye.'
> She was astounded.
> 'Pye?' she asked.
> 'Yes, to Pye,' he said. He stopped, turned away from her. 'That's the tragedy.'
> 'What d'you mean?'
> He could not look at her. He knew, if he did, that it would break down, that he would not be able to go on, that Pye would be nothing; because he now knew the whole experience was almost over. (ibid., pp. 195–6)

And a few pages later, at the book's close,

> He waited, watching his anger. Then he heard the verdict.
> 'I can't help it,' she said. 'I shall always hate him, and his beastly sister.'
> This was too much for the state he was in. He let go. 'God damn you,' he shouted, releasing everything. 'You get on my bloody nerves, all you bloody women with your talk'. (ibid., p. 198)

Green's commentary here seems to suggest that freedom may, in fact, be impossible, for Pye or for Richard, and that chance's operations have somehow become extended into a crisis of contingency. Either way, Green has failed, in *Caught*, to achieve the task he set himself: to create a character free from authorial determinants. The obsession with freedom constantly frustrated, or extended into meaninglessness, also works as a metaphor for

Green's writerly frustration at his inability to escape determining the action of his novel. And yet, as Jeremy Treglown has commented, in *Caught*:

> . . . among exaggerations, inventions, and cover-ups, the narrative wanders in fatalistically corrective mood: 'She was, of course, hopelessly wrong in this'; 'but he was wrong'; 'In this the men were wrong.' Green claimed to dislike too-knowing story-tellers, but what he really disliked was omnipotence, not omniscience. He knows what his people are doing but knows, too, that in an imaginatively truthful story, they can't be saved from it. (Treglown, 2000, p. 131)

In *Caught*, this precise articulation of Green's anxiety about the role of the author has been transmuted into a discussion about fate and free will among the characters. Green's sadness at Pye's submission to his fate is both a condemnation of the forces that conspire to bring it about, and a sophisticated rebuttal of his own limitations as a writer who aspires to a sort of narrative indeterminacy. *Caught*'s significance lies in Green's cool dissection of people's inability to determine the difference between moral actions and chance: once this distinction is elided, then what *Caught* articulates and describes is this very tension, both for his characters, and for his readers.

Back and the Second World War

As John Brannigan has argued, the post-Second World War act of imagining Europe as a composite identity, a place of civilization and culture, rather than of death camps and mass destruction, was a mammoth, and perhaps impossible, task (Brannigan, 2002). V. S. Pritchett anticipated this vision precisely when he wrote, as the continent ceased its firing, that 'to imagine Europe – that is the hardest thing we have to do. The picture comes to us in fragments and to piece it together and above all hold it in the mind is like trying to hold a dissolving dream and to preserve it from the obstinate platitude of our waking life' (Pritchett, 1945, p. 11). Europe was, of course, literally fragmented by the war into previously non-existent geographical entities, and this idea of disintegration and fragmentation was echoed again and again by individuals, and became a totemic collective articulation of emotion and experience. Elizabeth Bowen's decisive declaration of the putative link between this 'fragmentation' and literary stagnation was typical: 'these years rebuff the imagination as much by being fragmentary as by being violent' (Bowen, 1942, p. 340). The idea of fragmentation manifesting itself as an incompatibility between the times and artistic |creation is echoed by Stephen Spender, in his *September Journal* (1939), for whom the only solution to this incompatibility is, seemingly, an imaginative recourse to the past: 'During these first days of war I have tended to live in the past, partly because the present is so painful, partly because it is so fragmentary and undecided' (Spender, 1978, p. 122). Orwell, too speaks of the chaos of modernity in The Lion and the Unicorn (1941): 'And the diversity of it, the chaos!' 'How can one make a pattern out of this muddle?' (Orwell, 1968, p. 75). Orwell's exclamation is accompanied by an exhilaration that implies that the chaos spurred his literary imagination rather than stymied it, and his immediate impulse remains creative, to 'make a pattern' out of it – and thus to render the disorder ordered. Evelyn Waugh, rather more nihilistically, has Everard Spruce proclaim in *Unconditional Surrender* (1961), the final novel in his *Sword of Honour* trilogy about the war, that 'the human race was destined to dissolve in chaos' (Waugh, 1961, p. 41).

Hazard, uncertainty, chaos, anxiety – it is notable how many of the words and ideas that were brought close by the war are intimately related to concepts of chance. This closeness was perhaps made especially acute by the technological facts of the new bombs that Londoners, from the first moments of the war, were told to expect; the 'pilotless' missiles – whose very name suggests a wild, agency-less randomness, impossible to forecast – which became a terrifying totem of the unpredictability of death. Questions about the part that luck and chance played, then, were paramount, and we are reminded here of the connection between the root of the word chance with the idea of events that befall you, or things that fall on you, out of nowhere, or without a visible cause. If anxiety itself is understood as the anticipation of unpredictable events, chance can therefore have its equivalent as a state of mind, turned towards the future random event, the 'future of the next second' (Harrisson and Madge, 1940, p. 187).

This proximity of death was removed from the traditional conception of death as a *telos* or destination at the end of a temporally circumscribed life. Death in wartime is constantly proximate, and yet as a phenomenon it is also more subject to chance than ever, since its status as a randomly distributed risk is drastically enhanced. Before the bombs of the Second World War started, of course, they were constantly expected, and this state of expectation, experienced as a fearful sort of fatalism and constant expectation of the event, can be understood as a space dominated by thoughts of chance: a passive, uncertain waiting for the unexpected. In fact, bombs were anticipated by the civilian population almost as soon as hostilities had commenced, and, as Bernard Bergonzi remarks, in the years leading up to the war 'the idea [of the bombing of London] haunted the literary imagination' (Bergonzi, 1993, p. 1). The air-raids had been foreshadowed in Greene's *A Gun For Sale* (1936), and in Orwell's *Coming Up For Air* (1939), in which an RAF bomb is accidentally dropped on a village in England. The belief that the aerial bombardment of London was imminent was increased due to false alarm air-raid sirens that started within hours of Chamberlain's announcement of the beginning of the war, and the expectation of bombs was to instil an uncertain, searching fear in the British population for the duration of the war. Lyndsey Stonebridge describes the first and longest of the many 'Lulls', before the raids had begun in mid-1940: 'The interminably anxious time that came to be known as the Phoney War' represented, she suggests 'the irreal space between the declaration of war and the first air-raids on Britain', and the nature of this irreality depended on this sense of the expectation of action. Life was on hold: 'lines of civil defence were drawn and the papier-mâché coffins for the anticipated thousands of air-raid victims were made to order; for ten months the civilian population looked to the sky, but still the bombs did not fall' (Stonebridge, 2001, p. 49).

This indivisibility between chance, or the anticipation of its operation, and the chaos and anxiety of the Second World War was, Stonebridge argues, profoundly connected to the transition that the novel form went through.[5] During the war and in the immediately post-war period the population's appetite for totalizing, explanatory narrative novels waned drastically, subject to what she calls a 'lull in meaning' (Stonebridge, 2001, p. 125). This chronological space also perhaps functioned as a lull in determinism, where danger and hazard made chance the only ruler of circumstance. Chance could thus be described as the ruling spirit of the time, intimately connected to, and informing, the prevalent anxiety, confusion and haphazardness.

In *Mimesis*, Auerbach discusses the putative link between books that are concerned with the 'everyday occurrence' and a verisimilitude in the author's ability to represent chance:

> [T]here is a greater confidence in syntheses gained through full exploitation of an everyday occurrence than in chronologically well-ordered total treatment which accompanies the subject from beginning to end, attempts not to omit anything externally important, and emphasises the great turning points of destiny. (Auerbach, 1953, pp. 547–8)

This 'chronologically well-ordered' novel sounds much like the sort of novel which, as we have seen, rang so hollow during the war. A swing towards the disordered and the seemingly arbitrarily selected, then, can be seen as not merely a stylistic inheritance from the experimental modernists, but rather as a specific response to the war. Along with a reluctance to impose artificial structure, a desire to give equal weight to events of consequence and seeming inconsequence was a way to represent a certain chance-bound or chaotic element of life. The everyday not only increases realism, but can also deepen representations of character: 'Irrelevancy means so much,' as Green wrote to Neville Coghill (a friend and tutor from Oxford) in 1925, 'it shows you what a person is & how he thinks, & conveys atmosphere in a way that is inconceivable' (Treglown, 2000, p. 54). The fixation with the trivial and the everyday is noted by Michael North:

> . . . for the novelists of Green's age the basic political fact is the utter irrel-evance of the individual and his complete helplessness in the world of fact. The characters of Waugh, Powell, Isherwood, and Orwell are all at loose ends [and have] nowhere particular to go. The comic lack of conse-quences . . . is an index of their very lightness, their nature as extraneous beings. (North, 1984, p. 10)

Green's singular achievement is recognizing this characteristic helplessness in the face of the whims of chance and subsequently attempting to repre-sent it truthfully in his novels. Moreover, his wish that his characters could have that very lightness and verisimilitude that North notes as characteristic of the age was overtly linked to the sense of fragmentation that, as we have seen, was perhaps the most notable aspect of the historical moment. In 1954 Green acknowledged to Rosamond Lehmann the fecundity that the war, and the immediately post-war period, had inspired in him: 'The truth is, these times are an absolute gift to the novelist. Everything is breaking up. A seed can lodge or sprout in any crack or fissure' (quoted in Mengham, 1982, p. 71). The 'gift' to the novelist can be read as an environment sym-pathetic to Green's natural inclination towards narrative reticence, or as an invigorating tool to convey the character's freedom. During a period of dis-solution, when 'everything' is breaking apart, the writer, in his narrative representation of reality, is perhaps called upon to do less formulation. He can, in Green's hopeful vision, let his work grow freely; it can act as a con-duit for that which he wishes to represent. This is, of course, what Green has been advocating all along: the retreat of the overbearing author figure who seeks to 'create' a ghastly puppet show that has no bearing on the true nature of reality – which is, of course, full of discrepancy, irrelevancy and chance. The horrors of selective narrative, then, perhaps retreat during periods of instability, and the contingency and uncertainty of real life can find their narrative representation in more meandering, less determined forms whose relation to the wartime atmosphere is explicit.

Back was written directly after *Loving* and published in the year after the end of the war in Europe. It is saturated with anxiety about states of uncertainty, ignorance and the significance or otherwise of coincidence. The novel centres on Charley Summers, a diffident and damaged young man sent back from the war after his leg has been amputated, and on his attempts to readjust to life in England. Charley's lover Rose has died during the war, and her widower, James, has been left with their small boy, who Charley believes to be his son. Charley is damaged, paranoid and has little grip on a reality that even to the reader seems indeterminate; indeed, the novel's central ethical concern is how to act under a fog of uncertainty. At the beginning of the narrative, we see that Charley is effectively incapable of exercising his agency: he knows nothing, and is directed in almost everything by others. His speech is characterized by awkward pauses, *faux pas*, misunderstandings of people and situations, and is constantly contradicted by the perceptions of other characters. As the plot pivots and weaves between the twin pillars of coincidence and misunderstanding, Charley becomes increasingly helpless at the centre of a web of contingency that spreads until it threatens to envelop his agency altogether.

As Edward Stokes notes, 'coincidence is employed by Green even more lavishly in *Back* than in *Caught*. The whole plot is based on the accidental likeness of two half-sisters born a few weeks apart, and on the verbal coincidence that the name of a flower, rose, is also a woman's name, a colour adjective, and the past tense of a common verb' (Stokes, 1959, p. 121). In the midst of his grief for the dead Rose, Charley is beset by coincidence. He meets a man named Middlewitch, whom he dislikes, in a bar, who calls a waitress Rose, and happens to have digs in the same building as Nance, who turns out to be the illegitimate half sister of his dead love and her double. As a result of these coincidences Charley believes that Nance is Rose, though other characters cast doubt upon the extent of their physical resemblance. The word 'chance' appears constantly – someone will think of their 'chances for promotion', or will 'chance a kiss', or a cigarette. 'By any chance?' is the customary tag to any question and things are done when a character gets 'the chance'. Charley finds himself, 'by chance, within a few yards of the address Mr. Grant had given' (Green, 1946, p. 43). 'What are the odds!' is Charley's secretary Dot's favourite expression, and the slightly baleful epithet 'lucky' is applied to the most unfortunate of characters and situations: '"Here's luck," Charley said, to speak for the first time' during his uncomfortable drinking session with Middlewitch (ibid., p. 20).

Middlewitch declares to the waitress that 'He's stuck on a girl called Rose. Bit of a coincidence, isn't it?' (ibid., p. 112). In Charley's opinion, Nance's situation is down to 'Tough luck' (ibid., p. 140). Later on in the novel, Nance and Charley have this exchange: '"Only it was queer the way we met, and now here you are knowing so much I've no idea what you haven't learned." "It's luck," he explained. "Chance, that's all"' (ibid., p. 159).

In the midst of this anxious, chance-soaked narrative, the fear of the mental state of the returning servicemen is a constant presence: '"They're coming back nervous cases, like they did out of the last war," he repeated to himself, and thought that, in that case, then everything was hopeless' (ibid., p. 106). As Mr. Philips, Rose's father, explains to his wife: '"My dear, this is the war. Everything's been a long time. Why only the other day in my paper I read where a doctor man gave as his opinion that we were none of us normal. There you are"' (ibid., p. 84). Charley's inability to act is therefore clearly linked to the war's having forced him into a state of ignorance and fear that is inimical to the decisive exercising of his volition. The uncertainty and the state of 'not-knowingness' that characterize *Back*, and the descriptions of the fall-out from the war, are clearly connected. As Mr. Grant tells Charley: 'Because what you have to remember, Charley boy, is that you're one of the lucky ones. You're back' (ibid., p. 79). While Charley's 'luck' is consistently emphasized, it is imbued with a tragic irony since we can see that he has been stripped of any meaningful agency of his own. If one does not act, how can one be anything but subject to the vagaries of fortune and misfortune? The link between the sinister coincidences that flood Charley's existence and the view of the servicemen is here made obliquely as a contrast between interiority and exteriority:

> He fled Rose, yet every place he went she rose up before him; in florists' windows; in a second hand bookseller's with a set of Miss Rhoda Broughton, where, as he was staring for her reflection in the window, his eyes read a title, 'Cometh up as a flower' which twisted his guts; also in a seed merchant's front that displayed a watering can, to the spout of which was fixed an attachment, labelled 'Carter's patent Rose.'
>
> For she had denied him, and it was doing him in.
>
> A woman behind him said, 'They're like flies those bloody uns, and my goodness are they being flitted'. (ibid., p. 52)

In a resort to his customary preoccupation with the unknowability of the individual, Green ironically contrasts here Charley's interior landscape, which consists of panic and horror at the seeming infinity of the improbable occurrences that dog him, with an exterior view of his actions: to an observer, he is just another 'hopeless case', like a fly 'being flitted'. The woman's pathetic metaphorical comparison of the men to flies has its obvious antecedents in Tennyson and Shakespeare. The Tennysonian metaphor is couched in terms of the revelation of the lack of a plan for mankind:

> And men the flies of latter spring,
>   That lay their eggs, and sting and sing
> And weave their petty cells and die.
>
> (In Memoriam *A.H.H.*, L)

Similarly Shakespeare's men, described by Gloucester 'as flies to wanton boys are we to th' Gods', are volitionless, vulnerably subject to the whims and hazards of an indifferent and cruel divine force.

That the servicemen, and Charley in particular, are more profoundly subject to fortune than other people is a persistent theme. Luck, in fact, ebbs and flows in the narrative along with the presence of the war: the nearer one is to death, the more chance matters. Mrs. Frazier, Charley's landlady, who foresees in her bumbling and banal way much of what comes to pass, frequently tells Charley how lucky he is:

'. . . take what pleasure and comfort you can, because who is there to tell what may befall. When these new bombs he's sending over, turn in the air overhead, and then come at you, there's not a sound to be had. One minute sitting in the light, and the next in pitch darkness with the ceiling down, that is if you're lucky.' (Green, 1946, p. 28)

Mrs. Frazier's role as ironically cast seer is thus established. One should live as passively and pleasantly as possible, and accept chance's vagaries with aplomb. As she undercuts the significance of random phenomena – of a bomb turning and coming at you – she also poetically and subliminally reinforces the mysterious power of chance with her use of the archaism befall. The root of chance, *cadere*, is the verb 'to fall' in Latin: befall is therefore related to chance's original meaning, how the dice, or the bombs, fall for, or on, you.[6] As yet another improbable coincidence confronts Charley, she remains unmoved: '"Never knew the two were acquainted," Charley explained, aghast. "What is there strange in that?" Mrs. Frazier enquired, irritable still. "Once you start on coincidences why there's no end to these things"' (ibid., p. 30).

Mrs. Frazier's passivity contrasts here with Charley's disproportionate reaction to coincidence. He is 'aghast' at the improbability of all that happens to him. This is sustained throughout the novel: early on, when Nance reveals offhandedly that Charley's acquaintance Middlewitch lives in the same building as her, he reacts with comic disproportion:

> 'I'd never have done this, only I happened to know that Mr. Middlewitch was in across the landing.'
> 'Middlewitch?' He spoke out in real horror.
> 'Now then,' she said, beginning to look frightened.
> 'Middlewitch?' he repeated, absolutely bewildered.
> 'Just because I give you the name of someone who lives in these digs, don't you start wondering if you'll strike lucky twice,' she said.
> 'Me strike lucky?' he mumbled. (ibid., p. 46)

Charley's horror, bewilderment, and importantly, total ignorance of cause and effect are shown as both a product of chance and the cause of the misunderstandings that ensue. Coincidence rules his life, and he is terrified of it. The word 'lucky' here is charged with a double-edged irony: it is both a positive interpretation of the chance that is oppressing Charley, and entirely erroneous – at no point so far in the novel has Charley struck 'lucky' in the positive sense. His movements have been fated, not by a universal power, but by coincidence and by characters whose actions have malign effects on him for no discernible reason or meaningful cause; in other words, by chance. This chance is, however, so seemingly malign, that the word 'lucky', with its happy associations, becomes imbued with a cold irony. This example of the dialogue that floods the novel ably demonstrates the comic use of chance in Green's work. Arbitrary coincidence brings Charley and Nance together as a plot device, and then coincidence furthers the misunderstanding from which Green's aesthetic springs. In this sense, coincidence and the inherent meaninglessness of random happenings, whatever eventual purpose they are put to, are at the heart of Green's characterization. The concentration on misunderstanding emphasizes the essential ambiguity of all human communion, and subsequent loneliness, of each person, and in doing so, fulfils Green's prescriptive advocacy of freedom for his characters: this is how real people are.

In *Back*, chance fulfils this function of aesthetic well-spring as completely as blindness does in Green's first novel, *Blindness*, or as self-absorption does in his novel of the idle rich, *Party Going*: it is the basis of all action at cross purposes, and thus of all interaction between characters. Nance is the novel's believer in chance and luck: "'You see, I've thought about this more than you can ever. If you like to put it that way, I've been brought up with the problem. It's chance, is all, nothing more than bad luck. I've known since I was sixteen'" (ibid., p. 69). Yet she is also the one who denies chance's operation, and assumes that Charley's stumbling actions must be down to his agency; 'you'll strike lucky twice' refers to her erroneous belief that Charley is taking advantage of her good nature, when at this point he believes that she is Rose. Nance's faith in chance is what leads her to doubt Charley's intentions:

> 'Did he send Middlewitch?' He asked, jealous again as soon as Mr. Grant was mentioned.
> 'Of course not. I said, didn't I?'
> 'How did you come across him, then?'
> 'I'll not have these questions. I've a life of my own, haven't I? It's not my fault, is it? And if I'm being nice to you it's only that I've the responsibility. Even if he did send you along so things wasn't natural, like crossing one another in the street.' (ibid., p. 70)

She fears that chance's normal, and 'natural' operations have been fatally meddled with: if she had crossed Charley in the street, the chain of events would have corresponded to an idea of what is proper. Chance, to Nance's mind, is the natural order of things, an order that it is foolhardy, and perhaps even dangerous, to distort.

Andrew Gibson has suggested that Charley's horror of coincidence, far from being a paranoiac and disproportionate reaction to the normal course of events that life metes out, is in fact justified by the exterior view of the events in the novel:

> The numerous coincidences in *Back* . . . not only tax our credulity, but are, like coincidences in *The Trial*, quite blatantly implausible. . . . They shrink the gap between Charley's view of the world and that world itself. Yet it is a difference that the novel nonetheless insists on. Charley wrongly assumes the improbable to be the case, in a world where it sometimes is. He mistakes the different for the same, in a world which seems likely to encourage him in his error. (Gibson, 1984, p. 207)

This is a convincing argument, and one that allows for the possibility that although Charley's worldview might be essentially paranoiac, he might also be right. All relationships and events in the book conspire coincidentally so that the smallest trivial occurrence becomes imbued with suspected significance. Rod Mengham has also argued persuasively that these 'coincidences' could in fact be portents of a hidden coherence that Charley cannot quite perceive, while allowing for the explanation that it is all a product of Charley's confused mind. He suggests that the word 'rose' becomes a symbol for the interconnectedness of the paranoiac worldview, a 'talisman for coherence which is out of his control; its magic is endangered by every chance occurrence in the environment' (Mengham, 1982, p. 167).

Of course, the flipside of this fatalistic interconnectedness of all events is misunderstanding and incomprehension, as when Charley, in a desperate grab for meaning, makes up his mind about Nance: 'Then he knew what it was. She was an enemy.' (Green, 1946, p. 49). As Mengham points out, Freud's definition of paranoid delusion emphasizes chance, making, as it does, creative use of accidental, disconnected events, and deduces: 'the writing of *Back* is like an elaboration of Pascal's wager; it is the construction of a *working knowledge*, in the absence of what remains unknown and hidden' (Mengham, 1982, p. 179). This working knowledge is akin to the paranoiac worldview, as it assumes coherence where there is none. The suggestion by Gibson and Mengham that Charley is ignorant of the reasons why the many coincidences are connected is persuasive, and yet leaves little room for chance. Perhaps it is apposite to note that there exists an alternative significance to Pascal's Wager. By reducing the question of divinity to a probability calculation, the wager introduces a rational approach to chance, as well as a probabilistic attempt to ratify the irrational. In fact, far from being necessarily symbolic of the attempt to access a 'hidden order,' Pascal's Wager can equally be understood as anathema to a fatalistic worldview, in that it reduces and undermines the determinism it seeks to quantify. If *Back* can be further illuminated by mention of Pascal's theory then perhaps it is in the sense that the interconnectedness of events, or the idea of a 'hidden order' that directs one's fate, and to which we are not privy, does not, in the final analysis, matter; Pascal's Wager instructs us that whether there is or there isn't a God has no bearing on how one determines the meanings of events. Rather, one should assume nothing, and proceed through life rationally. *Back* articulates this passivity as illumination rather than as inaction or solipsism, just as Pascal does. Chance – largely rational – and fate – largely mystical – are continually seeping into each other, and are impossible to separate: and importantly, Green seems to suggest, there is no point in even trying.

The other defined paranoia at work in the book is a topical concern with the overwhelming bureaucracy with which the society of 1945 found itself flooded. One of the best running jokes in the book concerns the proliferation of nonsensical acronyms for countless useless government institutions. This contrasts with the description of the discovery of parabolam (made from bird lime) and stainless steel, which are both truly 'lucky' coincidences:

> 'It was an accident,' he began, 'like it was with stainless steel, when the heads were on inspection round the foundry yard and one of 'em spotted something he'd noticed before, a bit of bright scrap through the rain. So they had it analysed, and there you are. Now it's what you cut your meat up with . . . It was exactly the same with parabolam,' he went on, 'only this time it was bird's droppings'. (Green, 1946, p. 37)[7]

The idea of paranoia in connection with managerial systems identified by critics in *Back* here seems misplaced. The description of chance's operation, untainted by predisposition, paranoiac coherence or sinister inexplicability, is like a brief respite from the miasma of 'bad' chance that infiltrates the book. Science, work and the ensuing logical world of order where chance's operations are marginalized, are Charley's escape.

Lyndsey Stonebridge has commented interestingly on the distinction between fate and chance in *Back*:

> There is no space for interiority in *Back*: no imagistic memorialising as self-authoring. Charley's fate is wholly determined by the agency of the roses that relentlessly pursue him through the text. . . . Charley's life is scripted beyond his conscious desires. That script, in this sense, *is* what lies beyond Eros (or beyond Rose). To live a life in which one's history and one's fate are so cruelly beyond the limits of one's wishes . . . is painful, but the result is not always fatal. (Stonebridge, 2001, p. 65)

That Charley's fate is 'wholly determined' by the agency of the 'hidden order' that the roses represent is, I think, wrong. It is eventually Charley's ability to fall in love with Nance, as distinguished, albeit somewhat ambiguously, from Rose, that proves otherwise. If Charley's agency had not been restored to him then this romantic ending would make no sense. In fact, the slow process of regaining his agency is clearly shown to be linked to his social rehabilitation, and thus his growing understanding of the true nature of chance is what makes possible his ability to act as a free man:

> But what a night to choose. Wasn't it just like his luck the old man should have another bad turn, exactly when his own affairs promised better?

Then, with surprising intuition, he supposed that one crisis in this life inevitably brings on another, that she wouldn't have kissed him if Mr. Grant had not been having a relapse (either if neither of them knew), nor, and here he fell unwittingly on the truth, would she have asked him if it hadn't been for the doubly serious illness. All the same, so to speak in spite of himself, he began to have hopes. (Green, 1946, p. 179)

The illumination of his understanding of chance's place in the natural order of things is clearly identified as what brings about his ability to hope, and thus to love: Nancy would not have kissed him if the chain of events had been different. 'He put his arms around her, and luckily, was very gentle. . . . Again, more by luck than good judgement, he kept silence' (ibid., p. 180). This demonstrates the frailty of human relationships by revealing the extent to which their success depends upon on chance, but more importantly, it also reveals Charley's recognition of luck as just that, luck. It has been liberated from the oppressive, ironic undertones that it has carried through the bulk of the novel, and this liberation seems to have had the corollary of freeing him. *Back* ends in a sort of romantic quietude. Charley sees Nance naked; he cries 'Rose', and she shushes him. The word has been stripped of its meaning and of any status it might have had as totem of a hidden order of events to which Charley could not gain access – it is finally just a word. When Charley and Nance kiss in the rose garden, Charley 'could not speak, paralysed', and the possible allusion here to the Hyacinth Girl episode of *The Waste Land* (or, indeed, to the rose garden at the opening of 'Burnt Norton') again emphasizes the fact that communication is not only unconfined to its sensory bounds but entirely disconnected from them. Charley's 'usual state of not knowing, lost as he always was' transmutes, then, from the pathos-laden vulnerability of not-knowing, but, rather, his not-knowing has become a kind of state of grace.

As I established in my first chapter, there exists a long association between notions of ignorance and those of chance. If one lacks a causal explanation for an event, one is in ignorance – ignorance is thus the starting point for recognizing chance as chance: as mere coincidence or arbitrary randomness, rather than a series of happenings that speak, however obliquely, of a hidden knowledge of our fate of which we are for whatever reason unaware. What Green's best novels elaborate is akin to the Beckettian self-definition, quoted at the head of this chapter, of working around the unknown and the partial. It is this 'not-knowingness' that allows the free operation of narrative chance. *Back* seeks to examine the complex interrelation of chance and fate in the world of one vulnerable, damaged young man, where the probability of death has charged the idea of chance with a terrifying fatedness.

The recognition of chance as chance, and of a state of ignorance, at the end, is the beginning of Charley's ability to function normally as an agent in his own life, to exercise his free will and engineer his escape from the portents, the roses, and the coincidences that have dogged him so sinisterly for so long.

It is therefore mistaken to interpret chance in Green's *Back*, and in his work in general, as a metaphor for fate. Green's significance for the history of chance's representation in the literature of the twentieth century is that, for him, chance functions as a mode of existing in the world passively, and in this he represents a wholly new expression of literary chance, and a wholly new way of planting a profound indeterminism at the heart of the novel. Green's careful associations between the unexpected, the improbable and the coincidental, and his wartime setting, can be read as a commentary on the uncertain, contingent mood of the war. His characters in *Back* and in *Caught* are trying to live under an oppressive regime of extreme chance: expecting at any moment to die in *Caught*, and in a world made chaotic and paranoid by wartime in *Back*. The incidences of predetermination, foreknowledge and moments of sudden illumination that everything is connected that abound in *Back*, and which appear to push chance and randomness to the periphery, can also be read as harbingers of an anxiety about the perception of chance. In an historical moment at which life was lived under the rule of randomness, and where the fear of being hit by a bomb meant that probability was an overriding concern in everyday life, a preoccupation with the predetermined speaks forcefully of an anxiety of its opposite. The emphasis on circumstance and contingency simultaneously tells us that actions are the only engine of meaning in the world, and that there is no point in performing those actions as the web of circumstance is so intricate that one will never be able to predict the outcome of an event.

Green's formal and stylistic virtuosity similarly reflects this set of ideas about passivity, freedom and chance. As Auerbach has demonstrated so clearly, a suspicion of plot is a corollary to a concern about the accurate representation of the randomness of everyday life. Green's stylistic virtuosity is itself symbolic of this passivity. Why plot? Why not fiddle with beautiful images of flames and roses instead of imposing an order that does not really exist? What will happen, Green seems to suggest, will happen anyway, with no help from any of us. Images are also the most concrete expression of the randomness of the mind, coming as they do arbitrarily, connecting the unconnected, setting up associations and engendering chance digressions and parallels that bring meaning into being by the fact of their imposition, rather than being made necessary by an explanatory, deterministic framework. Green's contribution to the novel form is, at least in part, his recognition that narrative is inimical to chance's true operations, an observation which is closely related to the specific circumstances of the historical moment in which he worked. When read as part of a composite, coherent literary philosophy and critical diagnosis, Green's desire to create a real, free life in his characters amounts to a reordering of the dynamics of fate, free will and chance in the novel of the mid-twentieth century.

Chapter Three

'I admire the will to welcome everything – the stupid violence of chance': Samuel Beckett and the Representation of Possibility

The fetishization of chance by the existentialists as 'stupid violence' linked chance indelibly with that other 'stupid violence': the Second World War. The culture of chance that the existentialists were surrounded by was not a mere avant-garde indulgence, but was, and had been for the length of the war, a reality: chaos, randomness and instability were everywhere. Chance itself, it almost seemed, could do real damage; bombs that were impossible to predict, killed; uncertainty was made concrete. Anything could happen. It seemed for a while that chance was no longer part of the vocabulary of hope, but part of the vocabulary of terror.

The existentialists recognized this dilemma and recast it anew, so that the discussion about chance became transformed into a discussion about possibility and contingency.[1] For the existentialists, hope only became possible once despair about our existential situation had been acknowledged. The hope that springs from resignation, therefore, was a result of the acceptance of a random, meaningless universe, where traditionally causal explanations of events could no longer speak to us. Possibility was therefore essentially conceived of as a space in which anything might happen. As discussed in the previous chapter, V. S. Pritchett wrote in the final months of the war that:

> To imagine Europe – that is the hardest thing we have to do. The picture comes to us in fragments and to piece it together and above all hold it in the mind is like trying to hold a dissolving dream and to preserve it from the obstinate platitude of our waking life. (Pritchett, 1945, p. 11)

By the mid-1950s Samuel Beckett was echoing this sense of cultural uncertainty and fragmentation in the artistic sphere: 'art has nothing to do with clarity, does not dabble in the clear and does not make clear', he told one interviewer: 'One can only speak of what is in front of him, and that now is simply the mess' (Driver, 1961, p. 22). Beckett's refusal to impose a novelistic order on top of reality as he saw it, and his efforts to represent the 'mess', namely a contingent and uncertain modernity, aligns him with those novelists that, more than trying to merely represent chance, actively try to incorporate it into both their form and content.

Beckett's concern with questions of contingency and possibility, and their representability in fiction, are perhaps the aspect of his writing that are the most relevant to existentialist thought; and yet these are also the aspects of his fiction that have received the scantest attention. Many critics, when talking about Beckett and philosophy, construct readings based on his assumed philosophy of being or his affiliations with this or that movement. I am not attempting to do this; I do not merely wish to excavate his texts for references to, or parallels with, Existentialism. Rather, I will look at the ideas about possibility and chance that were current, namely existential ones, before moving on to examine Beckett's work, with particular attention given to his 1953 novel *Watt*, in the light of these, and acknowledge the formal ramifications this had for the novel in general. I am not trying to argue that Beckett is an existentialist, or to prove that he is not; rather, I wish to suggest that his recognition of life's 'mess' and his belief that a writer should perhaps represent it as it is, nevertheless echoes ideas that were feeding into the intellectual culture at the time – one that was, I believe saturated by notions of chance.

Narrative, the Novel and Chance

As we saw in my first chapter, Thomas Kavanagh has argued convincingly that the emergence of probability theory in the seventeenth and eighteenth centuries 'paralleled and in a very real sense sustained' the hegemony of the modern novel. 'Together they formed a single shift in how we saw and understood the world and how we represent our place in it' (Kavanagh, 1993, p. 11). His reasoning for this is essentially formal: 'The novel shares with probability theory the assumption that individuals act within a world of pre-existing causal sequences, of multiple determinisms compelling their reactions' (ibid., p. 118). The novel's traditional insistence, then, that moral character is roughly equivalent to fate is key. If probability theory 'tamed' chance, as Hacking has argued, then the novel effects a similar sleight of hand by containing it under larger movements of cause and effect. The reasons for a character's actions are fundamental to our understanding of the literary entity of a novel. Sartre's concentration on the aspects of narrative inimical to a representation of chance in *Nausea* (1938), therefore, mirrored Beckett's insistence on non-causal explanations for events in his fiction: both seek to counter this smothering, as they saw it, of the truly random nature of reality under a blanket of plot.

The novel form also adroitly reflects the ambiguity of chance's representation in literature, as it necessarily represents a deterministic universe: its events are ordered, predetermined, *written* by the author. Yet if the novel is to fulfil its mimetic function then moments, realizations, coincidences and events, all must come to the reader as unexpectedly as they do in life. The possibility of the author ceding his or her god-like control admits that perhaps events could become dictated by something else: if not chance itself, then perhaps something analogous to chance. The appearance of chance in the novel is thus aligned with spontaneity and modernity, and, in its refusal to accept cause and effect as the teleological explication of plot, inscrutability. As Sartre points out:

> A work is never beautiful unless it in some way escapes its author. If he paints himself without planning to, if his characters escape his control and impose their whims upon him, if the words maintain a certain independence under his pen, then he does his best work. (Sartre, 1950, p. 154)

In *Nausea*, Sartre's protaganist Roquentin also displays some writerly anxiety over this ambiguity: 'we forget the future was not there yet, that the guy was walking in a night without signs which offered him monotonous riches in a jumble and that he made no choices' (Sartre, 1965, p. 62). Rather, he argues, we read in bad faith if the character is stripped of a genuinely temporal existence: 'it all began with the end. It's there, invisible and present, giving these words all the pomp and value of a beginning' (ibid.). Throughout his literary career, Samuel Beckett showed an alertness to this narratological tension, and a desire to explore the possibilities for expressing it. In *Watt*, which will form the basis of my analysis which I shall come to later in the chapter, he highlights the idea of chance as a self-consciously mechanical cog in the narrative wheel: Mr. Hackett suspects that Watt finds the thought of leaving the city as painful as the thought of remaining in it, and that therefore he has left the decision to chance, or, as Beckett puts it, to 'the frigid machinery of the time-space relation' (Beckett, 1976, pp. 43–4). Of course, the frigid machinery here is actually a living, breathing Beckett, but this overt acknowledgement of the mechanistic and inhuman nature of causality ironically subverts the reader's suspension of disbelief, and simultaneously represents that which it is drawing attention to as unrepresentable: it adds a note of real, if logically impossible, freedom.

Existentialism and Chance: The Idea of the Possible

The mathematically informed, statistical idea of chance, as we saw in the first chapter, had changed the way that chance and the random were thought of. The idea that the future was entirely uncertain, and that predictable events only existed in terms of very large numbers – for example, if we imagine a population of twenty million, where three hundred thousand people a year are statistically likely to commit a crime – was now commonplace. The Leibnizian idea that it was possible to 'incline without necessitating' had been accorded new weight by the bankrupting of absolutely deterministic ideas by the developments in Quantum Mechanics in the 1920s and 1930s. Similarly the mathematical arm of probability theory, the study of statistics, was prevalent. In 1927, L. J. C. Tippet compiled a huge and hugely influential table of completely randomized numbers that were taken from parish registers' dates of birth and death for *Biometrika*, the journal run by Karl Pearson (Tippet, 1927). Some historians argue that there was no 'pure' theory of mathematical probability until 1933 (Gigerenzer et al., 1989, p. xiii), and Bennett attributes a radical, groundbreaking significance to the mathematician Richard von Mises, who, in 1928, wrote a book developing a theory of probability based on random selection which argued that where there is no predictability at all in the longest run, there is absolutely no rule that might help one devise a system (Bennett, 1998, pp. 20, 29–30). This method of long-run frequency, or random sequencing, was controversial, as it opened up the remarkable possibility that a sequence of random events could conform to no statistical rule whatever.

These ideas were taking hold in the period between the end of the modernist period and the end of the Second World War, and, coupled with the instability induced by the war itself, contributed to the 'mess' at the scientific and intellectual fringes of the culture, that Green, Beckett and Sartre, had, in different ways, all identified as the primary state of modernity. Culturally, too, as we have seen, the idea of randomness was breaking free of its previous incarnations as significance-freighted coincidence,[2] *fortuna*, or destiny, and was assuming the unsettling mantle and *modus operandi* of true uncertainty. The Dadaist and Surrealist experiments had introduced the idea of chance as a formal principle in art, and though the sense of these experiments as artistically vandalistic was always present, they, along with Mallarmé's groundbreaking poem *Un Coup de Dés*, had sown the seeds of possibility for the literary avant-garde to make their forms reflect the realities of chance in new and revolutionary ways.

The existentialists were influenced by these ideas about randomness and chance, both scientific/mathematic and cultural: Albert Camus, in 'Absurd Walls' in *The Myth of Sisyphus*, could now say 'no code of ethics and no effort are justifiable a priori in the face of the cruel mathematics that command our condition' (Camus, 1955, p. 21). And Sartre, in 'Determinism and Freedom', defines probability, or 'statistical prediction', as 'the result of a reasonable calculation about a pattern of behaviour' (Sartre, 1974, p. 245). His definition of possibility emphasizes the importance of pure chance, as it '*knows no conjuncture, that is, no connection* with antecedent causes'. He goes on to say '*pure future is neither knowable not predictable . . . which nothing has laid the groundwork for and nothing helps to bring about . . . makes it a future to be created*' (ibid., pp. 243–5; Sartre's emphasis throughout). The subsequent existentialist concentration on action, then, is dependent on a world that is subject to the fluctuations of chance. The largely existentialist conception of contingency, furthermore, attacked the very notion of causality, as Sartre has Roquentin muse: 'It is out of laziness, I suppose, that the world looks the same day after day . . . and in that case *anything, anything* could happen' (Sartre, 1965, p. 114); indeed, those people who believe in the 'proof' they are given that 'everything is done mechanically, that the world obeys fixed, unchangeable laws' are castigated as 'idiots' (ibid., p. 225). Sartre's fictionalized attack on causality here is anticipated by a speech given in 1931 to the school in Le Havre where he had been a teacher (presumably to a crowd of increasingly saucer-eyed children):

> You know that each instant depends narrowly on those which have preceded it, that any given state of the universe is absolutely explained by its anterior states; that there is nothing which is lost, nothing which is in vain; and that the present goes strictly towards the future. You know this because you have been taught it. But if you look within yourself, around yourself, you do not in the slightest feel it. You see movements arising which, like the sudden stirring of a treetop, seem spontaneous. You see others which, like waves on sand, are dying out, and in their dying seem to lose their vital force. It seems to you that the past is bound very loosely to the present, and that everything gets old in an aimless, sloppy, groping way'. (Merkel, 1987, p. 45)

In *Notebooks for an Ethics*, Sartre elaborated his preoccupation with the illusion of causality as a belief in the primacy of probability theory: 'Every human undertaking succeeds by chance and at the same time through human initiative. . . . In a word, possibles get realized *in terms of probability.* Freedom lives in the sphere of the probable, between total ignorance and certitude' (Sartre, 1992, p. 335). This emphasis interestingly associates possibility, or freedom, with probability theory (Barnes, 1959, p. 365).[3] Chance is no longer 'tamed' by probability, in the existentialists' understanding of it, but instead given its fullest possible rein.

This acute sensitivity to the possible was widespread in the thought and literature of the immediate post-war period, as we have seen. One of Sartre's favoured definitions for the possible was that it represents 'an option on being'; in other words life itself is, or has become, profoundly contingent (Sartre, 2002, p. 99). This idea also adds ambiguity to the distinction between chance and the existentialist emphasis on choice. If you are able to choose, and act according to your will, then you are free, and you therefore exist in a random universe where chance operates. The existentialist absurd is merely the revelation of this fact – the revelation that possibility, and therefore chance, is infinite. McBride calls the existentialist understanding of possibility 'existence turned towards the future' (McBride, 1977, p. 92). That the future is as yet unwritten, and entirely uncertain, is an obvious corollary to this. Subsequently, the existentialist's figuration of chance is as a premise and not a consequence of the absurd, a necessary tenet of our existence as self-creating beings. Chance, for the existentialist novelists, is the opposite of what we saw in pre-seventeenth-century culture. It is no longer a negative, or a lack, but rather it is possibility in its widest sense: what *could* happen.

However, Sartre's definition, 'option on being', provides us with another layer to the reading of the idea of possibility as a discussion of chance recast for a specific time: the idea, grimly well suited to the immediately post-war period, that life itself is profoundly contingent. As Roquentin says in *Nausea*: 'the essential thing is contingency. I mean that, by definition, existence is not necessity. To exist is simply *to be there*; what exists appears, lets itself be encountered, but you can never deduce it' (Sartre, 1965, p. 188). If existence is not necessity, and not necessary, then our whole being is based on chance, an awareness of which brings with it the spectre of non-being: 'For the future dimension is ignorance, risk, uncertainty, a wager. If each human being is a risk, humanity as a whole is a risk. The risk of no longer existing, the risk of indefinitely stagnating in one aspect of its history' (Sartre, 1992, p. 467). The bleakness of this vision for the individual is emphasized in *Nausea*: 'Every existent is born without reason, prolongs itself out of weakness and dies by chance' (Sartre, 1965, p. 191). Sartre's disquiet at the centrality of non-being to being is apparent when he contends 'that the world is suspended in not-being as the real is suspended in the heart of possibilities' (Sartre, 2002, p. 19). Possibility for Sartre, therefore, is an almost physically conceived space, analogous to not-being, 'a sort of geometrical place for unfulfilled projects, all inexact representations, all vanished beings or those of which the idea is only a fiction' (ibid.). This sense of possibility casts it not in the future realm of what could have happened, but in the present realm of what might have happened, and brings with it an elegiac sense of loss for vanished possible lives.

Early Beckett: *Proust, Murphy* and the Decline of Cause and Effect

Hans Arp, who was Beckett's co-signatory in 1932 to an aesthetic credo called 'Poetry is Vertical', which appeared in issue 21 of *transition*, was a poetic advocate of chance, along with his fellow Dadaists. In the manifesto was included this extraordinary passage:

> Chance opened up perceptions to me, immediate spiritual insights. Intuition led me to revere chance as the highest and deepest of laws, the law that rises from the fundament. An insignificant word might become a deadly thunderbolt. One little sound might destroy the earth. One little sound might create a new universe. (Motherwell, 1989, p. 294)[4]

There are a number of striking aspects to this: first, the significance accorded to chance in philosophical terms; secondly, his insistence on the connection between chance and 'intuition' and 'spiritual insights'; and finally, the markedly physical association of chance with the real world. It is no longer an instrument of the gods or a tool of augury, but, rather, has real physical presence; it can induce a 'thunderbolt', 'destroy the earth' or 'create a new universe'. Importantly, Arp's sense of chance as a catalyst for radically lopsided effects is also indicative of a new way of looking at cause and effect, and one that had not yet become common parlance in mathematics, foreshadowing as it does the idea of the butterfly effect in modern Chaos Theory ('One little sound might destroy the earth').[5] In 1932 Newtonian determinism and causal explanations for events were becoming scientifically unfashionable, and were being replaced gradually, as we have seen, by an increasingly statistical approach to prediction and a quantum approach to explanation.[6] Parallel to this was the acknowledgement of random phenomena, or uncaused events, necessary for the science of probability, demonstrated by the growth of probability and statistical theory. So although Arp's invocation of something close to the butterfly effect has no established scientific parallels in 1932, it poetically suggests an idea (in this case a cause inducing a wildly disproportionate and random effect), which, later in the century, will become common mathematical and scientific, as well as cultural and literary, parlance. The sense of unpredictability as terrifyingly absolute, then, if merely among the avant-garde, seemed to be gaining currency.

Beckett shared with Arp a longstanding disquiet about the Newtonian world of cause and effect which was reflected throughout his writing career, and which mirrored these scientific and cultural shifts. Although Beckett denied vehemently any specific alliance to any philosophical movement, idea or practitioner,[7] he nevertheless anticipated the later Sartrean attack on the notion of cause and effect[8] by frequently arguing against the domination of narrative by, as he saw it, overly simplistic causal explanations for behaviour and events, as well as attacking its dominion in the novel in general by downplaying its function in the machinery of his fiction.[9] In his first published work, the monograph *Proust* (1931), he says

[Proust] is almost exempt from the impurity of will. He deplores his lack of will until he understands that will, being utilitarian, and a servant of intelligence and habit, is not a condition of the artistic experience. When the subject is exempt from will the object is exempt from causality (Time and Space taken together). . . . As a writer he is not altogether at liberty to detach effect from cause (Beckett, 1931, pp. 69, 1).

Further, he argued that despair[10] in life was due in no small part to unpredictability, the only (ironically enough) reliable constant. This sense of despair in the face of possibility will become increasingly predominant, anticipating as it does Beckett's characters Murphy, Watt and Molloy, all of whom sit passively and painfully by while life doles out indignity after indignity.

Before I come to the period where my real interest lies, I would like to see how Beckett dealt with chance earlier in his novelistic career, by a brief examination of *Murphy* (1938), which deals with the idea of causality and chance thematically. Murphy himself is obsessed with ideas of freedom, and Beckett plays with ideas of chance and freedom on both a thematic and structural level. The plot turns on accident and chance encounters, and the word 'coincidence' is charged with a mocking tone throughout. Chapter Three opens with 'a striking coincidence': that the moon, 'full and at perigee, was 29,000 miles nearer the earth than it had been for four years' (Beckett, 1993, p. 19). Later, by another 'striking coincidence', the moon is again at the same location, only this time it is 'bathed . . . in an ironical radiance' (ibid., p. 70). As the narrative develops, Murphy becomes 'the contingent, as he himself would say, of a contingent' (ibid., p. 121). Murphy is a lackadaisical waster, with a circuitous mind bent on paradox and puns, and his fixation on the dialectic between complete freedom and absolute idle inaction is manifested in his favourite past-time: rocking back and forth as quietly as possible, in the half-light, naked, bound by the feet and hands to his rocking chair, which he positions so that he is staring at the wall. The story pivots on a number of missed chances: Murphy's lover, and love, the prostitute Celia, thinks he has left her; by chance, he comes back five minutes after she has given up and left him for good. The text is filled with Murphy's intellectual digressions while his life disintegrates around him. He has a revelation of sorts, while describing the five different biscuits that make up his lunch every day, 'a Ginger, an Osborne, a Digestive, a Petit Beurre and one anonymous'. He much prefers the Ginger biscuit, and so usually eats that first, and he despises the uncertainty of the anonymous, so eats it last. One day it hits him:

> On his knees now before the five it struck him for the first time that these prepossessions reduced to a paltry six the number of ways he could make this meal. But this was to violate the very essence of assortment, this was red permanganate on the Rima of variety. Even if he conquered his prejudice against the anonymous, still there could only be twenty-four ways in which the biscuits could be eaten. But were he to overcome his infatuation with the ginger, then the assortment would spring to life before him, dancing the radiant measure of its total permutability, edible in a hundred and twenty ways! (ibid., p. 57)[11]

The importance of possibility is demonstrated here by Murphy's stubborn avowal of it over any conception of taste or habit. What he must 'overcome' is his choice, his preference: the fact that he actually likes ginger biscuits the most. Get that out of the way, and the joys of possibility open up to him, even though he will find himself eating biscuits he doesn't much care for. It is, it seems, a good *in itself* to have expanded your possibilities, 'dancing the radiant measure of its total permutability', even if these very possibilities in reality lessen your enjoyment of life. This is a lightly limned indication of the fascination and neurosis surrounding the notion of possibility that will be a much more insistent, dominating presence in *Watt.*

Murphy's lopsided aetiology has become refined into farce by the end of the novel. Murphy dies as a result of an unlikely chain of events: as the coroner comments, one feels sardonically, it is 'a classic case of misadventure' (ibid., p. 147). Before his death he had found happiness, of a sort, while working in a home for the mentally retarded (the Magdalen Mental Mercyseat, or MMM). The minutely ordered life of the patients seems to provide Murphy with a feeling close to happiness; we are reminded of the times he spent bound to his rocking chair, and it becomes clear that it is perhaps only under constraint, or constraints, that he feels a genuine freedom. Someone in the home accidentally pulls a chain in the bathroom, which sets off the complicated system for the delivery of gas to Murphy's bedroom that he had insisted on, and his lit candle eventually ignites the escaped gas. Murphy's chosen past-time, that which made him feel free – rocking in his chair while bound – means he cannot escape the ensuing fire.

In Deborah J. Bennett's 1998 book, *Randomness*, she comments on Hume:

> In his 1739 work *A Treatise of Human Nature*, the Scottish philosopher David Hume discusses chance from a different perspective: its effect on the mind. He said that chance leaves the mind 'in its naïve situation of indifference'. That is, a set of equally likely outcomes produces a mental state of indifference among alternatives, and there is no reason to prefer one outcome over another. The belief that chance represents either insufficient knowledge or indifference is sometimes referred to as the subjective definition of randomness. (Bennett, 1998, p. 154)[12]

This idea of passivity in the face of contingent events, I would contend, is important in *Murphy* on several levels. First, the form of the novel and the narrative voice in particular pretend to eschew an overweening, heavily plotted tale: the first line of the book, 'the sun shone, having no alternative, on the nothing new' gives us no indication of why this day, rather than any other, is being reported (Beckett, 1993, p. 5). Or, similarly to the last line in his novella *First Love*: 'But there it is. Either you love or you don't' (Beckett, 1995, p. 45). In both texts, Beckett affects an indifference incapable of narrative judgement, which reminds us of Beckett's experimentalism; it consistently, and radically, reinforces his intellectual distaste for causality. In fact, causality's perceived inadequacy as an explanatory force in the traditional novel was something he determined he would get around, even if his avoidance of it at this point in his career meant nothing more than the drawing of the reader's attention to the writerly mechanism ('the frigid machinery of the time-space relation' (Beckett, 1976, pp. 43–4) and therefore creating its perceptible presence in the text. In fact, causation in Murphy, in a strikingly Sternean manner, almost seems to work backwards. As in *Tristram Shandy*, every cause seems to need an effect, with the story of how one became the other always dutifully, if ironically, explained later.

The second significance of passivity is that, for Murphy, it is perhaps the state closest to, or at any rate most analogous to, freedom. In a world where chance is felt to rule, and traditional ideas of cause and effect have been shown to be disingenuous, an affected indifference to events seems to be a new and radical mode of existence, and subsistence, for Beckett's characters. This reading is corroborated by Murphy's revelation of a condition where the random rules: the dark is equated with a 'willessness' and freedom, a 'perpetual coming together and falling asunder of forms' that we can neither conjure with nor comprehend (Beckett, 1993, p. 65). As a corollary to this, it seems that absolute freedom necessarily limits individual freedom, as individuality is meaningless, as the narrator comments: 'Here he was not free, but a mote in the dark of absolute freedom' (ibid.). Similarly, the patients at MMM with their 'indifference to the contingencies of the contingent world' perhaps understand how to deal with the 'mess' that is modernity better than the characters (ibid., p. 96). I think that this ability of the patients – or inmates – in particular is more than the fairly commonplace inversion and interrogation of the normal societal categories of sane and insane – the clichéd realization that it is the mad who are truly sane. Rather, this is a clear association between *contingency* and happiness: the 'self-immersed indifference to the contingencies of the contingent world which he had chosen for himself as the only felicity and achieved so seldom' (ibid.): it is, perhaps, the mad who are most aware of their unimportance and therefore the most likely to be truly happy. Indifference, or passivity, to the randomness around us is thus key if we are to achieve this tantalizing 'only felicity'.[13]

Watt and the 'Possibilities of Choice'

Beckett began writing *Watt* in Paris in 1942, and although the novel was largely complete by 1945 it remained unpublished until 1953, by which time Beckett was already famous for *Waiting for Godot* and for the first two books of what later came to be known as the *Trilogy*: *Molloy* (1951) and *Malone Dies* (1956, but published in French in 1951) (*The Unnamable*, the final book of the *Trilogy*, was also published in 1953). He commented nonchalantly a little later: 'it was written as it came, without pre-established plan,' (Beckett, 1984, p. ix) a comment, that, in itself, might impress upon us his identification with or view of the artistic importance of chance and his artistic rejection of an overarching authorial presence. David Hesla argues that *Watt* as a whole can be related to this first impulse – to give voice to, but, crucially, not shape to, the mess and confusion that we find around us (Hesla, 1963). In the course of an interview with Tom Driver, Beckett stated:

> . . . the confusion is not my invention. We cannot listen to a conversation for five minutes without being acutely aware of the confusion. It is all around us and our only chance now is to let it in. The only chance of renovation is to open our eyes and see the mess. It is not a mess you can make sense of. . . . One can only speak of what is in front of him, and that now is simply the mess. (Driver, 1961, p. 22)

And later in the same interview:

> What I am saying does not mean that there will henceforth be no form in art. It only means that there will be new form, and that this form will be of such a type that it admits the chaos and does not try to say that the chaos is really something else. The form and the chaos remain separate. The latter is not reduced to the former. That is why the form itself becomes a preoccupation, because it exists as a problem separate from the material it accommodates. To find a form that accommodates the mess, that is the task of the artist now. (ibid., p. 23)[14]

Beckett's increasing disquiet about the notion of the 'form itself' is self-evident on reading *Watt*, which consciously seeks to counter the 'domination of chance by narrative' that, as discussed, can be said to constitute no small part of the novelistic form throughout its history.[15] It is this primacy of Beckett's formal experimentation with novelistic causality that I take to be at the heart of the novel, and which forms the basis of my reading of *Watt*.

Watt extends and deepens the themes that had appeared in *Murphy*. Watt, the protagonist of *Watt*, is further removed from reality than Murphy. They share a solipsistic, essentially inactive view of the world, but this impulse, leavened by wit in *Murphy*, is exposed as a kind of nihilism in *Watt*. We meet Watt on his way to the house of a Mr. Knott, whose servant he is to become. Various misunderstandings and exploitations of him occur, largely to his bafflement. We get the sense of someone to whom things happen as misadventure and bad luck, and for whom events have obscure and murky causes. He offers himself up to work at the house without telling the reader why he is asked to or would want to, and does what he is told unquestioningly. Other than the plot's basic refusal to interrogate reasons for characters' choices or those for the inscrutable, 'imprevisible' (one of Beckett's favourite words) happenings in the novel, we can see a similar preoccupation with ideas of chance and possibility on both a narrative and a linguistic level. A chance event is 'a trifle and in all probability tractable obstruction' – that is, if it exists at all: 'as chance would have it, or some other agency'. The possibility of 'some other agency', though, is playfully dismissed: 'But that little was enough, for Watt the possibility was enough, that something other than he, in this box, was not intrinsic to its limits' (Beckett, 1976, p. 196). Uncertainty, in fact, is the primary mode of Watt's existence: 'his progress, though painful, and uncertain, was less painful, less uncertain, than he had apprehended, when he set out' (ibid., p. 234), and 'all he desired was to have his uncertainty removed' (ibid., p. 225). Furthermore, much of the novel is taken up with long lists of possible happenings, or 'demented pondering', to borrow a phrase from Alvarez's incisive anti-*Watt* critique (Alvarez, 1973, p. 45). The narrative, seemingly never-endingly, runs through every scenario that may form the outcome of any, usually banal, day-to-day event in Watt's life. After these lists of the mathematically figured, minutely altered calculations, which resemble the workings out of an equation, all we are left with is usually a bathetic, inconclusive result: 'it seems probable she was not' (Beckett, 1976, p. 138).

The prose itself in these cases can be seen to represent an understanding of the world as specifically contingent, and at every turn expresses a fraught relationship between this arbitrary, unpredictable reality and the confines of narrative. If every possible outcome is listed, then perhaps chance will be extinguished; or, in other words, perhaps the unpredictable will be predicted. The language is uncertain, digressive and attempts to cover every possibility: 'the possibility, if not the probability, is not excluded of our finding two or less than two or even more than two men or women or men and women as little bony and so on as fat and so forth eternally turning' (ibid., p. 60). Beckett is unwilling to allow his prose to take the easy route of providing 'the illusion of fixity' (ibid., p. 222), of stating that something is a particular way because something else made it so, and in this unwillingness we can see an implicit critique of the easy lies upon which fiction so often relies. Fixity is an illusion, and yet narrative 'fixes' reality. There should be no conclusions to be drawn about life, *Watt* insists, because all is uncertain, and all is up for grabs. It is these anxieties that I would like to suggest are encoded in the very sentence structure of the novel.

> . . . and Dick's ten years on the first-floor are not *because of* Harry's ten years on the ground-floor, or of the other's coming then, and Harry's ten years on the ground-floor are not *because of* Dick's ten years on the first-floor, or of the other's coming then, and the other's coming then is not *because of* (tired of underlining this cursed preposition) Dick's ten years on the first-floor, or of Harry's ten years on the ground-floor, no, that would be too horrible to contemplate, but Tom's two years on the first-floor, and Dick's two years on the ground-floor, and Harry's coming then, and Dick's ten years on the first-floor, and Harry's ten years on the ground-floor, and the other's coming then, are because Tom is Tom, and Dick Dick, and Harry Harry, and that other that other, of that the wretched Watt was persuaded. (ibid., p. 132)

The 'cursed preposition' he is tired of underlining, the fact that one event is not '*because of*' another, is once again a refutation of the efficacy of cause and effect in the novel, and, indeed, a similarly damning refutation of causal explanations for the linkages between events in real life. So, are we supposed to accept that each action and event is unrelated, and yet is accorded identical narrative weight, worthy of equal and passive reportage? Things are as they are, we are told, simply because 'Tom is Tom, and Dick Dick, and Harry Harry'. So will individuals always reject a rigid psychological or causal determinism, one that would seek to explain away their actions? And if things exist as they are because 'Tom is Tom', does that not imply that Tom is determined through his nature to act as he does, thus ambiguously embracing that very determinism?

These sorts of inconclusive formulations, typical of the novel, are distinguished by a prose that stumbles and retraces its steps at every turn. It goes round and round a subject with miniscule alterations, until every possibility, even of linguistic or semantic difference, has been stymied. Alvarez has noted:

> There are 250 pages of this pausing, devious, repetitive withdrawal from statement, 250 pages of qualification after qualification, a hesitant, slightly hiccuping timidity masquerading as precision. . . . It is like a squirrel running around his treadmill: an enormous expenditure of prose in order to say more or less nothing and go more or less nowhere; an expense of spirit in a waste of mannerism. (Alvarez, 1973, p. 43)

The idea that the autistic precision of Watt's perception of possibility is in fact 'timidity' is, I think, correct. As Richardson has said of Moran from *Molloy*:

> He is a willing component of that well-ordered system that is an integral part of a larger (though ultimately irrational) totality. When narrating, he displays an almost neurotic obsession with probabilistic thinking and causal explanation as he seeks to fit every element into a cohesive teleological order in which each cause unproblematically produces its intended and appropriate effect. (Richardson, 1992, p. 67)

The failure of cause and effect to gel so 'unproblematically' is thus what produces this uneasy, and we might say, obsessional (Alvarez calls it 'psychotic') obsession with cataloguing and categorizing reality, in this case, a description of a picture hanging on the wall consisting of a point and a circle:

> Watt wondered how long it would be before the point and the circle entered together upon the same plane. Or had they not done so already, or almost? And was it not rather the circle that was in the background, and the point that was in the foreground? Watt wondered if they had sighted each other, or were blindly flying thus, harried by some force of mechanical mutual attraction, or the playthings of chance. He wondered if they would eventually pause and converse, and perhaps even mingle, or keep steadfast on their ways, like ships in the night, prior to the invention of wireless telegraphy. Who knows, they might even collide. And he wondered what the artist had intended to represent (Watt knew nothing about painting), a circle and its centre in search of each other, or a circle and its centre in search of a centre and a circle respectively, or a circle and its centre in search of its centre and a circle respectively, or a circle and its centre in search of a centre and its circle respectively. (Beckett, 1976, p. 126)

And so on. The frequent, yet always funny, application of Beckett's bathetic wit here ('prior to the invention of wireless telepathy') is perhaps the reader's reward for trudging through these lists (which appear on almost every page of the novel) as is the presence of beautifully arresting images such as: 'blindly flying thus, harried by some force of mutual attraction, or the playthings of chance'. The personification of the circle and the point thus sees them figured as an allegory of man's position in relation to forces beyond our understanding. Their blindness to the root causes of their situation remains the same whether they are blind to some force of 'mechanical mutual attraction' or to the fact that their relationship to chance mirrors that of a fly to a wanton boy. We all, Beckett seems to imply, are similarly blind to the causes of our situation, and the ensuing pathos is both deeply felt and ironic.

Watt's neuroses, and the style of the prose that reflects them, are both reminiscent of the desire that Richardson identifies in Moran in *Molloy* – 'there is a frantic urge to eliminate the random and deprecate the inexplicable' (Richardson, 1992, p. 67). Alvarez notes the same impulse in *Watt*:

> He reacts to the mild occasions of his life like someone whose inner world is so terrifying that to contain it he must account in advance for every possible eventuality, like a man who can keep his demons out by blocking every chink in the floorboards. . . . More simply, Watt's demented pondering is a defence against the dangerous unpredictability of life. (Alvarez, 1973, p. 45)

Alvarez approvingly cites Hugh Kenner's description of the 'deliberate witty pedantry' of Beckett's style (ibid., p. 36). I would like to suggest that, as Alvarez states, this narrative obsession with possibility in *Watt* is intimately connected to an anxiety about unpredictability, and that the ensuing style has a deeper internal coherence and logic than most previous critics have argued. They have diagnosed the style, but have not seriously looked at the possibility that it represents a formal engagement with the same ideas that *Watt* examines thematically: namely, possibility and contingency.

The prose, it is important to note, while unarguably repetitive and mechanical, is nevertheless also firmly suggestive here of a kind of joyful linguistic inclusivity – no possibility ('two or less than two or even more than two . . .') is ever shut down, which not only leads to an *impasse* in the normal order of cause and effect, but also to an exponential increase in irrationality between one thing and another: there is, we could say, a cause, and then infinite possible effects. This dislocation of cause and effect in Beckett's writing leads to obfuscation, necessarily; to the unexpected and poetic beauty of surprising and illogical correspondences; and also to a – wilful, certainly – embracing and celebration of the contingent, the pointless and the exhilaratingly voluble. To rule nothing out is not, Beckett sometimes seems to suggest, to let any old thing in – it is to allow possibility its fullest rein.

As Hesla points out:

> [*Watt*] is Samuel Beckett's version of the human experience which
> Jean-Paul Sartre in *Nausea* and Albert Camus in *Le Mythe de Sisyphe* defined
> as the sense of the absurd. Existence off the ladder is Beckett's phrase for
> what Sartre calls 'contingency' and what Camus describes as life after the
> 'stage sets collapse'. (Hesla, 1971, pp. 83–4)

Existential absurdity thus appears as an ally of chance, of the uncertain and
of possibility. It also stands as the existential revelation that accompanies
the realization that the universe is meaningless, or, that we live in a world
ruled by chance. Yet again we can see that although existential conceptions
of possibility are unlikely to have influenced Beckett directly, we can nevertheless trace a literary and philosophical confluence of ideas: namely
Beckett's belief, as expressed in *Watt*, that possibility need not – indeed,
perhaps, cannot – be allowed to equal an easy and fallacious optimism.
Beckett overtly links the idea of absurdity to necessity, and expends a little
energy wringing it dry:

> But he had hardly felt the absurdity of those things, on the one hand, and
> the necessity of those others, on the other (it is rare that the feeling of
> absurdity is not followed by the feeling of necessity), when he felt the
> absurdity of those things of which he had just felt the necessity (for it is
> rare that the feeling of necessity is not followed by the feeling of absur-
> dity). (Beckett, 1976, p. 131)

The frustrating ability of the prose to examine every possibility, while shying away from anything approaching an interpretation or judgement on
the list that has gone before, is overt here: is absurdity, as we would perhaps imagine it to be, opposed to necessity, or are they aligned? Beckett is
equivocal. Edith Kern seems to suggest that the existential revelation of
absurdity is simultaneous with the revelation of freedom. She notes a
moment where Arsene has a momentary 'sensation of being both free
intelligence and contingency'. She comments: 'what happens to Arsene is
a realisation of the universe's being there . . . in its purposelessness and
total disregard for the logic to which man wants to reduce it' (Kern, 1970,
p. 187). This absurdity provides a further narrative reason for the minute
descriptive precision, and the paralysis of Watt's decision-making facility,
as he futilely tries to tether himself to the objective reality of any given
situation.

Further evidence of the meaninglessness of the novelistic universe in which Watt is operating comes from the mindless violence in which Watt and Sam (a character who may or may not exist inside Watt's mind, and may or may not be a narrative manifestation of Samuel Beckett) engage enthusiastically. After they have forced a rat to eat its own offspring, we are told: 'it was on these occasions, we agreed, after an exchange of views, that we came nearest to God' (Beckett, 1976, p. 170). In the essay 'Situation of the Writer in 1947' Sartre says 'they [French writers of the earlier generation] were all fascinated with violence, wherever it might come from; it was by violence that they wanted to free man from his human condition' (Sartre, 1950, p. 145). He returns to the chance / violence relationship in *Notebooks for an Ethics*:

> . . . all violence, beginning where force leaves off, implies a certain confidence in chance (taken as unknown laws). If I hammer harder and harder on a nail, there is no violence. But a moment arrives when I am no longer in control of my gestures. At this moment, I count on statistics: twenty blows of the hammer will fall somewhere by chance, but one will come that will strike the nail. I do not count on what is known but on what is unknown, there is *hope* in violence and *certitude* in a lawful operation. Recourse to magic. (Sartre, 1992, pp. 171–2)

As we saw in Chapter One, the link between danger and chance is, and always has been, overt. We are reminded of Kavanagh's observation that,

> . . . there is, consciously or unconsciously, a link between any meditation on chance, the less than certain, and the gamble of death. The truly fortuitous event, the event outside any causal chain through which we might control it represents an unacceptable scandal in the same way that the reality of our own death, the ultimate unthinkability of that death, is antithetical to any true living of life. (Kavanagh, 1993, p. 27)

This link between death or despair and possibility, mirrored in the existentialist ideas, is present in Watt's paradoxical statement that he was closest to God while committing acts of violence, and is key to my argument. In the insistent refusal of the text to let the linguistic inclusivity brought about by its attempt to represent possibility equal hope, Beckett ironizes the easy association of possibility with optimism. As we are told overtly, Watt 'abandoned all hope . . . while continuing to believe in the possibility' (Beckett, 1976, p. 45).

The need for an engagement with the idea of possibility and chance, in all of its aspects, is perhaps the primary underlying structural motivation for the peculiarities of Beckett's prose in *Watt*. There is a parallel, and related, neurosis about language in *Watt*, one related, as Edith Kern notes, to the presence of class in *Watt*: 'certainty prevails only among the "they": the Hacketts and the Lady McCanns' (ibid., p. 90). It seems that certainty about language, too, is a privilege available only to those for whom every choice is not agony: 'The realisation of the purposelessness and absurdity of the universe turns the certainties . . . into inanities. It affects the value given to facts, their explanation, and their expression' (Kern, 1970, p. 189). This suspicion of certainty and purpose extends to Watt's apprehension of language:

> Looking at a pot, for example, or thinking of a pot, at one of Mr. Knott's pots, of one of Mr. Knott's pots, it was in vain that Watt said Pot, pot. Well, perhaps not quite in vain, but very nearly. For it was not a pot, the more he looked, the more he reflected, the more he felt sure of that, that it was not a pot at all . . . he could always hope, of a thing of which he had never known the name, that he would learn the name, some day, and so be tranquilised. But he could not look forward to this in the case of a thing of which the true name had ceased, suddenly, or gradually, to be the true name for Watt. For the pot remained a pot, Watt felt sure of that, for everyone but Watt. For Watt alone it was not a pot, any more. (Beckett, 1976, p. 78)

This inability to call a pot a pot, here, is still extraordinarily disquieting.[16] Is reality, here, becoming arbitrary, or is it merely a disjunction between reality and the linguistic tools we have to describe it? Beckett had met Axel Kaun in 1937 and, under his influence, decided that rationalism was 'the last form of animism' and that chaos was a preferable alternative. Beckett wanted an assault against words, and specifically against the English language,[17] as they were getting in the way of what he wanted to say: 'It is indeed becoming more and more difficult, even senseless, for me to write an official English. And more and more my own language appears to me like a veil that must be torn apart in order to get at the things (or the Nothingness) behind it' (Pilling, 1997, p. 153). The dislocation of things and their names experienced by Watt amounts to a randomizing of perception, and reminds one of Sartre's protagonist Roquentin in *Nausea*, who says to himself, '"It's a seat," a little like an exorcism', but the word fails to do its job of naming the object: 'it refuses to go and put itself on the thing'.

The seat, he finds, 'called a seat . . . is not a seat. It could just as well be a dead donkey, tossed about in the water' (Sartre, 1965, p. 169). This is the terrifying obverse to the cool rationality associated with chance in its early-twentieth-century incarnation, that of the arbiter of a statistically ordered universe. If we can talk about chance in terms of probability then we have effected the taming of chance. Beckett's profound anguish at the excruciating arbitrariness of his character's relationship with language, in contrast, reveals a keen awareness of the old sense of chance as a lack of knowledge, and of the original Greek idea of the chaos that existed before the world came into being.[18] Experience, for Beckett, is now analogous to this terrifying sense of anarchy, of words and meanings cut free from their age-old tethers. Chance, here, is the enemy of meaning.[19]

In the middle of one of his many streams of consciousness, Watt says:

> And if I could begin it all over again, knowing what I know now, the result would be the same. And if I could begin again a third time, knowing what I would know then, the result would be the same. And if I could begin it all over again a hundred times, knowing each time a little more than the time before, the result would always be the same, and the hundredth life as the first, and the hundred lives as one. A cat's flux. (Beckett, 1976, p. 46)

Chance, and therefore possibility, is here marginalized, impotent. Nothing will ever happen that is not already laid out for us. This is, however, not a hopeful meaningfulness, one adjacent to ideas of destiny and purpose – there doesn't seem to be anyone to lay them out – but rather, a hellish vision of, and version of, a Nietzschean eternal return: 'a cat's flux'. Where chance's operation is thus curtailed, but not replaced by ideas of hope, purpose or religious meaning, we see a stasis in human endeavour: what is the point of existence if, by the force of your will, you cannot effect change on your surroundings? Beckett's concern with possibility and contingency has become embedded in the sentences themselves. *Watt* doesn't have to be about chance; by its very being it demonstrates at every turn a neurosis or anxiety about chance's very existence. In *Watt*, the narrative doesn't move towards anything so much as circuit itself, and, by doing so, erases the very possibilities it has so carefully and minutely built up. Buttner, one of Beckett's best critics, concluded that 'In face of the emptiness and spiritual aridity of existence, hope is always kept alive in Beckett's characters' (Buttner, 1984, pp. 151–2). But it is this very assumption, the easy linkage between possibility and hope, that I hope I have shown to be fallacious.

Leland Monk argues that Joyce's *Ulysses* marks the cut-off point of chance's representation in literature because it 'rejoices in things that happen by chance' and the resulting 'undecidability of pleasure' that is celebrated is an aesthetic that has:

> . . . a certain *pleasure*, the expression of a capricious whim, a vagary that is erratic and unmotivated. . . . It is finally undecidable whether such a 'throw beyond' is the function of a pleasure that transgresses the authorial will or the function of a will that legislates its own pleasures. (Monk, 1993, pp. 151–2)

Beckett throughout his career distanced himself from Joyce's very 'authorial will' ('He's tending toward omniscience and omnipotence as an artist. I'm working with impotence, ignorance' (Shenker, 1956, p. 1)), and on the topic of chance this was no different. Joyce's elaboration of chance as the 'undecidability of pleasure' has perhaps become, under Beckett, reversed. Thomas Kavanagh has depicted the history of chance's relationship with literature as follows:

> [a]gainst a vision of the world as a potentially finite series of knowable and ultimately controllable determinisms, chance implied a resolutely tragic vision. To recognize chance was, more than anything else, to recognize our inability to reason toward and become part of any natural order. (Kavanagh, 1993, p. 4)

Chance as a 'resolutely tragic vision' is the chance of the universe of Beckett's novels, peopled by those with an 'inability to reason toward and to become part of any natural order': of Murphy rocking himself to death to achieve some sort of freedom, and of Watt obsessively categorizing reality until it barely exists other than in a series of equally meaningless options. Chance is not a Joycean *voluptas*, an eroticized undecidability, but a painful taxonomy of being. What should be an image of exhilarating volubility, of fulfilment of possibility, of filling up life to its very seams, turns out to be the reverse. If every possibility is mooted, it is simultaneously stymied. The exploration of possibility, then, becomes its death, cancelling itself as it reproduces. When we hold *Watt* in our minds as a coherent achievement, we see possibilities expanding exponentially like dividing bacterium; but in a stark echo of the times, it has become an image not of hope, but one of panic.

Coda: *Lessness*

The final Beckettian fiction that I would like to look at is *Lessness* (1969), a long short story or prose poem from later on in Beckett's literary career, which in a minor way serves to consolidate my reading of *Watt*, while linking Beckett's experimental treatment of narrative chance to the 1960s genera- tion of aleatorical artists and writers that will form the subject of my next chapter. Like the Dadaist experiments of fifty years earlier, *Lessness* experi- ments with how chance could be incorporated into the form of the work, perhaps as a tentative, if not entirely successful, attempt to rid his fiction of the dreaded teleological predictability and therefore induce a 'purity of the will' of his own. Seemingly influenced by Dada, *Lessness* incorporated chance into the very fabric of its constitution. The important distinction here is that the constitutive parts were written phrases by Beckett (or 'image clusters'), and chance was left to dictate new and un-hoped-for or imagined associative links between them, unexpected interactions and correspon- dences unforeseen. Susan Brienza and Enoch Brater, in their 1976 paper 'Chance and Choice in Beckett's *Lessness*', defend the work from this seem- ing influence of Dadaism. The clear distinction, they point out, between the nihilism of those experiments and *Lessness* is the use of authorial choice: chance's role is reduced to deciding what goes where, but the 'what' is all Beckett's. Brienza and Brater describe this method:

> Writing his 60 sentences in six categories, Beckett had each grouping cen- tre on the following images: 1) the ruins as the 'true refuge'; 2) the endless grey of earth and sky; 3) the little body; 4) the space 'all gone from mind'; 5) past tenses combined with 'never'; 6) future tenses of active verbs and the 'figment' sentence about dawn and dusk. He then composed units of repetitive melody within each category. He wrote each of the sixty sen- tences on a separate piece of paper, mixed them in a container, and then drew them out in random order twice: the resulting sequence became the 120 sentences. Beckett then wrote the number 3 on four separate pieces of paper, the number 4 on six pieces, the number 5 on four pieces, the num- ber 6 on six pieces, and finally the number 7 on four pieces. Again drawing randomly, he ordered the units into sentence blocks according to the number drawn, finally making 120. (Brienza and Brater, 1976, pp. 245–6)

They then go on to argue that although the ultimate arrangement of sentences is left to chance, it is not chance, but Beckett, who has chosen what the words and phrases will be. This emphasis is undoubtedly right, although the distinction between the Dada experiments, which in fact used varying measures of aleatorical composition, and were rarely conducted without any selection at all, and the minutely controlled and controlling *Lessness* is perhaps overstated. Nevertheless, speculation on the exact division of labour of the authorial decision-making process between Beckett and chance, is not, as I see it, the main point of *Lessness.*

The story is in fact remarkably unified in purpose and effect, and as a formal and structural experiment it is at one with its lyrical and thematic content. The cumulative effect of the text is deadening: while it feels like a comprehensive exploration of poetic and imaginative possibility, with each combination of words and phrases being given full rein and expression, it ultimately returns no sense of hope to the reader. The repetition forces the reader to confront the meaning of the phrases, but then because of its cyclical nature it nullifies hope for a progression of thought, or hope of an escape. As the circularity of the repetition decreases, the 'Lessness' of the title seems redolent of a poetic prediction of the reader's experience, that of ever-diminishing returns.

This deadening effect is reflected in the subject matter. Beckett describes the 'lessness' of a being who is less than alive because he was still-born: 'Blacked out fallen open four walls over backwards true refuge issueless' (Beckett, 1984, p. 255). This might well serve to remind us of the ever-present link between chance and mortality, since our original prospects and chances of life at all, *Lessness* insists, are bleak. This acute sensitivity to the divorce between possibility and hope, and the overt parallels with Sartre's discourses on being and non-being is instructive. We are reminded of Roquentin's stark confrontation of the logical extension of a world governed by chance in *Nausea*: 'Every existent is born without reason, prolongs itself out of weakness and dies by chance' (Sartre, 1965, p. 191). Which, in turn, reminds us of one of Sartre's definitions of possibility in *Being and Nothingness*, where he calls it 'a sort of geometrical place for unfulfilled projects, all inexact representations, all vanished beings or those of which the idea is only a fiction' (Sartre, 2002, p. 19). The 'vanished beings' here, though, bring to mind not ghosts of the newly war dead, but grief for those who never were, for whom existence was only ever an 'idea' or 'a fiction'.[20] *Lessness*, then, as an experimental piece of short fiction, is less interesting perhaps for its limited formal use of the principles of chance, and rather more so for its ever greater radical disengagement with the idea of meaningful possibility.

Chapter Four

'Let's Celebrate the Accidental': B. S. Johnson, the Aleatory and the Radical Generation

Well, the grand thing about the human mind is that it can turn its own tables and see meaninglessness as the ultimate meaning. . . . Let us say Yes to our presence together in Chaos.

John Cage

Karl Miller, in a 1968 summation of the literary landscape of the 1950s and 1960s, concluded that the period had not been a fertile era for literary experimentation:

> That the search for new form hasn't prospered in Britain lately is not very alarming: a great deal of the new form that *has* been found, here and elsewhere, is an illusion (William Burroughs' collage technique, for example), and the original abstention from experiment strikes me as having been both comprehensible and rewarding. (Miller, 1968, p. 26)

In retrospect, Miller's judgement looks a little pre-emptory. In fact, rather than being a period characterized by 'abstention from experiment', the period under scrutiny in this chapter, from the mid-1950s up until the end of the 1960s, saw writers and artists return to the avant-garde, obscurantist and experimental aspects of early twentieth-century modernism (especially Dada), that had been in retreat in the 1940s and early 1950s.[1] Once again, formal fragmentation was being celebrated for its ability both to undermine the authority of texts, and to cast doubt on the very idea of the text as pronouncement from a god-type figure. The innovation, too, that had characterized aspects of high modernism, was back: as Stuart Laing has commented, this was an era in which 'Joyce was allowed to come down from the bookshelves' (Laing, 1983, p. 251). In fact, as we get further away from the 1950s and 1960s, it seems a period particularly characterized by an awareness of the possibilities of new forms, and a desire to move away from the conservatism that had distinguished the art of the immediate post-war era.

One tendency that seems retrospectively characteristic of the period, and one that is closely related to the impulse to experiment, is a preoccupation with the aleatory. A fascination with chance and randomness was now endemic across the artistic disciplines, and emerged as both a thematic and formal concern in as diverse areas as the visual arts, poetry, the novel and music. Bernard Bergonzi's observation, made in 1970, was typical: 'I have become discontented with the customary academic notion of the novel as a complex but essentially self-contained form, cut off from the untidiness and the discontinuities of the world outside' (Bergonzi, 1970, p. 7). Once again the constant motion and unpredictable, senseless bustle of life is seen as being impossible to re-create on the page: it resists order, and is, at base, unplottable. The incomprehensibility of chance, its refusal to be subsumed into the ordered world of art, is the aspect of our understanding of chance that became firmly entrenched during the period. Consequently, in this chapter I will argue that pure chance can rarely be fully present in narrative, and that the combination of the two, when it is attempted, is combustible and potentially destructive. I define pure chance, as outlined at the beginning of the book, as chance that plays a part in the procedures that determine the composition of the work of art, either through arrangement or selection, or (in terms of the novel) by letting the reader decide the order in which elements of the text will be read. This is the only way that chance can operate in narrative as it does in life – other representations are necessarily subsumed into narrative determinism, for reasons previously discussed. This definition necessarily entails a mingling of the arbitrary with the creative process itself, whether in fiction, music or visual art: formal intervention is the only way that chance can be fully present. This randomness does not signal a meaning that we are merely unable to grasp, nor the significant coincidences familiar to us from the nineteenth-century novel; it is not the chance-as-mysticism which so often prevailed in modernist literature, nor probability as 'statistical fatalism': it is randomness that has no meaning other than that which we futilely try to assign to it, and which in fact problematizes the idea of meaning altogether. Once this randomness is introduced as a collaborator it joyfully and anarchically denies the supreme power of the author, and thereby subverts and complicates the idea of 'art' altogether.

Chance, for many artists in the 1960s, in this way became a means of forging an artistic identity that was concerned with freedom and possibility away from the constraints of form; as such, it undermined the very idea of a possible coherent artistic identity. To embrace chance is to commit to those very subversive capabilities that eventually lead to the failure of its representation. To what degree shades of individuality and identity affect the work of art in conjunction with chance, or even are amplified by them, is a moot point, but not necessarily a problematic one; as we will see, the elision of chance and choice is in part what invigorates the artwork, and, as in the novels of B. S. Johnson, there is a significant degree of interplay between individual artistic authorial choice and the submission to absolute unpredictability.

The post-war representation of chance elsewhere had, as I have shown, so far presented itself in diverse and sometimes oblique ways. Writers still, for the most part, engaged with chance as a thematic or philosophical concern, albeit one that was starting to nag at the confining and stultifying effects of Bergonzi's 'essentially self-contained form' that had consistently failed to accommodate it. As we saw with Beckett, an examination of novelistic possibility therefore necessarily affected the very sentences that attempted to describe it: a proper engagement with chance, I have argued throughout this book, always bodies forth formal or structural implications. So in the work of Henry Green, an apparently conservative novelist of the pre- and immediately post-war era, the thematic engagement with chance, which amounted to a delineation of what it is to live under the rigours of randomness, through a depiction of characters living under a fog of uncertainty while statistical bombs wended their way towards them through the limiting strictures of probability, eventually seeped into a post-existential and finally self-defeating preoccupation with a desire to free the novel's characters from the control of their creator. After his expansive masterpieces of the 1940s, he increasingly, and, eventually, solely relied on dialogue as a means of recording, without explaining, his characters.

Rudolph Arnheim, in his essay 'Accident and Necessity in Art', has linked chance, when dealt with as subject matter, to the growth of realism:

Accident always refers to relation, and when we call a relationship accidental, we express our belief that it did not come through a direct cause and effect connection between the parties concerned. The stylized Byzantine features are more closely controlled by the primary concept of man than is the Rembrandt figure, which shows the intrusion of extraneous, individual encounters. The difference may be expressed also in the language of the statistician by saying that with increased realism, the solution offered by the artist becomes a less probable one. (Arnheim, 1972, p. 167)

Arnheim's analysis, then, suggests that the inclusion of accidental relation-ships in the representation of a scene enhances realism, just as unlikeli-hood enhances the ability of art to convince. Similarly, Harriet Watts, in her book on chance and Dada, notes that in art accidental relations are often depicted by means of the crowd scene – again, emphasizing that where the pictorial emphasis is on the accidental nature of how the elements of the artwork have been drawn together, there exists a greater realism than in a more stylized, over-determined composition (Watts, 1975, p. 2). As noted in my first chapter, David Trotter has made a similar argument about crowd scenes in his book on nineteenth-century art and literature, *Cooking With Mud*. An increasing amount of chance-as-subject-matter in the novels of the writers I have studied can also be linked to a particular strand of realism that was in the ascendant – one that sought to represent life with a minimal amount of authorial intervention. This is certainly true of Green, and it is also true of the novels of B. S. Johnson. My contention is that, eventually, chance-as-subject-matter inevitably bursts through the inbuilt limitations of its own representation and engages directly with the form of the work, as a serious engagement with chance must confront the paradoxical nature of its representation in a determined form. The formal engagement of alea-torically experimental fiction is therefore an oblique commentary on chance's uniquely uncomfortable relationship to the literary forms that seek to contain it – experimentation is, and has been all along, the logical conclusion of chance-as-subject matter. This formal engagement with what I have throughout termed 'pure' chance is, I suggest, a direct response to the specific challenge mounted by the incompatibility of chance with narrative.[2]

This chapter seeks to contextualize the interplay between the avant-garde and chance in the cultural history of the late 1950s and 1960s, and then to analyse as a case study the British novelist who perhaps engaged most seri-ously with the ramifications of pure chance and its compository potential – B. S. Johnson. The chapter will examine the extent to which the art and literature of the period radically undermined the notion that, as Bernard Bergonzi had it, 'Art must essentially be the impression of form on flux' (Bergonzi, 1970, p. 210), and, rather, strengthened an alternative vision of post-war literature. Helmut Heissenbuttel encapsulated this alternative view of the relation between literature and chance, or between the form and the flux, when he commented that: 'Chance is a favourite weapon of the twen-tieth century against the seduction to always the same kind of sentences' (cited in Watts, 1975, p. 3).

Chance in the Literature of the 1950s and 1960s

The notion that chance was the dominant mode of the era, as the disperser or destroyer of the attraction to 'always the same kind of sentences' meant that, by implication, chance was the key to the increasing predominance of formal experimentation. This experimentation manifested itself as a reinvigorated awareness of other cultures: as Stuart Laing notes, during the 1960s there existed 'a new openness to European and American influences, a reawakened interest in novels' formal properties' (Laing, 1983, p. 252). As such this section is a necessarily incomplete attempt to convey the astonishing breadth of engagement with ideas concerning chance among writers of the period, and an attempt to show that this specific engagement often took the shape of an anxiety about how best to represent the random in an essentially non-random form. The American post-war generation of novelists were, in the 1960s, beginning to reach the peak of their powers: Pynchon, Vonnegut, Barth, Bellow; but there remained, equally, a strain of literature in Britain and Ireland more concerned with the continental legacy of Existentialism and with an anxiety about how this should be translated into a formal questioning of the determinism that a novelistic structure requires. Emblematic of this was Beckett's assertion, quoted above, that: 'To find a form that accommodates the mess, that is the task of the artist now' (Driver, 1961, p. 23).

The explosion of aleatorical art in the 1950s and 1960s constituted a mass, almost collective attempt to find a form that would 'accommodate the mess'. B. S. Johnson – who used this specific quote from Beckett to justify his radical and indeed notorious 'novel in a box', *The Unfortunates* (1969) – was perhaps typical in this sense. Almost certainly influenced both by Dada, and by the French writer Marc Saporta's 1963 experiment with random order (but with pages rather than chapters) *Numero 1*, as well as by Samuel Beckett who was at this point writing in French, Johnson's major work was a hybrid of continental and early twentieth-century influences. Alan Burn's 'cut-up' compository innovation in *Babel*, also of 1969, bore a close relation to William Burroughs' similar 'cut-ups' in America in the early 1960s, where sections of prose were dismembered and reassembled to re-create better the randomness and fragmentation of perception. As Burroughs describes the method in terms of its relation to art:

Now montage is actually closer to the facts of perception than representational painting. Take a walk down a city street and put down what you have just seen down on canvas. You have seen half a person cut in two by a car, bits and pieces of street signs and advertisements, reflections from shop windows – a montage of fragments. . . . Writing is still confined in the sequential representational straitjacket of the novel, a form as arbitrary as the sonnet and as far removed from the actual facts of human perception and consciousness as that fifteenth-century poetical form. Consciousness *is* a cut up. Every time you walk down the street or look out the window, your stream of consciousness is cut by random factors. (Burroughs, 1986, p. 61)

As Douglas Patey has argued, formal fragmentation need not impinge on the reader's ability to make sense of the whole. He comments that 'the individual episode may as reading paradigm of penetration embody all the patterns of signification of the longer work in which it appears, itself and associative sequence of episodes. Each episode stands in relation rather of synecdoche rather than metonymy to the work in which it appears' (Patey, 1984, p. 246). Patey quotes Isaac D'Israeli as saying, in an oddly close echo of Henry Green, 'A well-chosen anecdote frequently reveals a character, more happily than an elaborate delineation; as a glance of lightning will sometimes discover what had escaped us in a full light' (ibid., p. 247). Bernard Bergonzi has expressed the contrasting, sceptical view of the use of cut-ups to induce an experience of randomness, which he described as 'the desperate expedient of William Burroughs' "fold-in" technique, an attempt to achieve by random means . . . atemporality' (Bergonzi, 1970, p. 27). In fact a great deal of aleatory art is still dismissed by critics today, even by theorists of chance. Leland Monk notes the examples of Julio Cortázar's *Hopscotch* (1966), William Burroughs' cut-ups and Chance the gardener in Jerzy Kosinski's *Being There* (1970), but goes on to comment that:

[i]ncorporating chance elements into the creative activity certainly problematizes the agency and intentionality of the creator; it does so, however, by the imposition of another kind of narrative, the story of the work as process. The music or the text that is composed on aleatory principles does not anymore represent chance simply because it is the result of chance. (Monk, 1993, p. 147)

I suspect that it does. If narrative itself is what has elided chance with fate, then narrative's disruption is subversive of that suppression. The alternative 'kind of narrative', the story of the 'work as process', quite simply does not fulfil the same function as teleological narrative. As such, in terms of the representation of chance, it does not pose the same manner of problem. There are, nevertheless, other kinds of problems which it does pose – namely, how to combine aleatorical methods or structural elements with the universal need for a coherent narrative?

Doris Lessing's *The Golden Notebook* (1962) achieves a tension between form and order by allowing the 'chaos' in her protagonist's life to dictate the terms of its own arrangement. Anna Wulf writes her life into four separate notebooks, each of which has a different purpose and which together make up the meta-narrative of *The Golden Notebook*. The function of the notebooks is explicitly described by Wulf, Lessing's protagonist, as a means of controlling the unpredictable and chaotic nature of reality. When asked what is in her notebooks, Anna's reply is succinct: "'Why the four notebooks? What would happen if you had one big book without all those divisions and brackets and special writing." "I've told you, chaos"' (Lessing, 1962, p. 272). This ordering of experience into artificial categories is, we are led to conclude, a method of dissembling, of avoiding reality. As Earnshaw notes, Anna 'needs to compartmentalize facets of her life into manageable portions to provide some sort of order, and thus avoid her own disintegration' (Earnshaw, 2000, p. 58). Tom, her best friend's teenaged son, points out to Anna: "'If things are a chaos, then that's what they are. I don't think there's a pattern anywhere – you are just making patterns, out of cowardice"' (Lessing, 1962, p. 273). This chaos that must be so carefully calibrated by Anna is perhaps a product of her wartime experiences, which seem to induce visions of infinite hazard, and yet also of freedom, in a passage that could be a direct echo of Henry Green's description of the war in *Caught*: 'And the intoxication, as I knew even then, was the recklessness of infinite possibility, of danger, the secret ugly frightening pulse of war itself, of the death we all wanted, for each other and for ourselves' (ibid., p. 163). Neil Nehring has noted the prevalence of this anxiety about freedom in post-war literature, citing examples from Anthony Burgess and Kingsley Amis. In *The Right to an Answer* (1960), Burgess's Denham makes the point more pessimistically, from an entrenched and fearful conservative position: 'the post-war English mess . . . that's made by having too much freedom . . . the great democratic mess in which there's no hierarchy, no scale of values, everything's as good – and therefore as bad – as everything else.' This can be seen as an appeal against the anarchic, redistributive powers of chance, where wealth and advantage was no longer predetermined but allocated haphazardly, and a hankering after the comforts of social determinism. Amis, in *Lucky Jim* (1954), had declared that luck, that seemingly frivolous totem of a positive encounter with chance, was now, in fact, the only social force (Nehring, 1993, pp. 244, 190).

John Fowles's *The French Lieutenant's Woman* (1969) similarly addressed this very point through its inculcation of what Patricia Waugh calls the novel's 'doctrine of hazard' (Waugh, 1995, p. 75). Fowles uses mid-twentieth-century conceptions of existential freedom and chance to suggest that the decline of God in our society is a projection of a deeper human need to outgrow 'mystery', and the form of the novel echoes his prescriptive advocacy of a painful uncertainty as the path to freedom by having an alternate ending. This attempts to convey openness of outcome by mirroring the way we experience it. As such, *The French Lieutenant's Woman* represents one of the most literal-minded examples of the novels of the 1960s to deal with the determinism inherent in the idea of a plotted story, though not one without its own tensions. According to Patricia Waugh:

> The existentialist Fowles saw the need to repudiate God as an illusory projection of human desire for comfort and certainty. Only without such illusions may we embrace the painful condition of freedom which alone confers full human responsibility. . . . Appropriately, the novel is an existential labyrinth with no final *telos* or significance. . . . Fowles's ethical position, however, creates aesthetic difficulties. If your message is the goodness of mystery, contingency, and the need to avoid belief in redemptive orders, it would seem inconsistent to bow to an aesthetic requirement that moral paradoxes be resolved and hermeneutic endings neatly tied up. However the open-endedness of *The Magus* seems obfuscatory to a pointless degree. Fowles's non-doctrinaire doctrine of mystery creates an aesthetic and ethical abyss: in relativising every frame and position offered, it undermines even as it embodies the authority of its own ethics of hazard . . . (Waugh, 1995, p. 75)

This use of the fragmentary and contingent as a fig-leaf for a underlying order and meaning again serves to emphasize the tendency to connect randomness with its opposite, or as Beckett had it, as quoted above: the impulse that will 'try to say that the chaos is really something else', a tendency which, incidentally, will later find a potent scientific metaphor in Chaos Theory.

The critical landscape, for the most part, responded to some of the same philosophical and literary anxieties surrounding a retreat of order, hierarchy and the other comforts provided by the certainties of determinism. Raymond Williams, among others, argued for a democratization of culture based on its ordinariness, concentrating on The Movement – writers like Philip Larkin, Kingsley Amis and John Wain. According to Gary Day:

'The achievement of the Movement was to confer a sense of cultural worth on the ordinary things of life. The meaning of culture was no longer quite so strongly identified with the sort of "high" culture that was characteristic of Modernist art' (Day, 2000, p. 13). It was 'the expression of welfare capitalism' according to Day that instigated this 'ordinariness' (ibid.). The effect of this democratization on the idea of chance was two-fold, and contradictory. On the one hand, chance is the great democratizer – there is nothing more subversive of deterministic power structures. On the other hand, as Norbert Wiener interestingly notes, chance, when understood as probability, its democratic, rational form, can actually lessen the likelihood of new ideas: '[I]t is possible to interpret the information carried by the message as essentially the negative of its entropy, and the negative algorithm of its probability. That is, the more probable the message, the less information it gives. Clichés, for example, are less illuminating than great poems' (Wiener, 1954, p. 21).[3] And as Earnshaw points out, the avant-garde remained impervious to Williams's conception of democratization anyway: 'A number of writers continued this tradition [the modernists' avant-garde streak] in Britain. . . . However, as with the Dadaists and Surrealists, the more avowedly "experimental" writers produced work regardless of whether there was an audience for it or not' (Earnshaw, 2000, p. 63). Chance's split loyalties to two intertwined and almost inseparable impulses continued: to realism and to the aim of representing the fabric of life democratically and without selection on one hand; and the obscurantist avant-garde that denies those aspects of art that actually appeal to a mass audience – storytelling, form and order—on the other.

The prevalence of literature replete with chance, and with examinations of its implications, was thus wide-ranging. That this engagement with chance necessitates a movement towards aleatorical innovation is perhaps what signals its own failure – a truly random reading experience would very likely not be worth having, and chance will always be secondary to the demands of narrative. Nevertheless, and contrary to Leland Monk's view of the failure of aleatorical art in finally representing chance, the attempts to introduce aleatorical elements into the novel, poetry and art have achieved no small task: namely, the re-creation of the human experience of disorder and the unexpected. And is it not eventually, perhaps, a failure of the texture of *all* reality to be absorbed into its mimetic re-creation? W. H. Auden, in his essay 'The Poet and the City' (1963), draws attention to the disjunction between art and life. A life could never be anything like a poem, he posits, since it would be 'a nightmare of horror for, given the historical reality of actual men, such a society could only come into being through selective breeding, extermination of the physically and mentally unfit, absolute obedience to its Director' (Auden, 1963, p. 248). Auden's emphasis on the disorder of life, and the mutilation necessary to transform it into art, reminds us once again of the power of chance to subvert artistic intention. In this sense the elision of accidental phenomena with an increased level of realism is entirely accurate – if the novel must attempt to teach us how we live, then true randomness is perhaps the element that is able to show us that aspect of life that is so often ignored by literature: that we live randomly, fitfully, among the disorder.

One of the formative notions that predominated in the art, music and literature of the 1960s, particularly, was *bricolage*. Claude Lévi-Strauss's *The Savage Mind*, which established the term as part of the critical vocabulary, was first published (as *La Pensée Sauvage*) in 1962 and was translated into English in 1966. Jessica Maynard defines bricolage as:

> . . . an *ad hoc* making-do, a cobbling together, an ingenuity in the face of the resources readily to hand. At the heart of the word, and the activity, is the sense of deviation, a redistribution of energy, an unpredictable swerve away from the normal course of things, and also, it should not be forgotten, a sense of constraint or circumscription. . . . The successful *bricoleur* responds with a certain measure of guile to the contingencies of what is available. (Maynard, 2000, p. 32)[4]

Bricolage, then, combines chance selection with control – the building blocks, originally randomly chosen, are subsequently assembled according to the choices of the artist. The differing emphasis in the concept of bricolage adds another layer to our understanding of chance, as the constraints placed on the artist/author by their passivity in the process of selection necessitate a *greater* creativity. Artistic guile and imagination, then, appear as the fruits of constraint. In this sense chance does the opposite of undermining the author; rather, chance enters the scene as an active and inspiring collaborative partner. This is an understanding of the function of compositional chance that the Dadaists were very familiar with, and one that has always been at the heart of 'pure chance': compositional chance is not merely destructive of the idea of artistic form, but is also actively capable of inspiring creativity.

British art's reliance on chance in the 1950s and 1960s was also in large part due to its being in thrall to American post-war abstract artists. Among these, perhaps the most significant was Robert Rauschenberg, who published his 'manifesto' 'Random Order' in the art periodical *Location* in 1963. This manifesto consisted of a mixture of fragmented poetic observations and images, strung together in careless random fashion. Rauschenberg's interest in random phenomena and his utilization of them in his work was in part fed by an intense connection with John Cage,[5] whose work, albeit in a different field, was exploring similar ideas, and whose profound connection with chance can indeed be seen as emblematic of the 1960s generation of aleatorists. Cage, who composed the first extended composition determined by purely chance procedures, *Music of Changes* (1951), was a clear inheritor of the tendency inculcated by the Dadaists, and Cage's radical act of aleatorical engagement can be read as a starting point of the definitive rebirth of aleatorical art.[6] Nineteen fifty-one stands as a break from late modernism as well as from the stultifying immediate post-war austerity, and also as a re-welcoming of those disordered, iconoclastic aspects of the Dadaists' work that sustain such a close association with chance and randomness. This reaction against the artwork as discrete, created object – a missive from its creator – in part welcomed chance events as collaborator and also let natural phenomena stand as art, no matter how disordered or messy. This subversive move away was characterized here by British artist Victor Burgin: 'Modernism stood for *order* . . . everything in its proper place, doing its duty fulfilling its preordained role in patriarchal culture' (Burgin, 1986, p. 47). In contrast, the 'neo-Dadaists'[7] of the 1950s and 1960s relied on the idea of bearing witness to chance happenings and accidental collisions, observing the resulting form, or anti-form, and allowing what it appears to represent to speak for the artist; or constraining the artist's options by means of letting chance select the building blocks of the artwork. The predominant themes of this approach to art could thus be categorized as an undermining of artistic authority, humility in the face of nature and its ability to create beauty, and an interest in silence, ignorance and nothingness. Chance, for Cage, was a means of access to the chaos that surrounds us, a technique to dampen down the distractions of noise and form. As he wrote in 'Experimental Music':

And what is the purpose of writing music? One is, of course, not dealing with purposes but dealing with sounds. Or the answer must take the form of a paradox: a purposeful purposelessness or a purposeful play. This play, however, is the affirmation of life – not an attempt to bring order out of chaos nor to suggest improvements in creation, but simply a way of waking up to the very life we are living, which is so excellent when one gets one's mind and one's desires out its way and lets it act of its own accord. (Cage, 1961a, p. 12)

The ontological status of accidental phenomena was thus important to Cage: his utilization of chance as compository element is a collaborative technique, but one that aspires to a mode of being. As he commented, 'the idea of relation . . . being absent, anything . . . may happen. A "mistake" is beside the point, for once anything happens it authentically is' (Cage, 1961b, p. 59). Silence, then, is intimately connected to the accidental – anything *may* happen, during it, or equally may not. Similarly being itself is not necessary: rather, anything that 'is' is automatically a product of chance.

This humility in the face of the natural world and the unwillingness to distort it for artistic purposes evinced by Cage was one of the predominant modes of engagement with chance among the neo-Dadaists on both sides of the Atlantic. To this end some expressed an attraction to a movement away from form all together. David Masters quotes the minimalist Carl Andre, 'I don't want the detail of a structure to be interesting, you know, beautiful effects and so forth. This doesn't interest me at all. I want the material in its clearest form' (Masters, 2000, p. 214). Rauschenberg produced a series of 'dirt paintings', one of which he dedicated to Cage. Cage commented on it: 'The message is conveyed by dirt, which, mixed with an adhesive, sticks to itself and to the compass upon which he places it. Crumbling and responding to changes in the weather, the dirt unceasingly does my thinking' (Cage, 1961c, p. 99).[8] Masters relates a talismanic episode in Britain that echoes this in its radical advocacy of random technique.

> The British abstract artist Robyn Denny (b. 1930) was a student at the Royal College of Art in 1957 when he and some friends had a confrontation with their tutor John Minton. Denny had begun to produce large boards on which paint and bitumen had been dropped, dribbled, smeared and finally set alight. When shown at the college's 'Sketch Club' Minton had satirised and ridiculed the work. To him it was meaningless and irrelevant. 'Why', he said, 'you could call it anything'. (Masters, 2000, p. 204)

This tendency towards the unadorned and inartificial elevated to the status of art because of the nature either of its presentation or our observation, reminds us of the Dadaist Hans Richter's 'collaboration with nature' which was overtly a necessary condition for the operation of chance:

> It is the erotic pleasure of an unknown gift . . .
> But to follow this surprise – sensation with an alert mind,
> with instinctive feeling, inspiration, help and direction

That makes of 'chance' a creation of yours . . . in
collaboration with nature
That is what Arp meant:
'When you follow chance you create real life'. (Richter, 1971, p. 98)

Two differing and seemingly dislocated conceptions of chance thus co-existed. First, chance was understood as emptiness and silence, a means of allowing the artist or writer far to abdicate control. This is perhaps best exemplified by Cage's silent work and Rauschenberg's white paintings, and also finds expression as a willingness to co-exist with mess and accident, in the case of the artistic co-option of the natural world. The second sense is chance-as-composition, an active transformation of the random into artistic substance, as seen in the idea of bricolage and the aleatorical writers of the 1960s, and which was mirrored on the continent by writers such as those of the Oulipo group. The marginalia around the piece of art, or the blank canvas upon which it would be created, were suddenly held to be as interesting as the art itself. Similarly, there was a revival of what is, as Hans Richter had it, the crucial mixing of human choice with chance. It is this mixing that makes it 'a personal matter', thus bringing back the impress of the individual self of the artist into the artistic process:

> Randomness, chance, of course! It is the experience and sensation of our age, but it occurred to me that, because of this fact, the problem and necessity arises to integrate it into our everyday experience . . . to interpret the possible meaning of this disorder, randomness, chaos, cosmos or whatever you want to call it. . . . Chance is not a thing of itself. As Cocteau said in his most beautiful film *Orphée*, 'Everyone has his own death.' So is chance a personal matter. An arrangement without cause is, as Jung calls it – Chance – but it is still the individual, the author, who accepts this offering at the moment. So chance can be offered to you a hundred times, and you don't make anything of it. And then, another time, it clicks. (ibid., p. 108)

This versatility that lies at the heart of chance springs from this curious absence – when you examine it as a discrete phenomena, it disappears. It is, in a way that will prove metaphorically close to the scientific principle of uncertainty, nothing but what we observe it to be: as Richter states above, 'it can be offered to you a hundred times, and you don't make anything of it'. This elusiveness serves effectively to reveal the ambiguity at the heart of much of our experience, and to our falsely certain views about the distinction between art and life, chance holds up a mirror that reveals the crumbling of all certainty.

This understanding of chance as capable of an agency of its own was complemented by a literary period uniquely willing to explore 'pure chance' – as the evident limitations to chance's representation so often forced the chance-inclined author or artist (or composer) into formal dead-ends or novelistic paralysis. This examination has so far served to show how a result of this has been chance's subsequent alliance with the experimental: letting chance play a part in the composition of the artwork being one method of genuinely acknowledging it. It is no coincidence that the most significant aleatorically experimental works were novels; as David Lodge has remarked, the novel, 'of all literary genres, is the one most firmly fixed in the Gutenberg galaxy. It is the characteristic literary product of the printing press' (Lodge, 1979, p. 38) and as such, had perhaps the most determinism in it to shake out.

Chance, Typography and Experimentation in the Novels of B. S. Johnson

B. S. Johnson, the man described by his recent biographer Jonathan Coe as 'the one-man literary avant-garde of the nineteen sixties' (Coe, 2004, p. 3), was a self-consciously radical novelist. Writing in the 1960s and early 1970s, Johnson saw himself as the inheritor of the avant-garde tradition, and was unique in the decade, and indeed in his generation of post-war novelists, for the extent of his formal experimentation. As such I would like to examine his work as the most literal, and experimentally radical, example of the period's attraction to the aleatorical, although this attraction remained, much like B. S. Johnson's novels, a largely avant-garde concern. His formal techniques ranged from the playfully allusive – he borrowed Laurence Sterne's black page from *Tristram Shandy*[9] to stand for death in his first novel *Travelling People* (1963) – to the alienatingly uncompromising in their radicalism, such as his 1969 novel *The Unfortunates*, which was cut into pieces that his readers were encouraged to shuffle like a pack of cards before reading.

He had his crosses to bear as a result of this unapologetic formal experimentation: a national newspaper returned a review copy of his first novel, *Travelling People*, complaining that it must be a faulty copy because its pages were black; the Australian Customs seized *Albert Angelo* (1964), which has a hole cut through several pages, convinced that obscenities had been excised, and refused to release it until Johnson had told them what they were; and his 1966 novel *Trawl*, a collection of reminiscences conducted almost entirely in interior monologue, was found, by a fuming Johnson, in the angling section of his local bookseller.[10] Johnson's fundamental contrariness, for which he suffered these humiliations, stemmed from his dissatisfaction with the state of the novel in its post-war incarnation. He felt that his fellow novelists, writers such as Kingsley Amis and William Cooper, were all endlessly rewriting the 'nineteenth-century narrative novel', which after the innovations of Joyce and Beckett and the war was 'exhausted, clapped out' (Johnson, 1985, p. 5).

Johnson's formal experimentation could be described as a sort of typographical sensationalism, but was distinguished in every instance by his conviction that each represented a wholly justifiable and necessary response to a particular problem he had perceived. He wrote in *Albert Angelo* that:

> A page is an area on which I may place any signs I consider to communicate most nearly what I have to convey: therefore I employ, within the pocket of my publisher and the patience of my printer, typographical techniques beyond the arbitrary and constricting limits of the conventional novel. To dismiss such techniques as gimmicks, or to refuse to take them seriously, is crassly to miss the point. (Johnson, 1964, p. 176)

Johnson's concern with typography, or with the use of type or other graphical signs as visual rather than purely semiotic devices, is mirrored by his eagerness to use other extra-textual devices, whether these involve making physical changes to the book's format as described, or the importing of visual depictions of aspects of the text into the pages of the book. These forays beyond the 'arbitrary and constricting limits' of the novel always have their genesis in Johnson's unswayable conviction that these devices were solutions and responses to specific literary problems:

> Where I depart from convention, it is because the convention has failed, is inadequate for conveying what I have to say. . . . So for every device I have used there is a literary rationale and a technical justification; anyone who cannot accept this has simply not understood the problem which had to be solved. (Johnson, 1985, p. 8)

It was, I contend, chance, contingency and randomness that constitutes the major 'problem which had to be solved' for Johnson, and it was his preoccupation with their formal representation that called forth the visual innovation in his oeuvre. One of the ways in which chance can be confronted is typography, as it is the novel's very conventions, its 'bound-ness', that prevents it from being able to represent this aspect of life; so typographic innovation and technological experiments designed to circum-vent the linearity of the reading experience can thus stand as attempts to visually enact chance on the page.

Johnson firmly situated himself among the avant-garde tradition in his attempts to represent the unrepresentable. This, to Johnson's mind, was randomness. Life's essential chaos, as he saw it, was the truth that needed to be conveyed in fiction, and his awareness of the disjunction between narrative and chance gave Johnson a desire to free the novel from its constraints so that it could represent the randomness of reality. In *Fat Man on a Beach* (1973), the film broadcast three weeks before his death, at his own hand, at the age of forty, Johnson states:

> [life is] really all chaos. . . . I cannot prove it is chaos any more than any-one else can prove there is a pattern, or there is some sort of deity, even if it is all chaos, then let's celebrate the chaos. Let's celebrate the acciden-tal. Does that make us any worse off? Are we any the worse off? There is still love; there is still humour. (Johnson, 1975, p. 169)

With his typical rhetorical volubility, this statement's central exhortation, to 'celebrate the accidental', represents a direct impetus for Johnson's typo-graphical and visual outbursts. This is apparent not only in the aspects of his oeuvre where randomness is overtly alluded to, but can be seen as an implicit motivation for much of the experimentation in Johnson's novels: his desire to circumvent the predictability inherent in the conventions and unspoken assumptions about the nature of the book is itself a response to this specific anxiety about chance's representability.

The first Johnson text I am going to examine is his second novel *Albert Angelo*, the story of a young architect who works as a supply teacher in order to pay his rent and fund his desired career. The novel repeatedly uses visual aspects of the text as analogues for, or shortcuts to, the aetiological aspects of reading. So when Albert finds a fortune-teller's card in the street 'it is further from the truth to describe it than simply to reproduce it' (Johnson, 1985, p. 10), and both sides of the pamphlet advertising the services of the fortune-teller, Madame Mae, therefore appear on a double spread. The first is headlined 'Are You Unlucky?' and the second, 'Do You Wish To Know?' (Johnson, 1964, pp. 120–1). This second teasing question alludes to Johnson's frequent disavowal of the reader's desire to know what happens next, what he calls 'that vulgar curiosity' that impels the reader forwards, which he associates with the Victorian novel and the conservative fiction of his peers. It is worth quoting Johnson's description of this novelistic impulse in full:

> In any case, surely it must be a confession of failure on the part of any novelist to rely on that primitive, vulgar and idle curiosity of the reader to know 'what happens next' however banal or hackneyed it may be, to hold his interest? Can he not face the fact that it is his choice of words, his style, which ought to keep the reader reading? Have such novelists no pride? The drunk who tells you the story of his troubles in a pub relies on the same curiosity. (Johnson, 1985, pp. 5–6)

Johnson's contempt for the narrative suspense that inspires the curiosity of the reader subverts the meaning of the 'Do You Wish To Know' of Madame Mae's card. It now assumes a taunting air, satirizing the intentions of the reader, as well as turning the conventions of the book itself into a metaphor for the mystical discourse of divination. Of course, wishing to know what happens next in life, as well as in narrative, is a suppression and denial of chance. Perhaps making the point that this denunciation of narrative suspense cannot be made forcefully enough in writing, Johnson crucially chooses again to represent his commentary visually, and once more the resort or retreat to the extra-textual becomes firmly linked in the reader's mind with the avoidance of, or ironizing of, linear predictability.

At the end of *Albert Angelo*, in a section marked 'disintegration', the narrative breaks down irreparably. Johnson whips away the thin curtain between the author and his protagonist, and admits that 'telling stories is telling lies' (Johnson, 1964, p. 167). He later echoes this statement in the introductory essay to 'Aren't You Rather Young To Be Writing Your Memoirs?'

> Life does not tell stories. Life is chaotic, fluid, random; it leaves myriads of ends untied, untidily. Writers can extract a story from life only by strict, close selection, and this must mean falsification. (Johnson, 1985, p. 5)

This fundamentalist fealty to the truth acknowledges overtly that chance and randomness, synonymous with chaos in Johnson's terminology, are inimical to fiction. Truth and chance thus become allied, as the act of fictionalizing life means that it truncates this one important component of that life: the messy, random, contingent part. *Albert Angelo* represents Johnson's first serious attempt to circumvent this narrative determinism, and the disintegration of the narrative therefore comes to stand for uncertainty made textual.

Further evidence of Johnson's linking of the desirability of narrative indeterminacy with the points of the text that cannot be expressed adequately by narrative conventions comes on page 149 of *Albert Angelo*, perhaps the most interesting physical change to the book's format for my purposes. Johnson has cut a hole through the paper so that the reader is given a peek, literally, at what is going to happen in the future of the book. What is going to happen in the future, it seems, is violent death: a murder seems to take place in the page that is yet to come, though we are not told whose. The hole in the page effectively cancels the reliable solidity of the book, while inevitably making us look anew at that very thing: the novel's status as an 'object'. As Nicholas Tredell has pointed out, the hole also gives material form to prolepsis.[11] In the materialization of the idea of foreknowledge we can detect a further commentary on the unrepresentability of randomness: the narrative assumes an anticipatory purpose that would seek to elude the narrative unpredictability wrought by chance – in other words, it is merely a different way of inducing suspense in the reader. But Johnson playfully subverts this, making the oblique commentary that as we do not know what will happen next in life, so we shouldn't in books; our desire to know what comes next, fed by this sensational glimpse, is thwarted when we reach the page glimpsed through the hole and the death is properly contextualized. The death described is not that of any character in the novel, but the stabbing of Christopher Marlowe in 1593; thus a death we assumed to be happening in the future of the story in fact has already happened in an extraneous, distant past.

Trawl (1966) Johnson's third novel, consists of a loosely grouped series of reminiscences made while he spent three weeks as a passenger on a deep-sea trawler. He hopes that the isolation, and indeed the act of trawling itself will, in a gauchely literal interpretation of his central metaphor, 'shoot the narrow trawl of my mind into the vasty sea of my past' (Johnson, 2004, p. 9). To this end he recounts episodes from his life, from his oft-thwarted romantic history to his childhood as a wartime refugee, all interspersed with his life on the boat.

The typographical variance is defiantly odd in *Trawl*. Johnson uses dots in the middle of the line at different spacings (3 em, 6 em and 9 em) to indicate that the narrator is reflecting, remembering or commenting on his own thoughts and descriptions. Short sentences in groups interconnected by means of dots replace paragraphs, and he seems to use different varieties of dots, in the centre of the line, to mean different things. Interestingly, his anxieties about chance seem to call forth a category entirely of their own: two dots, with three em spaces in between. When describing the uncertainty of his wartime experience, he says: 'someone gave me a map of the Ruhr marked with bombing targets into which I stuck little flags with bombs pictured on them: at random. · · ' (ibid., p. 49). In fact these dots appear quite often in between random recollections; they are less flowing and more distanced than ellipses, and it is easy to assume that Johnson was trying to introduce a way to represent the arbitrariness of the mind – although the specificity of this typographical oddity makes it tempting to read the resonance between chance and typography here as unconscious, like a visual manifestation of a deeper anxiety.

Either way, the examples start to pile up: 'perhaps I delude myself: perhaps I am what I would always have been. · · ' (ibid., p. 72). And later: 'perhaps there were American aircrew in that audience that night who would die in the air the next— · · ah, that is fanciful, smacks of fictional speculation. · · ' (ibid., p. 81). Similarly, the two dots occur when Johnson discusses the possibility of causes for any of his recollections. When he remembers Mrs. Davies, who took him in, he muses: 'though she must have felt a need out of her own lack of children: but having found a motive, a reason, so what? · · ' (ibid., p. 82), and later, as he tries to evade finding reasons for why things in his life happened the way that they did: 'Compensating—though, again, what use are bloody reasons? · · ' (ibid.), and again, as Johnson muses on causality: ' · · What use are analyses, reasons, causes?' (ibid., p. 94), and then goes on to dismiss its validity: 'all I am left with are just things, happenings: things as they are, happenings as they have happened and go on happening through the unreliable filter of my memory' (ibid.). In this oddly oblique way, *Trawl* reveals a resonance between its formal oddity and experimentation, and its thematic concerns of causality and chance. In a similar marrying of formal interests with his thematic subject matter, Johnson again tests the boundaries of prolepsis, the literary and narrative equivalent of foreknowledge. Near the end of the novel, Johnson as narrator tells us: I peer at this entrail, watch its life beating away, interested and disgusted yet moved: and think of several different omens this particular sacrificial object could portend. · · (ibid., p. 134). Omens, of course, repel chance and guard against the contingent. Here, that distinction means that the augury of bird's entrails has been transmuted into a secular, literary forecast; no longer a way to divine the gods' will, but, rather, a primarily narrative device. The hoped-for anticipatory effect of 'several different omens' that Johnson could think of is for the reader's benefit, to instil that 'vulgar curiosity' that he supposedly abhors, and to invoke the mystery that he has condemned as spurious.

The Unfortunates is Johnson's most radical attempt to literalize the relation between his manipulation of the material fact of the book, and his thematic understanding of chance. The material format of *The Unfortunates* is, overtly, a direct response to the problem of randomness and the book. As Johnson described it,

> [t]he main technical problem with *The Unfortunates* was the randomness of the material. That is, the memories . . . interwove in a completely random manner, without chronology. This is the way the mind works, my mind anyway. (Johnson, 1985, pp. 10–11)

He comes to the realization that 'this randomness was directly in conflict with the technological fact of the bound book: for the bound book imposes an order, a fixed page order, on the material' (ibid., p. 11). This suggested that his solution needed to reverse the process: he needed to impose the randomness of the material on the form. The pages of *The Unfortunates* were therefore arranged into twenty-seven chapters of varying lengths, which were unbound, and arranged in a box so that the reader could read them in any order he or she chose, or in the order that chance presented them. The first and last sections were labelled as such, after a skirmish with his publisher, to give the reader some orientation and to limn a rough time frame. In between, the chapters are simultaneous, in the sense that they are temporal at all: as Johan Thielemans has commented, '[the loose chapters] are an exercise in what film language calls "parallel montage"' (Thielemans, 1985, p. 85). The relationship between aleatorical composition and linear time was under scrutiny elsewhere in the period. Alain Robbe-Grillet criticized 'the unconditional adoption of chronological development, linear plots, a regular graph of the emotions, the way each episode tended towards an end'. New ideas about randomness also impacted on our concept of time and linearity: 'why should we try to reconstitute the time that belongs to clocks in a tale that is only concerned with human time? Isn't it wiser to think of our own memory, which is *never* chronological?' (Robbe-Grillet, 1965, p. 63). Echoing this sentiment, Johnson wanted to get around the sequentiality that pagination necessitates and the inescapable sense that there is a temporal order to events in any novel: however episodic or fragmented your prose, it is always read in the same order, the order that the author has chosen. Johnson wanted to let chance take dual responsibility, at least – to actively participate in the experience and thus reduce his agency. This, he believed, would re-create the randomness of reality, and crucially, of memory. *The Unfortunates* is thus aleatorical in the most fundamental sense. It stands as perhaps the most serious attempt, at least in Britain, to engage with the problem of the representation of chance in the novel in the twentieth century.[12]

It is this tension in *The Unfortunates* between randomness and narrative that, as well as earning the book its deserved fame, has also been the main source of frustration for its critics. Johnson wanted *The Unfortunates* to truly engage with pure randomness, and yet he was not always successful, according to the majority of his critics, in keeping narrative in abeyance. As Coe has pointed out, his scheme was vulnerable to accusations of compromise: 'even then, a longish, twelve page section, for instance, would impose its own narrative sequence', and the inescapable result of this, Coe argues, is that 'any attempt at conveying randomness would be suspended for a good span of reading time' (Coe, 1999, p. x). David Lodge has commented with perspicuity that:

The random flow of sensation and association in the narrator's mind is imitated by the words, clauses and sentences *within each section* – a stream-of-consciousness exercise in the manner of Joyce. The randomness only affects the narrative presentation of this consciousness in time. It makes explicit the almost infinite choice a writer has in representing a particular sequence of events by refusing to commit itself to any one choice. Such is the nature of the human mind, however, that, working with the key of the marked first section, we mentally rearrange the events of the book in their chronological order as we read; and the puzzle or game element thus introduced into the reading experience has the effect (ironically, in view of the author's declared intentions, but also advantageously in my opinion) of putting the painful, personal, 'real' experience of the book at an aesthetic distance. (Lodge, 1969, p. 114)

Johnson's solution, for Lodge, is therefore unsuccessful in the terms he has set himself, although he concedes that in *The Unfortunates* he may eventually have achieved something entirely different. Other critics, including Frank Kermode, have pounced on the concession to his publisher that resulted in the labelling of the first and last sections, seeing it as a blatant and eventually fatal weakening of his project (Kermode, 2004). The tension is the familiar one between a randomness whose terms are originally chosen by the author, and the chance selection where the randomness is a product of a non-random initial premise. As we saw in the general discussion, reservations about the extent of randomness have always accompanied aleatorical art. The tension is inbuilt, as John Cage points out in 'Experimental Music': 'chance ought to be very controlled' (Cage, 1961a, p. 186). Rosemarie Waldrop in her discussion of chance in *Against Language?* typically discusses the compromises inherent in the concept of chance selection: 'chance selection is nearly a contradiction in terms . . . it is selection at several removes, but still selection. It can be called chance only in relation to meaning, to logical continuity' (Waldrop, 1971, p. 64). It is undeniable that narrative can never co-exist with absolute fealty to the concept of pure chance, though this is more an inherent facet of narrative than it is a disingenuousness on the part of the author, who pretends to be using chance but secretly retains control. As I have suggested throughout, though, it is in the intermingling of the two, between the author's intention and the introduction of random formal elements, that pure chance is detectable. Also, while it is true that, in a strictly formal sense, Johnson's concessions reduced the randomness of the reading experience, it is also true that, seeing as Johnson's loyalty is always, rigorously, to the 'truth' of any experience or representation of the workings of the mind, it doesn't eventually matter that much. Memories and recollection of experience do not return to us in a linear, tightly plotted, traditionally novelistic way; but neither do they come to us as entirely disjointed flashes, or individual images. It is common enough to remember whole events and with them their significance, but not to remember these discrete entities in the correct, chronological order. Memories are not necessarily analogous to single words or even single sentences, but they are often episodic, and fragmented: much like the sections of *The Unfortunates*. The randomness is in fact perfectly weighted in terms of fulfilling its stated aim: to provide a mimetically truthful representation of how memory is experienced randomly.

The subject of these memories is Johnson's close friend Tony Tillinghurst, and his illness and eventual death from cancer. Memories of Tony started coming to Johnson when he found himself back in Nottingham, the city that was the main site of their friendship, to report on a football match for *The Observer*. The newspaper report of this match was reproduced on the inside of the box, lying underneath the loose sheets and individually bound memorials to Tony. The report is subtitled 'Wasted chances' – the chance an obvious allusion to the randomness that he is commenting on, and wasted both in the sense of loss for his friend's early death and for the physical state of cancer that he catalogues so assiduously, as well as missed goal opportunities. The language, too, mirrors the preoccupations of the novel: it is a 'lucky match' for one player, again, his 'luck continues', he describes 'chances' missed and so on. The prose that makes up the bulk of the novel is evocative and sparse, which adds to the atemporality of the middle sections and emphasizes the melancholic, elegiac quality of the memories:

> He had such a great mind for detail, it crowded his mind like documents in the Public Records Office, there, a good image, perhaps easy, but it was even something like as efficient, tidy, his mind, not as mine is, random, the circuit-breakers falling at hazard, tripped equally by association and non-association. (Johnson, 1999, 'first', p. 3)[13]

This description of the mind as a circuit board, with 'hazard' reminding us equally of contingency and of danger, is a neat replica of Johnson's mind as a conduit for the lightning-quick randomness of memory.

And yet there is only so far that this reading gets us. Johnson himself stated explicitly that he wanted to re-create the randomness of experience, and of memory, and to let the novel itself stand as an expression of these. But I would like to suggest that the randomness is more concretely expressed, not in this straightforward metaphor, but in Johnson's total refusal to let one happening function as an explanation for another, and the implicit criticism of the traditional novel's limitations that comes from the rendering in physical form of this refusal. The literal ripping apart of necessarily closely related memories in *The Unfortunates* serves not just as a protest against the technological determinism of the book, or as a tangible metaphor for the cruelness and irrevocability of chance and cancer, but as a subversion of cause and effect that radically alters the supposed predictability of the reading experience. Contingency is thus denied: the memories do not necessitate each other, but pile on top of each other, each one sprung from nothing but its own need to be remembered. This broadens the possibilities of the operation of chance in the novel, and the theme of randomness that we are rather clumsily directed towards by the book's physical format is suddenly experienced by the reader as a visceral and powerful reality. Terrible and unlikely things happen, and they have no reason to do so. Events, and memories, are thus chaogenous, or as the narrator says, tripped equally by association or non-association.

For Johnson in *The Unfortunates*, the ultimately chaogenous event was death. In a world ruled by uncertainty, where accident is the only meaningful agent, the inevitability of decay, dying and death assumes the significance of the only determinism; and yet its inexplicability remains absolute. As it is expressed in the novel, the inevitability of death is nevertheless related to chance as it represents the ultimate defiance of causal explanations: 'That this thing could just come from nowhere . . . I still do not understand' (ibid., 'for recuperation', p. 2). 'This thing', of course, is specifically cancer, a word that, as Nicholas Tredell points out, is itself absent from the text (Tredell, 1985, p. 39). *The Unfortunates* speaks eloquently of the overwhelming unfairness of luck: the cancer appears for no reason, grows uncontrollably and in an unpredictable manner, and assumes the terrifying power of the truly random: that which has no cause and answers to no explanations. Johnson writes of 'the explosive, runaway, zealous, monstrous cells of the tumour' (Johnson, 1999, 'just as', p. 8), and it is here that his conception of chance as an ultimately terrifying universal force finds its fullest and best expression.

However, also present in the description of Tony's illness is Johnson's characteristic contrary impulse. At the same time as the illness is drawn as the ultimate expression of randomness, it is also shown to be mystical, mysterious, shrouded in failure. The implied 'fault' would necessarily deny the cancer's status as the ultimate expression of bad luck, or ill fortune, and transmute it into part of the discourse of divine (or otherwise) punishment; either way, the spectre of agency is introduced to the chaos. To return to Kavanagh's history of chance and the novel, I would like to briefly remember his description of chance's potential significance, a quote that found resonance with the novels of Samuel Beckett and, I believe, similarly illuminates the best work of his acolyte over twenty years later:

Against a vision of the world as a potentially finite series of knowable and ultimately controllable determinisms, chance implied a resolutely tragic vision. To recognize chance was, more than anything else, to recognize our inability to reason toward and become part of any natural order. (Kavanagh, 1993, p. 4)

Chance as a 'resolutely tragic vision' is, as much as it was for Beckett, exactly right for *The Unfortunates*. Peopled as it is with the unlucky, the novel is suffused with the idea that the presence of bad luck represents some kind of essential failure. Whether this failure is personal, or is evocative of a wider failure of modernity to allow explanations for events, the admittance of chance here calls into being a fundamental, and moving, vulnerability. After Tony's cremation, as the narrator looks back, he sees 'a straight column rising from the chimney of the crematorium, it went straight upwards, as far as smoke can ever be said to move in a straight line, into the haze, the sky, it was too neat, but it was, it was' (Johnson, 1999, 'we were', p. 1). It is tempting to read this as an epiphanic revelation of the pleasures of linearity, or to understand Tony's column of smoke as a parallel line to the narrative one which Johnson has performed so acrobatically to avoid. As he would object, probably apoplectically, 'life is not like that'; although, perhaps if we are in the realm of the truly random, sometimes it is: sometimes life, in all its messy arbitrariness, occasionally produces a pure narrative line.

I nevertheless hesitate to conclude my reading of Johnson's approach to chance, and the aleatorically experimental tendency of this period in general, on such a note. Johnson often seems to inspire a wistful critique, one that wishes he was another sort of writer, and his novels are often read as expressing an unconscious desire for those aspects of the novel that he has publicly renounced, just as aleatorical art is easily dismissed by the highlighting of its inevitable compromises with narrative. I would like, rather, to emphasize a corollary, and motivation, of Johnson's radicalism that has been understated by his critics, and a corollary that applies to all aleatorical art: that what underlies it is a serious attempt to represent chance in the only way that is genuinely, mimetically possible: by letting it formally participate in the construction of the narrative. His desire to represent the contingent, accidental and random aspects of life with fealty to the impossibility of their representation in narrative, and the subsequent calling forth of extra-narrative devices to serve this end, therefore represents a logical progression from recognizing the aspects of chance that are inimical to narrative. Johnson's endeavours with conventional printing boundaries, typography and image, thus emerge as literary strategies capable of delivering an implicit, but unmistakeable, critique of the novel's specific limitations, namely, its inability in its conventional incarnation to re-create the reality of the human experience of chance. Above all, Johnson, just like the Dadaists, acknowledged that, although pattern and order are necessary for human perception and understanding, too much stultifies, and if the substance of art could be stripped of conventional order, our perception could be freshened and reinvigorated.

Chapter Five

'The incomprehensible operation of grace': Mess, Contingency and the Example of Iris Murdoch

For Green, Beckett and Johnson, a pretension towards omniscience and omnipotence was the worst writerly sin. They all shared the view that the impulse to impose one's idea of form too rigidly inevitably results in a suppression of narrative's ability to represent the loose ends of life. The result of an engagement with the philosophical implications of chance is, as we have seen, subversive of the idea of the novel as a vessel for meaning and value. Narrative's inability to be assimilated to chance, and chance's resistance to its own representation, have induced writers such as Beckett and B. S. Johnson to formulate a kind of poetics of chance; an introduction of formlessness into form. As David Trotter describes it: 'we might want to imagine a poetics of mess, whose topic is the practice, in modernity's name, of a degree of "formlessness": the invention of complicities with and figures for contingency' (Trotter, 2000, p. 31). *The Unfortunates* represents an attempt to illustrate Johnson's belief that a verisimilitudinous retelling of the randomness of our everyday experience is a sufficient artistic end in itself, without recourse to the 'form' which, while it might, he conceded, be necessary for narrative art, would undermine the purity of his engagement with the aleatory. Two decades earlier Henry Green's work, in a very different way, had been stymied by this same paradox, and his desire to avoid a false over-determination in his fiction eventually led to stalemate as he struggled with the problem of literary free will. A desire to look upon chaotic and formless muddle or mess, to examine its effects on the human psyche, and even to introduce it as a formal principle into literature, is shared by all the authors I have so far discussed. A particular strain of British fiction since the war had been preoccupied by the implications of overweening authorial power, and for many novelists this was intimately connected with the problem of chance. Insofar as an engagement with contingency and, by implication, chance, necessitates and is a result of a formal awareness of the novel's limitations, an awareness of chance was characteristic of the time.

Iris Murdoch is firmly in this camp. Murdoch was perhaps the post-war novelist who thought the most deeply about contingency and its implications for the novel form, and she was certainly the post-war novelist who showed the greatest desire to do it justice in both philosophical and artistic terms, as her biographer Peter Conradi notes: 'the ability to learn openness to contingency is a virtue her philosophy and fiction alike are famous for commending' (Conradi, 2001, p. 279). Uniquely, and crucially for this study, she also drew parallels between contingency and *goodness*, that I believe represent an entirely new development in how chance was viewed in the twentieth century. David Trotter, in *Cooking with Mud: Mess in the Literature of the Nineteenth-Century*, coins the term 'mess-theory' in connection with depictions of contingency in nineteenth-century literature and painting. Trotter distinguishes between illusion-sustaining and illusion-destroying mess, between good and bad messes. However, for Murdoch, mess is almost without exception good. Muddle, and an ability to bear it, as her characters often illustrate, define a person: resistance to muddle, which is expressed throughout her novels in a variety of ways, is consistently shown to be destructive. An affinity with mess, with aspects of the natural world and its paradigm of formlessness, or with the accidental, are all consistently shown to be a path to the elusive good. Murdoch thus introduces a radically new kind of ethical dimension to the discussion. Chance in the novel no longer purely describes to us how we *do* live; it now, however partially and falteringly, demonstrates to us how we *should* live, and instructs us how this may be possible.

Chance's presence in the novel has always been indicative of a tension between the need to represent it as an inevitable aspect of life, and the novel's inherent reliance on form, and thus its profound resistance to the contingent. Whether in making us question our ideas about meaning, or about novelistic authority, or about the truthfulness of art, chance's subversive power remained intact. Murdoch's obsession with the contingent, and her discussion of an ethical dimension of contingency and its implications for the novel form, spans her entire career but is at its most attentive and philosophically complex in the 1970s. Her novels of this period accept that our confrontation of the contingent nature of things generates an element of genuine fear, an heir of the existential horror which is seen as a natural reaction to chance's power to subvert and render meaningless the belief that there exists value and purpose in the universe. Rather than transmuting this fear into a nihilistic embrace of the horror of contingency, or even to a Sartrean relish and delight in chance's ability to inspire an awestruck horror, she instead prescribes acknowledging chance's power as undeniable and non-negotiable, and then submitting to it. Goodness, she contends, gives up the search for meaning; it co-exists with meaninglessness, is illusionless and brave. In this 'giving-up' she transmutes an apprehension of chance into an ethical good – into an opportunity for a secular version of grace.

This shift from chance being seen as an ethically neutral concept, in post-existential thought, to a position in which contingency is seen as a new component of how to be good, is not merely a philosophical change but a literary one. If, at points in chance's assimilation to narrative, we can still hear an echo of chance's age old, pre-twentieth-century negative connotations, Murdoch's proposal of an acceptance of the contingent as good worked as a distinct literary prescription that would allow contingency into the novel without going to the avant-garde reader-unfriendly extremes of B. S. Johnson. In this chapter I aim to look at the discussion of contingency in Iris Murdoch's philosophy and fiction, and analyse its contribution to – and effect on – the wider discussion of chance that has formed the basis of this study. As the chapter progresses I will have more to say on this subject of Murdoch's insistent and systematic allying of contingency with goodness, but first I need to look at the term contingency in more detail, both in Murdoch's work and in context.

As a philosophical idea, contingency was fashionable in the post-existentialist British circles of the 1960s and 1970s. That events are contingent means that they are profoundly subject to the vagaries of chance; it also implies something of the future element – if the future is contingent, we do not yet know what it consists of. It can perhaps be best understood as an interpretation of reality as dependent on something else, as provisional, and tied up in a multi-faceted, dense system of cause and effect. Uncertainty, and an embrace of the impossibility of determinism in our lives, is always somewhat turned towards the future event – it is anticipatory of what has not yet happened. Adam Phillips describes contingency as follows, emphasizing its closeness to chance:

> It can be called luck, fortune, accident, coincidence, and is sometimes experienced and described as a kind of non-intentional or random agency. There is actually nothing behind it making it happen – though we can personalize it by projection – and its presence, in and of itself, says nothing about our power. It neither diminishes nor enlarges us, though we can use it to do both. (Phillips, 1994, p. 20)

That it 'neither diminishes nor enlarges us' is emblematic of the mid-twentieth-century view of chance, as I have explored it. Chance, and therefore contingency, is morally and ethically neutral; it has been absorbed into the sterile environs of scientific and mathematical discourse. Though 'we can use it to do both', contingency, within the bounds of its own operations, is amoral.

The anticipatory quality of contingency also means it is connected intimately, if often subconsciously, to the erotic. As Phillips suggests, uncertainty is an essentially flirtatious state:[1] as a mode of being which is uncommitted to any one course of action, the contingent is always ready and able to change course depending on a number or combination of random coincidences. If we take Phillips's point about flirtation, contingency means never quite shutting off any possibility: it means never, really, for once and for all, saying no. An openness to contingency, and a readiness to respond to its manifold suggestions, is analogous to living in a state of constant, ever-present possibility. As a corollary to this, an acceptance of the contingent means seeing the world through a prism of protective, distancing scepticism, a scepticism that is a refusal to commit to, or to believe in, any one thing – the scepticism of the terminal flirt.

The obverse of limitless, eroticized possibility, however, is muddle and mess, the confusion that comes with accepting ignorance about the future. David Trotter argues that mess is in fact the footprint of contingency, its vital sign, and posits that mess, as an idea and as a literary trope, both sustains and destroys illusion. Messes destroy illusion because they 'subtly corrode the idea of yourself that you have prepared for the world's inspection' (Trotter, 2000, p. 2). They can also, however, sustain an illusion; he uses the example of Fred Vincy's muddy trousers in *Middlemarch* (1871) making him happily realize he is cut out for working the fields. Trotter clearly demarcates 'mess' as a product of chance: 'the association [sustained by the idea of mess] which will for the most part concern me here . . . is the association with chance' and 'this much is clear: in a manner free from determinisms of all kinds, "messes just happen"' (ibid., pp. 9, 2). In fact, their very lack of any meaningful agency helps us to develop a mature equanimity, limned as disillusionment, with which to face the events of the world: 'the sharpness in the disillusionment they induce is the knowledge it brings of contingency. Chance, rather than shortcoming or lapse, is narcissism's worst enemy' (ibid., p. 2). The negativity of 'disillusionment' here is balanced by the reward that this disillusionment brings: an undercutting of narcissism, and a sober, reflective ability to see the world as it really is. Knowledge of contingency, then, invokes a sort of sceptical wisdom. As Trotter puts it:

But the meanings and values thus ascribed [to mess] are ones which envisage the very limit of meaning and value itself. The version of their own habit they most fiercely resist, both in descriptions of experience in general, and in descriptions of the history of culture in particular, is the most widespread and deeply felt of all: a determinism hell-bent on the excavation of cause from effect. Determinism, while it may demand a prodigious expenditure of energy and intelligence (indeed, precisely *because* it demands all of that), is the easy option: the choice we make without knowing we have made it. It gives us plenty to do, as human beings and as cultural historians, and the doing (the excavation) has a meaning and a value of and for itself, whatever its outcome. Determinism is never not productive, and we should be grateful for the bounty it brings. But the hardest thing of all to think about is chance, which denies the very form and purpose of thought itself. (ibid., p. 10)

This addresses the very problem that I have identified throughout this study. Chance is the hardest thing of all to 'think about', and more so for novelists, who are engaged in a process that would seek to contain or deny chance. As David Gordon says: 'the novel, because it includes so much of what would be counted contingent in other forms, allows us to see how our dreams of significance are mocked' (Gordon, 1995, p. 93). For Trotter, this difficulty is assuaged, at least partly, by artists' metaphorization of chance and contingency into mess: for mess, as literal muddle, or as the depiction of states of disorder or chaos, works as a transformation of contingency into a novelistic mode. Or as he puts it: 'writers and artists think *with* mess as well as *about* it' (ibid., p. 8).

Trotter goes on to say there is much fertile ground for mess theory in the twentieth century, although it is not within the scope of his study. In fact he specifically mentions Iris Murdoch as the exemplar of mess-friendly twentieth-century writers, and quotes from her 1959 essay 'The Sublime and the Beautiful Revisited' her serious affection for 'whatever is contingent, messy, boundless, infinitely particular' (Murdoch, 1999a, p. 174). Although I do not have scope here to take the baton proffered and offer a 'mess-theory' reading of Murdoch, nevertheless, mess and its associated ideas may offer us an instructive way into looking at her creative and literary use of contingency. Her depictions of mess, in other words, can show us the creative uses to which contingency is put.

The implications of contingency, and thus mess, in the novel are wide-reaching, sometimes contradictory, and can be positive or negative; mess can be a creative and interesting maelstrom; equally it can, as a signifier of chaos in its purest form, function as the source of horror, violence and confusion. In 'The Sublime and the Beautiful Revisited' Iris Murdoch famously concluded her essay with the following passage:

> We may turn at last to what finally differentiates art from life, the question of form. Form is the temptation of love and its peril, whether in art or life: to round off a situation, to sum up a character. But the difference is that art has *got* to have form, whereas life need not. And any artist both dreads and longs for the approach of necessity, the moment at which form irrevocably crystallises. There is a temptation for any novelist, and one to which, if I am right, modern novelists yield too readily, to imagine that the problem of a novel is solved and the difficulties overcome as soon as a form in the sense of a satisfactory myth has been evolved. But that is only the beginning. There is then the much more difficult battle to prevent that form from becoming rigid, by the free expansion against it of individual characters. Here above all, the contingency of the characters must be respected. Contingency must be respected because it is the essence of personality. And here is where it becomes so important to remember that the novel is written in words, to remember that 'eloquence of suggestion and rhythm' of which James spoke. A novel must be a house fit for free characters to live in; and to combine form with a respect for reality with all its odd contingent ways is the highest art of prose. (ibid., pp. 285–6)

Form, then, at least in its 'crystallised' aspect, is the enemy of contingency. The fact that life is contingent, messy, unpredictable, is familiarly difficult to comprehend,[2] and Murdoch limns it as antithetical to the artistic impulse – the temptation to create form, narrative, myth, story. Murdoch's preoccupation with contingency did not, however, lead her to ever more alienating forms of experimentation, nor to a state where she was afraid to impose a narrative shape on her characters at all: instead she found a way to balance these ideas in harmony. Partly this came from her philosophical engagement with the same ideas that sustained the best of her novels; partly because of the realization that while 'novels have got to have form', this form must be challenged and pushed against by contingency itself:

> What is feared [by the proponents of Romanticism] is history, real beings, and real change, whatever is contingent, messy, boundless, infinitely particular, and endlessly still to be explained; what is desired is the timeless non-discursive whole which has its significance completely contained in

itself . . . the symbol is known intuitively to be self-contained: it is a making sensible of the idea of individuality under the form of necessity, its contingency purged away. (Murdoch, 1999a, p. 174)

Nevertheless it is the artist's greatest responsibility to try and represent contingency, or a version of contingency that is compatible with form, truthfully, as to do otherwise is to lie – indeed the reassuring lies of art damage our very reality: 'our sense of form, which is an aspect of our desire for consolation, can be a danger to our sense of reality as a rich receding background' (Murdoch, 1961, p. 20). Contingency is necessary as a weapon with which the novelist can do battle against the temptation of form, which has its equivalent in life, as above, which she describes in 'The Sublime and the Beautiful Revisited' as 'necessity': contingency is its enemy, for it resists artificial pattern. Murdoch imagines a tussle between contingency and form in which neither dominates, but both are held in a harmonious balance: 'the literary work itself is not in the grip of necessity – how soon we sense this in the cases where it is. The great novelist is not afraid of the contingent; yet his acceptance of the contingent does not land him in banality' (Murdoch, 1999a, p. 271). This is achieved primarily through character: 'the individuals portrayed in the [great] novels are free, independent of their author, and not merely puppets in the exteriorisation of closely locked psychological conflict of his own' (ibid.). As Elizabeth Dipple has it in her 1982 critical study of Murdoch:

> . . . let us note that she again uses the word 'accidental' to try to convey the quality of structure, of autonomy of character and action she aims to produce by removing her will from the scene . . . she specifically applies the word 'love' – the love of a creative mind concentrating on something outside of itself and its own satisfactions. This attribute of love allows random and 'accidental' behaviour in complex, constantly surprising characters. (Dipple, 1982, p. 40)

Richard Rorty similarly emphasizes the importance of the contingent self in what he calls self-creation – the process of coming to know oneself. He describes a tension between:

> . . . an effort to achieve self-creation by the recognition of contingency and an effort to achieve universality by the transcendence of contingency. The same tension has pervaded philosophy since Hegel's time, and particularly since Nietzsche. The important philosophers of our own century are those who have tried to follow through on the Romantic poets by

breaking with Plato and seeing freedom as a recognition of contingency. (Rorty, 1989, pp. 25–6)

Contingency, then, is clearly opposed to universal truth. It is what we are left with after the breakdown of the grand narratives, and the failure of the search for truth. It allows for a multiplicity of truths, of subjective interpretations of the same thing, to co-exist. The individual, for Murdoch as for Rorty, must strive to recognize his own essential contingency, and this task is, as we have seen, a matter of ethical self-awareness. Given that this is how people are, the re-creation of this contingent self in the novel is a practical matter of literary verisimilitude, as well as of evoking an edifying vision of a particular mode of being and its possible consequences. Murdoch's idea of character became a constant struggle to re-create a measure of the true contingency that resides in each individual. As quoted above, Murdoch says: 'There is then the . . . battle to prevent that form from becoming rigid, by the free expansion against it of individual characters. Here above all, the contingency of the characters must be respected. Contingency must be respected because *it is the essence of personality*' (Murdoch, 1999a, p. 285; my emphasis). The 'contingency' of the characters stands for a verisimilitudinous representation of the true nature of human beings as unpredictable and unknowable, each capable of random and contradictory acts. This 'essence of personality' is the aspect of humans most unimaginable by a creator figure, as it refutes the determinism necessary to predict its actions in novelistic form. So character, alongside contingency, subverts and contradicts 'form' when it is threatening to overwhelm the work, as form corresponds to pattern, to the lies or to the narratization of the self that is always, eventually, a dishonest imposition.

Murdoch's understanding of contingency was much influenced, later negatively, by her flirtation with Existentialism. She is able to say in fully Sartrean mode in 1953: 'Man lives amongst a world of things alien [and] senselessly contingent' (Murdoch, 1987, p. 10), and her sense of contingency always fully incorporated the existentialist understanding of it as that chaotic aspect of reality from which we recoil. Although the Sartrean view of the self takes the knowledge that we live in a chancy universe as *a priori*, so as to show how we are free to act, to Murdoch's mind it consistently underestimates the forces of causality and chance that reduce the individual's choices. However, she came to criticize Existentialism for this simplification, as Peter Conradi points out:

For Murdoch the faults of liberalism are to a large extent the faults of Existentialism. Both oppose, too simply, an innocent self to a guilty society, an inheritance they share from Romanticism. For her the question is posed not in terms of the mischievous default of history to make us secure and happy, but in terms of our own deep unacknowledged unfreedom and irrationality, our complicity in 'life-myths' we unknowingly construct and live by, and our deep defencelessness, which we wrap up in various ways, to history, chance, and contingency. (Conradi, 1986, p. 17)

For Murdoch, then, our complicity, our lack of innocence, is key. The self is the site of a sort of passive unfreeness, which can only be defeated by attention to the good. We are not free, as the existentialists would have us believe, because, although in reality we are ruled by chance, we are unwilling to accept this; for this reason we lie to ourselves, and construct narratives that are mere self-indulgent props of, and products of, the ego. Contingency, for Iris Murdoch, in a clear echo of the literary philosophy of Henry Green, is the abstract condition of the random universe, but is also the most private and particular site of the self. In 'Against Dryness', she says she imagines her characters as 'substantial, impenetrable, individual, indefinable and valuable', and adds that the character is 'free and separate . . . related to a rich and complicated world from which as a moral being he has much to learn' (Murdoch, 1961, pp. 16, 18). This is where the unknowability and privacy of individuals resides, as, of course, real people are unpredictable and contain vast, dark, areas of motivation that we, as onlookers, can never entirely comprehend.

In a further parallel to Green, and to Bakhtin, whom Conradi tells us Murdoch read enthusiastically in 1942 (Conradi, 2001, p. 529), this takes on theological overtones, and indeed Murdoch took seriously the responsibility that accompanies the author/creator metaphor that I examined in relation to Henry Green, believing, as Gordon points out, that 'persons should not be coerced' (Gordon, 1995, p. 76). To Harold Hobson she said 'God, if He exists, is good because He delights in the existence of something other than Himself' (Hobson, 1962, p. 28). In fact, the imagining of another discrete human being is the definition of ethical good, as it breaks through human egoism and solipsism that are the primary instruments for evil in the world. This ethical dimension to the novelist's art corresponds to the literary good, happily: as Murdoch said, in conversation with Frank Kermode,

. . . one isn't good enough at creating character. One starts off – at least I start off – hoping every time that . . . a lot of people who are not me are going to come into existence in some wonderful way. Yet often it turns out in the end that something about the structure of the work itself, the myth as it were of the work, has drawn all these people into a sort of spiral, or into a kind of form which is ultimately the form of one's own mind. (Kermode, 1963, pp. 63–4)

Murdoch wants to write like a realist, one that strives to evoke the messy nature of reality while acknowledging its own role in the possible defeat of the same. But this approach also mounts a challenge to other, more continental post-war ideas about 'character', especially the structuralist idea that defines traditional literary representations of persons as particular, independent and with a clearly defined 'self' that remains consistent from one moment to the next as unworkable, even as undesirable, and instead sees the self merely as a site for competing social determinisms. In fact in Britain a reading or reaction to certain existential ideas could be defined in terms of this difference – for Henry Green, and later for Iris Murdoch, the freedom of the self was contested but the particularity, and contingency, of the self was not. A passive acceptance of chance and contingency, rather than an emphasis on will, choice and agency, came to define the way existentialist thought had filtered down from continental philosophy to the British novel. Indeed, Murdoch's affinity with the indeterminate, the messy and the formless in her work, I suggest, is a key component of her ability to think, as Trotter would have it, *with* contingency rather than just to think *about* it.

Does Murdoch, in her thinking *with* contingency, allow mess and contingency to sustain the associations of flirtation and scepticism suggested by Phillips? Or does she argue that the 'contingent self' is uniquely modern, *à la* Rorty? While keeping these ideas in mind, I would also like to suggest that she insistently figures certain types of person, or certain modes of experience, as affiliated with, or somehow uniquely able to bear, mess and muddle. Her ingenious, neat characters, those who adopt the artist's desire to direct action and who hate contingency, are always men, for instance, from which we may extrapolate that femininity is perhaps better equipped to deal with a messy reality, or even that it is inherently aligned with the same. A femininity, which manifests itself as mess, shows us more about the male subject's inability to perceive the good about mess, and thus his inability to perceive good at all. The feminine itself, then, is something akin to what Trotter identifies as 'good mess' (although I should stress again that for him this never quite encompasses the ethical dimension that it acquires in Murdoch – 'good' for Trotter means 'positive'; for Murdoch it means the Good). In looking at these questions, the Murdochian novels that are most relevant to us here and which contain the most insistent explorations of the themes that are relevant to this study of contingency are *The Sea, the Sea* (1978), and *The Black Prince* (1973). Before getting to those, however, I would like briefly to discuss two earlier novels that foreshadowed Murdoch's later exploration of these ideas.

In *A Fairly Honourable Defeat* (1970), Murdoch uses the distinction between different sorts of messes, and the differing aptitudes of her characters to live with mess, as instructive of the difference between goodness and evil. In fact, 'muddle' becomes indicative of an exemplary state of being. Evil, for Murdoch, is the result of the exertion of one's ego to the detriment of others – it flourishes through not truly seeing that other people exist. Among her primary characters we find Morgan, a self-absorbed, superficially charming egotist, easily seduced by her own idea of herself as forever at the centre of some emotional drama. After leaving her husband, the saintly Tallis, Morgan embarks on an affair with the older, powerful and mysterious Julius, but is then rejected by him. She seeks domestic solace by going to stay with her happily married sister Hilda, her husband Rupert and their teenaged son. Julius, with whom Morgan is hoping to prolong their petering-out affair, is the central instrument of plots in the novel. He is a slightly absurd character, a cliché of the charming, mildly dangerous sophisticate; elegant, and seemingly entirely impervious to emotion and messy human entanglements.

Throughout the novel Julius is closely associated with the word 'ingenious', and it is this quality of directing action that is his primary function in the novel. In fact, he is reminiscent of the figure of Joyce's God in *A Portrait of the Artist as a Young Man* (1916); indifferent, paring his fingernails in the face of the human misery he creates.[3] This creative impulse finds its expression in his setting up of plots in his circle to expose the shams of human vanity and love as being no more than extended creations of individual egos. He achieves this by taking on, as a sort of amusement, the task of proving his point, which throughout has been that people are no more than mere 'puppets'. Rupert complains: "'You make human beings sound like puppets.'" Julius replies "'But they *are* puppets, Rupert. And we didn't need modern psychology to tell us that'" (Murdoch, 2001, p. 216). These 'puppets', Julius believes, are controlled by the competing forces of contingency and human ego:

Human beings are roughly constructed entities full of indeterminacies and vaguenesses and empty spaces. Driven along by their own private needs they latch blindly on to each other, then pull away, then clutch again. Their little sadisms and their little masochisms are surface phenomena. Anyone will do to play the roles. They never really see each other at all. (ibid., p. 224)

Julius's counterpoint in the novel is Tallis, one of the most straightforwardly 'good' characters in the whole of Murdoch's oeuvre. Tallis is insistently allied with mess and clutter. His flat is 'littered with filthy junk' (ibid., p. 20), refracted through the perceptions of the other characters – as Hilda says 'Wherever Tallis is there's always a muddle! Then she thought, this is unjust. Wherever there is muddle, there Tallis is' (ibid., p. 178). In fact, Tallis is a paradigmatic Murdochian 'saint', a figure that recurs throughout her novels.[4] In *The Sovereignty of Good* (1970), Murdoch's emblematic 'Saint' figure is shown to be good because he can apprehend formlessness without desiring to impose form on to it, but neither does it submerge him. As Gordon points out: 'it is his ability to bear the mess rather than be subjected to it that distinguishes him' (Gordon, 1995, p. 36). He is, in this way, egoless, and this contrasts to what Murdoch dismissed as the 'existential' hero of much contemporary literature – as she describes him:

the lonely brave man, defiant without optimism, proud without pretension, always an exposer of shams, whose mode of being is a deep criticism of society. He is an adventurer. He is godless. He thinks of himself as free. He may have faults, he may be self-assertive or even violent, but he has sincerity and courage, and for this we forgive him . . . he might do anything (Murdoch, 1970b, p. 18).

Tallis's mode of existence thus critiques human existence in firmly Murdochian mode, and is proved right: all human endeavour in the novel seems to spring from egotism. Here she disseminates Morgan's pathetic delusions, after she has been the subject, along with Peter, of an experiment by Julius to demonstrate how easy it is to manipulate two people into falling in love:

Happiness is free innocent love. It's so different to almost everything else I've been up to almost all my life. The rest remains, tangled, awful, the decisions to be made, the pain to be caused and suffered, the unpredictable edicts of the gods, the machine. But this is outside the machine. This is felicity, blessing, luck, sheer wonderful utterly deserved luck. It can come to me after all. Oh *good*! (Murdoch, 2001, pp. 184–5)

Morgan's egoism inhibits her ability to understand chance – 'sheer wonderful utterly deserved luck', where the 'deserved' undercuts the randomness of the luck – but in his artistry Julius of course makes the same mistake, writ large; he too elides the external world with his own ego in refusing to recognize that other human beings each have their own real existence. For him they are puppets, and so he is unable to quantify the consequences of his mistreatment of them. In fact, the feeling that contingency itself has somehow punished the small world of characters for Julius's meddling is hard to escape. These meta-narrative concerns are the most problematic, and the most radical, aspect of the book: as Gordon notes, 'the most fascinating thing about [the novel] may be the complicity between its villain and its author' (Gordon, 1995, p. 431), and the idea that Julius is a guilt-free proxy for achieving the sort of novelistic plotting that Murdoch tries to resist is an arresting analogy.

I would like to argue against this supposition, which I think is too neat, and which eventually refuses to pay Murdoch the compliment of taking her at her word. I do not think she was attracted to what she was critiquing, though she was clearly aware of the human susceptibility to power. I believe this can be seen through the clear distinction not just between good and evil in the novel, but between Julius's self-descriptions as an 'artist' and Murdoch's own narrative descriptions of him, which are consistently as 'ingenious' or cunning. His artistry, in other words, does not amount to art. Murdoch wrote in *The Sovereignty of Good* that 'the only genuine way to be good is to be good "for nothing" in the midst of a scene where every "natural" thing, including one's own mind is subject to chance, that is, to necessity' (Murdoch, 1970a, p. 63). A few years earlier, in *The Time of the Angels* (1966), Murdoch had foreshadowed this insight when she wrote: 'there is only chance and the terror of chance . . . all altruism feeds the fat ego. . . . People will endlessly conceal from themselves that good is only good if one is good *for nothing*' (Murdoch, 2003a, pp. 163–5). Being good for nothing certainly implies a passive, permissive attitude, but it also goes further – to be good for nothing is to be unable, in some profound way, to exert one's will at all. A passivity and equanimity in the face of the true, chaotic nature of things could thus equally be interpreted as a paralysed inability to act in the presence of the same. Through her depiction of Tallis's perception, Murdoch interestingly explores this conception of good, and its ability to exist in the world: 'the accident was deeply the product of its circumstances. Tallis did not try to unravel these nor did he speculate about the guilt of any person, not even about his own. He grieved blankly over something which seemed, in its disastrous compound of human failure, muddle and sheer chance, so like what it was all like' (Murdoch, 2001, p. 409).

In stark contrast to this, Julius denies the possibility of being 'for nothing'. Everything must have meaning, and mess must be viewed as matter waiting to be ordered by a directing consciousness. As he says to Tallis: 'As things are, what does your life amount to? I suppose it's always like that, but it does pain me. After all, I am an artist. This is just a mess' (ibid., p. 422). The word 'mess' here, as elsewhere, acts as a talisman of contingency; as Gordon puts it, mess is 'the salient quality of the world around us when perceived by a selfless consciousness' (Gordon, 1995, p. 65). Julius's rejection of it is decisive – as the supreme ego in the novel, his novelistic desire to plot, and thus to subvert contingency, is felt with immediacy as a kind of evil. Indeed this 'evil' is shown to be productive, and yet ultimately uncontrollable, even by an ego as authoritative as Julius's: it ends in the foreseen consequence of the breakdown of Hilda and Rupert's marriage, but also in the unforeseen consequence of Rupert's death by suicide, and it fails in its secondary aim of bringing about the end of Axel and Simon's relationship. That this quality of ingenuity is destructive of Tallis's goodness, and of his mess, which are inseparable, is instructive. Ingenuity is tantamount to devising and analysing situations to one's advantage, an epistemological category – those that are ingenious use the contingency of the world around them creatively; they transform mess into an ordered and sequential interpretation of reality. The fact that this is signalled to us through his choice of the word 'artist' is also further evidence for Julius as Murdochian proxy. And yet I think that Murdoch makes a clear distinction between the artist that Julius thinks he is and Murdoch's own art. In as much as *A Fairly Honourable Defeat* explores the operation of evil and the desire to impose form on reality, one could assume an affiliation between Murdoch's view of her own aesthetic task and this evil. However, we see straight away that evil is not merely the misuse of power, but also the creative impulse as *separated* from art. As Gordon says, 'Murdoch characteristically finds the danger of egoism not in the crudest human expressions but in what are generally considered the highest – religion, love, and art' (ibid., p. 9), and he argues that Julius is identified as a metaphorical novelist – indeed, that he is identified with Murdoch's own impulse to form, throughout. However an artist, Murdoch stresses, must respect his characters' consciousnesses. Her insistent use of the word 'ingenuity' in connection to Julius stands for the temptation to shape, without creating real free characters, which, in an echo of Henry Green, is her aspiration. In other words, those that are 'ingenious' attempt form, but crucially without the respect for separate consciousnesses that would, as if through a process akin to alchemy, transform the resulting manipulated reality into art.

What *A Fairly Honourable Defeat* eventually leaves us with is an imprint of the ethical dimension of contingency, an area that Murdoch will creatively expand upon later in her career. Tallis's saintliness and his sanguinity about mess, both literal and metaphysical, are the same thing. His ability to bear the horror of contingency amounts to a refusal to impose his ego on the world in a way that would underestimate the reality of others' existence. Murdoch described this urge in existential terms in 'The Sublime and the Beautiful Revisited': 'According to Sartre, a desire for our lives to have the form and clarity of something necessary, and not accidental, is a fundamental human urge' (Murdoch, 1999a, p. 269). So Tallis's goodness can be seen to be somehow inhuman, as a desire for neatness and form is human. And yet, our attraction to chaos, seen as a constant urge to revert to a primevally messy state, is also human. We could thus be said to be constantly in conflict over the two, and in this sense again Murdoch's writing takes on a prescriptive hue.

An Accidental Man (1971) develops this position interestingly by examining the implication of a contingency that has become alienated from the idea of goodness. The novel takes as its antihero a man whose frequent accidents have become obscured from their causes; for whom the very idea of the 'accidental' has stopped being about luck and has become a sort of determinism. Valentine Cunningham's 2003 introduction to the Vintage edition emphasizes the complex 'accidentalism' of the novel. As Cunningham points out, this is shocking in its iconoclasm towards Murdoch's own sacred theme:

> . . . shocking not least because being 'accidental', making do with the accidentalism of the world, with what Iris Murdoch continually hailed as the 'contingency' of life, is normally for her the essence of the moral, of moral thinking and moral action and crucial to a novel's being what she thought a novel should be, namely an agent of the good. Personal goodness . . . comes through accepting and coping with, not seeking to evade or adjust, the muddle and mess of the world in all its rebarbative detail, its confusing particularity. (Murdoch, 2003b, pp. vii–viii)

This aspect of goodness – the acceptance of the contingent – which we saw in *A Fairly Honourable Defeat*, is only present subtextually in *An Accidental Man*. Here, contingency as a good functions as both unknowable and somehow suspect, while chance reigns over the characters' lives like a malevolent God. As Frank Baldanza points out, in *An Accidental Man*, structurally, 'chance takes over the function of Julius in the preceding novel' (Baldanza, 1974, p. 64).

Unusually for a Murdoch novel, there is no-one who is uncomplicatedly 'good', no-one who suffers for their sins and no-one who has any sort of spiritual breakthrough – this could be read as a commentary on the idea of the meting out of novelistic justice as deterministic, or as a further illustration of the ethical ambiguity of the accidental. Austin Gibson Grey is the accidental man, a selfish destroyer whose deeds are seemingly accidental but also the product of a monstrous ego, trailing the messy debris of human relationships and, interestingly, lots and lots of death behind him. Austin, who is described as 'always doing things he didn't mean or want to do' (Murdoch, 2003b, p. 25), is an example of how those who superficially give themselves up to contingency passively, in a crude satire of the saint figure, are perhaps the greatest egoists of all, for they expect other people to clean up in the wake of their abdication of responsibility. As we have seen, Murdoch's conception of the Good was twofold – her perception of goodness and contingency rest on character in a way that must respect the absolute particularity of persons as we saw above. Goodness for the novelist, then, is essentially the same as goodness in life – the realization that other people's centres of consciousness are as legitimate as one's own. The suppression of the worst excesses of one's ego, or as Gordon has it, the 'unselfing' process, is thus vital.[5] In 'The Sublime and the Beautiful Revisited', Murdoch wrote: 'Virtue is not essentially or immediately concerned with choosing between actions or rules or reasons, nor with stripping the personality for a leap. It is concerned with really apprehending that other people exist. This too is what freedom really is' (Murdoch, 1999a, p. 284). Some of the dense particularities of this formulation are teased out in *An Accidental Man*. The effort to perform ethically aware acts, for instance, is an abiding theme, and the problems of 'really apprehending that other people exist' are demonstrated amply in a novel peopled with ego-bound, blind, selfish, wasters. How to reconcile these two aspects of goodness – if we really understand that people exist we must intervene to help save them from chance itself – is perhaps the primary lesson of the novel: a lesson that remains ultimately unlearned, but a lesson nonetheless.

Chance and accidents batter down on the characters until they all mistrust the very idea of agency; until, indeed, it becomes apparent that 'bad luck is a sort of wickedness in some people' (Murdoch, 2003b, p. 11). Or as Adam Phillips would put it, until they have taken the 'luck out of accidents' (Phillips, 1994, p. 13). Accidents, from the farcical to the lethal, permeate the narrative. In this way, the shadow of a complex sort of determinism is ever-present in the novel. As Cunningham says, 'and all these terrible real accidents are shadowed by possible accidents, by questions about accident and accidentality . . . and these people do seem predestined to awful fates, if only by their novelist' (Murdoch, 2003b, p. xi).

The paradox of Murdoch's belief in contingency as a literary good and her supreme, almost dictatorial authorial control remains unresolved in the novel. Indeed, if the idea of the 'accident', which should be the purest sort of contingent event, has become an 'awful fate', what possible relationship could that bear to the contingent? Does Murdoch invest 'accidentalism', the idea that events have no identifiable cause, and are not in any real way dependent on any other aspect of our reality – with a determinism of its own?

Trotter comments on accidents as follows: 'Freud, as Phillips says, wanted to take the luck out of accident. According to him, accidents at once gratify and disown forbidden desires. To put it another way, they connect us to the person we might have been, the person we still might be. What looks like chance is actually a hidden necessity, a life demanding to be lived' (Trotter, 2001, p. 11). Freud's fullest discussion of chance and his attitude to it is in *The Psychopathology of Everyday Life* (1901, first published in English in 1914), in which he describes the psychoanalyst's aims as being clearly opposed to superstition:

> I believe in external (real) chance, it is true, but not in internal (psychical) accidental events. With the superstitious person it is the other way around. He knows nothing of the motivation of his chance actions and parapraxes and believes in psychical accidental events; and, on the other hand, he has a tendency to ascribe to external chance happenings a meaning which will become manifest in real events, and to regard such chance events as a means of expressing something that is hidden from him in the external world. (Freud, 1966, pp. 257–8)

For Freud, chance was a matter of matter. As for Murdoch, the tendency to ascribe significance to chance events was a function of an overweening ego. Trotter's analysis of Freud, whereby psychical chance works as a linking device between us and our own unlived possibilities – lives that could have been lived, desires that could have been fulfilled – evidently reconnects chance back to its association with the future element discussed above. The idea of possible lives unlived is, in fact, later explored by Murdoch in *The Sea, the Sea*:

> What a queer gamble our existence is. We decide to do A instead of B and then the two roads diverge utterly and may lead in the end to heaven and to hell. Only later one sees how much and how awfully the fates differ. Yet what were the reasons for the choice? They may have been forgotten. Did one know what one was choosing? Certainly not. There are such chasms of might-have-beens in any human life (Murdoch, 1999b, p. 85).

The temporally specific nature of chance, that it cannot exist retrospectively, is of course also what imbues an apprehension of its fleeting presence with such power, as Garth, Austin's son, suddenly realizes one day:

> The contingent details of choice disturbed him. Everything that was offered him was too particular, too hole and corner and accidental, not significant enough, though at the same time he realised with dazzling clarity that all decent things that human beings do are hole and corner. (Murdoch, 2003b, p. 137)

'Hole and corner', 'accidental' – this is the revelation of the meaninglessness and insignificance of one's own life, including even 'the decent things' we might do. The novel constantly equivocates between an interpretation of 'accidentalism' as pure randomness and an interpretation of it as imbued with determinism, and in construction after construction Murdoch elides the two or denies that they are opposed at all: 'Of course Austin had not really done this "on purpose". It had all been, like so many other things in the story, accidental. . . . The stage had been set by whatever deep mythological forces control the destinies of men' (ibid., p. 438); '[t]here were connections, but could they work in his life? Because a child could step into the road and die there was a certain way in which it was necessary to live. The connections were there, a secret logic in the world as relentlessly necessary as a mathematical system.' He continues: '[p]erhaps for God it was a mathematical system, the magnetism of whose necessity touching the here and now was felt as emotion, was felt as passion. He had recognised, at times, that touch and trembled at its awful certainty, being sure that he could not now be otherwise contented. It was an eternal doom. These deaths were merely signs, accidental signs even' (ibid., p. 187).

The association of necessity with passion in the mind of Garth here is an obscene parody of the revelation that is associated with apprehension of the Good, but later on in the mind of the agnostic and tortured Charlotte a truthful and consolation-free recognition of the true chaos of the world is perhaps a sign of madness:

> Why should she kill herself in a fit of envy, and then again why should she not? It was all one. Whether this despair made it easier or harder to act, whether it would finally carry her off, mere chance would decide. She had always been the slave of chance, let it kill her if it would by a random stroke, She would not die gladly, but then she had not loved gladly either. Her swansong would be made of words smashed into nonsense against a

cracked world, exploding with it into the chaos upon which everything
rested and out of which it was made. (ibid., p. 261)

This is not a submission to contingency, like Tallis's, that is necessary for an
understanding of the good. This is a perversion of the interconnectedness
of cause and effect into the terrifying reverse aspect of chance – that which
makes a 'nonsense' of language and is the chaos of anarchy. It permeates
the description of the death of Austin's troubled wife Dorina: 'the thing was
pure chance and yet weighted with a significance of horror which he could
not bear to contemplate' (ibid., p. 317). The word 'horror' here seems specifically Sartrean – the horror at the contingency of the universe, which is
the proper human reaction to formlessness – but in Murdoch, that horror
must be transmuted into a sort of grace. That the transformation into this
state of grace, which is an apprehension of the Good, has failed to occur in
the novel at all can be read as Murdoch's disgust at the susceptibility of
humans to the consolatory power of turning away from that horror instead
of accepting it. In *Metaphysics as a Guide to Morals* (1992) she wrote: '[the
novel contains] the invincible variety, contingency and scarcely communi-
cable frightfulness of life' (Murdoch, 1992, p. 96). This is akin to what
Sartre would call nausea: the horror provoked by an awareness of contingency. In *The Black Prince*, she would write that life 'is horrible, without
metaphysical sense, wrecked by chance, pain and the close prospect of
death' (Murdoch, 1975, p. 73).

   It is clear that alertness to accident has here become transformed into the
obverse of the characteristic Murdochian awareness of the contingent. In
any case, as Phillips points out, 'accidents' always tend to be bad: 'that our
lives might simply be a series or collection of coincidences seems peculiarly
unacceptable (though it could, of course, be comforting). Indeed, the word
"accident" usually signifies something going wrong' (Phillips, 1994, p. 17).
So in this sense, *An Accidental Man* is an examination of the relationship
between the accidental (negative) and the contingent (positive), in a world
where, sadly, the contingent is found wanting.

The Black Prince: Causality and the Erotics of Mess

The Black Prince is generally considered to be, along with *The Sea, the Sea*,
one of Murdoch's very finest novels. It is the story of Bradley Pearson, a
58-year-old, ascetic writer, whose degree of success, in both his life and
his literary career, has been minimal. He is divorced, and lives alone,

unencumbered by either literary productivity or a functional social life. He spends much of his time trying to remain detached from the mess and dirt of other people's human relationships, which he views with distaste. Bradley's friend and rival, Arnold Baffin, is a successful writer whose life is the reverse of Bradley's – his family life is unimaginable; chaotic, but a source of joy, and his literary profligacy inspires a similar mixture of envy and disgust from Bradley. The narrative that Murdoch constructs around these two contradictory figures revolves around the human desire to extinguish contingency and the temptation to impose form on one's life. Bradley, indeed, is firmly in the tradition of the Murdochian male ascetic. He fears contingency, trains for him representing 'object lessons in the foul contingency of life' (Murdoch, 1975, p. 66). The proximity of this contingency-denial to a kind of neurosis is exemplified by Bradley, and I would like to suggest that in *The Black Prince* Murdoch consistently allies resistance to, or fear of, contingency to madness of various types. This further impresses upon us Murdoch's belief that the opposite state must be attained, one that can recognize muddle and mess as part of the natural process of being and as part of the process that will lead us to the good.

As in most Murdoch novels, love is transformative, if transitory. Bradley falls in love with Julian Baffin, Arnold's daughter, and runs away with her briefly, but then she changes her mind and returns to her parents. It is an affair with disastrous consequences, eventually culminating in the death of Arnold. The novel opens with Bradley being called upon to enter the dark, unknowable confines of this family life when Arnold asks him to come over as he thinks he may have killed his wife. Bradley arrives to find an alive, but humiliated and distraught, Rachel in bed. His description of her is worth quoting in full:

> There was a dark reddish bruise under one eye and the eye was narrowed, though this was hard to see because the eyelids of both eyes were so grossly red and swollen with weeping. Her upper lip was also swollen on one side. There were traces of blood on her neck and on her dress. Her hair was tangled and looked darker as if wet; perhaps it was literally wet with the flow of her tears. She was panting now, almost gasping. She had undone the front of her dress and I could see some white lace of her brassiere and a plump pallor of flesh below. . . . I got a whiff of alcohol from her panting breath. She knelt upon her dress and I heard it tear. Then she half ran half fell across the room to the disordered bed, where she flopped on her back, tugging at the bed-clothes, ineffectually because she was half lying on them, then covering her face with both hands and crying

in an appalling wailing manner, lying with her feet wide apart in a grace-
less self-absorption of grief. (ibid., pp. 34–5)

Rachel's humanity, her very physical being, inspires disgust and horror in
the neurotic and fastidious Bradley. Her injuries are perceived aesthetically
as slights upon Bradley's sight. Mingled with this horror is an unmistakeable eroticism, perceptible in the relish with which Bradley describes what
disgusts him: 'her hair was tangled and looked darker as if wet; perhaps it
was literally wet with the flow of her tears. She was panting now, almost gasp-
ing. She had undone the front of her dress and I could see some white lace
of her brassiere and a plump pallor of flesh below'.

In fact, the eroticization of mess is a primary theme of *The Black Prince*,
suggesting that Bradley's asceticism is perhaps related to repressed sexual
desire. The question of repression is addressed in the text itself, by
Bradley's continual return to Freudian tropes, such as his fixation with
London's Post Office Tower; he admires its clean lines and forceful, phallic
imprint on the sky. We are led by the text to contemplate the possibility that
Bradley is in fact a repressed homosexual, and that his distaste for the feminine is connected to his falling in love with a boyish girl (with a boy's name)
and experiencing a sexual epiphany that overrides his previous impotence
when he sees her dressed as a Shakespearean prince. A sense that male
desire is affiliated with artistry, and with the imposition of form onto the
debauched and louche idea of the feminine , is the clear subtext here.

Male sexuality throughout the novel is in fact complicit with the desire to
extinguish a more natural, messy state of being. In a parallel to the Rachel
scene, Bradley is later called upon to deal with another middle-aged woman
in dire straits who also lies in bed prostrate but who is similarly incapable of
evoking pathos in Bradley. His sister, Priscilla, has turned up at Bradley's
house after leaving her husband on suspicion of an infidelity that is later
confirmed in the narrative:

> I did not know what to do, I felt fear and disgust at the idea of 'mental
> breakdown', the semi-deliberate refusal to go on organising one's life
> which is regarded with such tolerance these days. I peered into the room.
> Priscilla was lying in a sort of abandoned attitude on her side, having half
> kicked off her bedclothes. Her mouth was wet and wide open. A plump
> stockinged leg stuck rather awkwardly out of the bed. (ibid., p. 75)

The 'fear and disgust' is a clear echo of the scene in Rachel's bedroom,
where objects and flesh alike evoke horror:

The room has the rather sinister tedium which some bedrooms have, a sort of weary banality which is a reminder of death. A dressing table can be a terrible thing. . . . The plate glass 'table' surface was dusty and covered with cosmetic tubes and bottles and balls of hair. The chest of drawers had all its drawers gaping, spewing pink underwear and shoulder straps. The bed was chaotic, violent, the green artificial silk coverlet swooping down on one side and the sheets and blankets creased up into a messy mass, like an old face. There was a warm, embarrassing smell of sweat and face powder. The whole room breathed the flat horror of genuine mortality, dull and spiritless and final. I do not know why I thought so promptly and prophetically of death. . . . I felt the soft warmth of the brown stockinged foot. A pungent sour odour joined the vapid smell of the room. I wiped my hands on my trousers. (ibid., pp. 38–9)

In fact objects, here, have become metonymically inextricable from the true subject of this description – Rachel. She is present merely in her accoutrements and a pervasive smell, and, finally, a 'brown stockinged foot', which is corpse-like in its immobility. David Trotter identifies objects as having an affinity and complicity with contingency itself:

Messes often involve a mutually defining collision between a person and an object: a man knocks over a vase, a woman touches a freshly painted gate. Since they promise a meaning and a value that has little to do with conscious or unconscious intent, such encounters might be thought to provoke one of modern philosophy's most enduring fantasies: that suspension of the mind's search for significance would somehow make possible an account of the way the body inhabits the world. (Trotter, 2000, pp. 14–15)

Objects are inherently chancy as they are distinct from any human intent, and thus our communion with them can tell us much about our existence in a contingent reality. Murdoch herself certainly felt an affinity with the inanimate, as she commented to Harry Weinberger: 'How nice objects are – I'm glad we live in a thingy world' (Conradi, 2001, p. 588). For Bradley, that we live in a 'thingy' world is an occasion for fear and disgust, and the erotic possibilities afforded by the spectacle have been reduced to the 'embarrassing' intimacy of what he is witnessing. And yet the submerged possibility that the violent chaos of the scene could be transmuted from one that evokes mortality to one that contains the suggestion of eroticism, is present. This eroticism depends on the scene's essential unpredictability;

its chaos. Trotter makes explicit the tripartite affiliation between chance, sex and death:

> Chance is potentially the matrix and occasion both of desire and of death
> . . . it may bring about, in an especially poignant way, the end not only of
> all possibility, but of all thinking about possibility. Chance presides over
> ultimate determination: over events in the face of which, when they come,
> we are helpless; over an effect whose cause we can barely conceive. . . .
> Illusion-destroying mess, actual or represented, enables us to understand
> contingency as the matrix and occasion of an exemplary death: not the
> death which happens as the outcome of an identifiable sequence of cause
> and effect, but the death which need not have happened at all, the death
> which is pure death. (Trotter, 2000, p. 9)

This is an extension of Phillips's useful description of uncertainty as erotic: 'disfiguring the difference between innocence and experience, intent and opportunity, flirtation does not make a virtue of instability, but a pleasure. It eroticizes the contingency of our lives by turning doubt – or ambiguity – into suspense' (Phillips, 1994, p. xxiii). It is the scene's messiness, and its contingency, that brings to Bradley's mind both the suppressed sexual associations and his sudden apprehension of death. The mess itself is the cause and the effect: it is contingency at its rawest. The possibility of death itself is eroticized as the ultimately gratuitous act – a flirtation with death becoming merely one further embrace of possibility.

The Black Prince is also a novel mired in the tension between causality and chance, and between the differing ideas of the self as a possible site determined by the operation of both. If we are helpless in the face of external events, and our essential self, and the reasons for that self's disfigurement, can be traced back through our behaviour and thereby explained, then this is both an elaboration of the self as a construction of causes beyond our control and a denial of the same. If every 'accident' or 'coincidence' can be explained away, if everyone is who they are for a set of ultimately explicable reasons, has the self not become an over-determined way to deny contingency? Gordon has argued for Murdoch's view of causality as a departure from any previous understanding of aetiology:

> She is postulating a system of 'moral' or 'spiritual' causality based on the
> cosmological forces of Chance and Necessity, a system that may be identi-
> fied with God understood as a power that impinges on human conscious-
> ness but that cannot be identified with human will or choice. (Gordon,
> 1995, p. 97)

This is a sophisticated analysis, but one that places too great an emphasis on necessity. Murdoch did not believe that necessity was a cosmological force. Indeed, in Murdoch's novels, a belief in necessity, or in any sort of compelling force that stands outside character, is usually a sign of madness, and for this reason I would argue that Gordon overstates his case when he claims that 'Chance and Necessity, then, are equally aspects of the Good' (ibid., p. 105). Other critics have noticed Murdoch's treatment of cause and effect but interpreted it rather differently. Elizabeth Dipple, for example, emphasizes the interaction of causality and contingency: 'her novels attempt the talk of discriminating, of showing how the tenure of certain ideas affect behaviour, how cause and effect operate, what power chance has' (Dipple, 1982, p. 39) and 'the causality of Bradley Pearson's punishment in losing Julian is part of the larger pattern of cause and effect which governs this book' (ibid., p. 125). Patrick Swinden goes further, and underplays the role of causality, suggesting that Murdoch 'does not believe that motive and consequence, cause and effect, are as firmly connected with each other as they have usually been represented in fiction', and 'the network is gradually revealed (to the reader as well as the character) to be an artificial environment. It is unreal, and its unreality tends to diminish the character's sense of his own reality as well as that of other people' (Swinden, 1973, pp. 235–6). This reading, however, wrongly necessitates the sort of clear-cut distinction between contingency and cause and effect that Murdoch, unlike Johnson or Beckett, is at pains to elide. Contingency, in *The Black Prince*, is profoundly linked to cause and effect – one makes things explicable and the other makes things inexplicable, but both are implicated in the 'dense mesh of interconnections' (Murdoch, 1975, p. 125) that the good feel constitutes being, and both subvert Bradley's attempt at directing others' lives as art: as Gordon points out, 'truly good art shows us the defeat of human wishes by contingency' (Gordon, 1995, p. 105). He goes on to suggest that Murdoch's novels work as an elaboration of a specific theory of causality. Detectable in her work, he argues:

> . . . is a creatively reactive argument against psychoanalysis and against the idea that 'character' and its 'deep' conflicts determine our fate. She would show that, to a greater extent than we know or say, Chance and Necessity rule our destinies, that we are absurd creatures rather than protagonists who struggle against destiny with tragic seriousness. Such an argument is hardly congruent with a humanistic philosophy, but practice is less extreme than theory, in part because the novelist's obligation to invest human characters with the understanding of these truths, to dramatise the wisdom of self-responsibility even if the content of that wisdom

is the recognition of one's limits in the scheme of things. Then, too, some of her novels, pitched in a more genial key, lean towards the generous-humane rather than the severe-ascetic end of the tragic-comic spectrum. These novels smile at human vanity and at our moral pretension in thinking ourselves free choosers and masters of destiny, showing as they do that choice and responsibility remain important in an extended view of human values. (ibid., p. 97)

The Black Prince, though, shows a more subtle engagement with Freudian psychology than a characterization of the psychoanalytic approach as deterministic, and opposed to the meta-psychological agency of chance, would allow. Bradley's elaboration of certain Freudian tropes are certainly emphasized – the obsession with the Post Office Tower, his neuroses, his homoerotic competitiveness with Arnold and the fact that his sexuality is only unleashed in the novel when he sees Julian dressed as Prince Hal. The Freudian interpretations of these aspects of Bradley's behaviour, however, are given to Francis Marlowe, consistently shown to be an egocentric, repellent character, and thus, I suggest, are simultaneously dismissed by Murdoch. Marlowe's personal sensationalism and desire for gossip elaborate his Freudian readings of Bradley's behaviour as superficial and titillating surface correspondences, that serve to diminish whoever puts them forward as explanations for human behaviour. Marlowe is a buffoon, whose inability to understand people or their real motivations at all is a source of comedy and pathos throughout the novel, and which reveals itself in his monologic postscript as a set of misreadings so severe as to edge into evil.[6]

In fact, we intuit, the reality of people is so complex and contradictory and particular that all versions of a person can be simultaneously true, and that to limit one's characterization of another to one aspect of their character is to misunderstand everything about the person. The bastardized version of Freud represented by Marlowe is a straw man argument, knocked down easily, to reveal a more profound allusion to psychoanalytical ideas in terms of causality. As Phillips comments, 'acknowledgement of the contingency of the self – and the contingent self that lives this acknowledgement – need not be exclusively a disillusioning or depressive experience, because somewhere one has never had illusions about it; in adult life it is contesting one's contingency that is productive of disabling illusion' (Phillips, 1994, p. 20). Although, as Phillips points out, the Freudian slip 'is the accident that is meant to happen' (ibid., p. 9), Freud's attachment to chance complicates and shields this formulation from any easy determinism, or, as Phillips formulates it, 'It may not be that all accidents are meaningful, but that meaning is made out of accidents' (ibid., p. 11). Freud indeed, was no determinist. As he wrote in 1910:

> If one considers chance to be unworthy of determining our fate, it is simply a relapse into the pious view of the universe which Leonardo himself was on his way to overcoming when he wrote that the sun does not move . . . we are all too ready to forget that in fact everything to do with our life is chance, from our origin out of the meeting of spermatozoon and ovum onwards. . . . We all still show too little respect for Nature which (in the obscure words of Leonardo which recall Hamlet's lines) 'is full of countless causes ("ragioni") that never enter experience.' Everyone of us human beings corresponds to one of the countless experiments in which these 'ragioni' of nature force their way into experience. (Freud, 1957, p. 264)

The ragioni represent not the explicability of cause and effect, but the inexplicability. That causality can be antithetical to the superficial desire to know why one thing happened over another thing belies the easy characterization of it offered by Marlowe. Richard Rorty traces this paradigmatic change that sees the self as contingent back to Nietzsche, who scorned the notion of some universal truth, and instead 'saw self-knowledge as self-creation. The process of coming to know oneself, confronting one's contingency, tracking one's causes home, is identical with the process of inventing a new language' (Rorty, 1989, p. 27). He goes on:

> . . . only poets, Nietzsche suspected, can truly appreciate contingency. The rest of us are doomed to remain philosophers, to insist there is only one true lading-list, one true description of the human situation, one universal context of our lives. We are doomed to spend our conscious lives trying to escape from contingency rather than, like the strong poet, acknowledging and appropriating contingency. (ibid., p. 28)

Because of Freud's detailed explanations of things, 'he leaves us with a self which is a tissue of contingencies' (ibid., p. 32).

Murdoch's elaboration of causality in the novel emphasizes the contingent self and endows it with ethical value, while refusing to oppose it to chance. The good have an awareness of the contingency of events that can transform the operation of chance into grace, while the wicked unthinkingly ignore the 'dense mesh of interconnectedness', which represents cause and effect, and thus their ability to comprehend the world of chance, or reality, is severely limited:

A serious kiss can alter the world and should not be allowed to take place simply because the scene will be disfigured without it. These considerations will no doubt seem to the young unutterably prudish and fussy. But precisely because they are young they cannot see how all things have their consequences. (This thing had consequences, including some very unexpected ones.) There are no spare unrecorded encapsulated moments in which we can behave 'anyhow' and then expect life to resume where we left off. The wicked regard time as discontinuous, the wicked dull their sense of natural causality. The good feel being as a total dense mesh of tiny interconnection. My lightest whim can affect the whole future. Because I smoke a cigarette and smile over an unworthy thought another man may die in torment . . . the past must be justly judged. Whatever marvels may have sprung out of one's faults through the incomprehensible operation of grace. *O felix culpa!* does not excuse anything. (Murdoch, 1975, pp. 124–5)

Murdoch's understanding of contingency does not rest on the idea that reality is *provisional*, but rather that it is essentially *dependent*. One event, one chance occurrence, is merely the product of a 'dense mesh of interconnections'. Thus reality is apprehended as a vast sea of contingency, comprehensible to us only in tiny portions. As we saw in the first chapter, causality has long been understood and assimilated in opposition to chance, as it allowed in Newtonian physics for the idea of determinism, but in the twentieth century causality has been distinguished by its sense of being cut off from these old mechanistic cause and effect ideas. Events have not become randomized, but causality allows for and embraces the random. Causality is therefore a way of both acknowledging that chance is worthy of determining our fate, and, for Bradley, another path away from the 'good muddle' and into paranoia. 'Everything is connected' cannot be understood as a rational response to aetiology – the butterfly effect, in other words, is no way to live one's life. Bradley's 'embrace' of contingency, then, where he believes that 'my slightest whim can . . .' is an illusion. The pathos of these messy Murdoch novels, indeed, is that no one ever learns – and even if they do, they forget again.

Contingency as the Good – *The Sea, the Sea*

Charles Arrowby, the male first person narrator of *The Sea, the Sea*, tells us early on, 'I hate *mess*', thus establishing himself as another masculine denier of contingency (Murdoch, 1999b, p. 38). However he is more attractive than Bradley, and more complex than Julius. Through him, Murdoch investigates the exercise of power and its relationship to contingency and the good. Charles' power is partly that of the artist, and partly that of the charismatic male manipulator. The narrative, more so than any other Murdoch novel, meditates on the connection between the abuse of power and 'form'. 'Lies, lies, almost all art is lies. Hell itself turns to favour and to prettiness. *Muck* . . . All art disfigures life, misrepresents it' (ibid., p. 164). This is reminiscent of Murdoch's formulation that 'form is the great temptation of art, because it threatens to become an end or stopping point in itself, rather than serving to illuminate that reality which always exceeds our descriptions of it' (Murdoch, 1961, p. 20). For Murdoch, we know that the dangers of form extend to life: 'Form is the great consolation of love, but also its great temptation' (Murdoch, 1959, p. 55). Charles is perhaps the personification of the impulse or temptation to form, not as an 'artist', as we saw with Julius, but, rather, he tries to create a narrative of his life by the exercise of manipulative power. The coincidence of his meeting his first love again, in the tiny village where he has come to retire, is recast as fate: 'I mean what incredible luck to meet her again like that, it's the hand of destiny' (Murdoch, 1999b, p. 177). And this extends to his view of all coincidence: '"I don't understand you, you're babbling. Why did he come here?" "I don't know, it was an accident, it was a chance –" "Funny sort of chance. My God, you're clever, it's the one bloody thing that would torment me more than anything else"' (ibid., p. 195). He doesn't believe in chance, because chance is what would work against and undo his tenuous control of the world.

Charles' hatred of mess and muddle defines him. After Hartley runs away from him, and Charles fears she is lost on the rocks, he follows her:

> It was extremely difficult to keep any pace over the rocks since they were so unpredictable and devoid of reason. Their *senselessness* had never so much impressed me. I kept trying to get near to the edge of the sea but the rocks kept defeating me, not by malign interest but by sheer muddle. (ibid., p. 234)

Titus, Hartley's son, echoes Bradley in an ominous foreshadowing of his eventual swallowing by the primary symbol of 'muddle' in the novel, the sea: '"I left home so as not to be bothered by muddles like that, I *hate* muddles, and I've had them all my life with those two, muddle, muddle, muddle. They're not bad people really, they've just got no sense of *how to live* a human life"' (ibid., p. 376; emphasis mine). The instructive, ethically prescriptive aspect of Murdoch's prose is thus ironized heavily. In contrast to these men, Hartley, in her quotidian, feminine, unassuming sanity recognizes muddle as her *métier*: "'of course it's a muddle, but it's my muddle, it's where I live and what I am. I can't run out of it and leave it all behind all jagged and loose like a broken shell'" (ibid., p. 302).

Throughout the book, Charles's attempts to master the world – his exercise of power in all spheres of his life, his corrupt and egotistical manipulation and control of others – is consistently contrasted with the 'mess' of the natural world and specifically of the sea. Charles' cousin James, who is a Buddhist, is set up by Murdoch as Charles' opposite number in how they react to and use contingency and muddle. As Charles says to James: "'I didn't ever believe you'd put yourself in this sort of squalid muddle. It's a kind of ordinary sly human stupidity which I was foolish enough to imagine you didn't suffer from. You've behaved like ordinary people do who can't imagine consequences'" (Murdoch, 1999b, pp. 409–10). James also, tellingly, admires the sea. He says to Charles just after Hartley has been trying to get him to let her leave, "'Charles, just look at the force of that water, isn't it fantastic, isn't it terrifying?'" (ibid., p. 330). Charles, in contrast, and while he is shown to be attracted to the sea's formlessness, projects his own neuroses onto it in the form of a sea monster which functions as a metaphor for the sea's terrifying power, because he cannot truly apprehend it – though his artistic descriptions of its formlessness imply otherwise. Charles is eventually pushed into the 'cauldron': 'I actually saw, in the diffused midsummer darkness-light, the creamy curling waves just below me, and the particular spiral of their movement in the confined space. Then I was in the water whose intense cold surprised me with a separate shock, and I made the instinctive swimmer's movement of trying to right myself; but my body was aware that no swimming could take place in that vortex' (ibid., p. 365). The vortex in its destructive chaos rebuffs all attempts to swim. In fact, the manner of the description of the 'cauldron' fulfils a similar function to Murdoch's use of fog in earlier novels. As Conradi says, 'fogs feature in Iris's novels as a concrete metaphor for obfuscation, or a bewitchment of the intelligence' (Conradi, 2001, p. 351). Throughout the novel swimming has functioned as an expression of Charles' individuality, and of his individual exercise of power, which he imposes on the sea. Swimming is an act of will that creatively transforms vast chaotic areas of matter into purpose and directed movement; that it is eternally frustrated is Murdoch's elaboration of the ability of the contingency of reality to eventually undermine man's volition.

In the postscript to the novel, Murdoch describes this impulse of Charles's, in a manner that could stand as a final description of this paradox at the heart of all of her most important novels:

> That is no doubt how the story ought to end, with the seals and the stars, explanation, resignation, reconciliation, everything picked up into some radiant bland ambiguous higher significance, in calm of mind, all passion spent. However life, unlike art, has an irritating way of bumping and limping on, undoing conversions, casting doubt on solutions, and generally illustrating the impossibility of living happily or virtuously ever after. . . . I might take this opportunity to tie up a few loose ends, only of course loose ends can never be properly tied, one is always producing new ones. Time, like the sea, undoes all knots. Judgments on people are never final, they emerge from summings up which at once suggest the need of a reconsideration. Human arrangements are nothing but loose ends and hazy reckoning, whatever art may pretend otherwise in order to console us. (Murdoch, 1999b, p. 477)

The sea that undoes all knots stands as a beautiful metaphor for Murdoch's understanding of life. That we must continue to try and resist the temptations of consolation is her great lesson, whether it remains unlearnt or not. She advocates that we must try and bear the loose ends, without explaining them away by an oppressive obsession with causality, or imposing a dishonest artistic structure on top of them. As Peter Conradi says, 'Her work abounds in iconoclasm, books left incomplete, torn-up, china or glass smashed' (Conradi, 2001, p. 549). Similarly, in an interview with John Barrows in 1961, she called her work 'an investigation that never ends, rather than a means of resolving anything' (Barrows, 1961, p. 498). In the end, her decisive allying of contingency, mess and chance with a prescriptive and instructive ethical philosophy – this is how we *should* live – is what saves chance in her work from scientific neutrality or existential horror, or Beckettian ignorance. Contingency, for Murdoch, represents openness to possibility, and a rejection of the scepticism that was the corollary of chance and uncertainty: rather, it is a way of being open to all things.

Conclusion

In conclusion I would like to return briefly to an idea that has run, covertly, alongside this (and, I would argue, every) examination of chance, and which I touched upon in Chapter Three, above: the idea of freedom and its relation to the individual. Freedom's relation to chance is at once straightforward and oblique; it is the condition for chance, it is its *a priori*, but it also bears a heavier conceptual burden: freedom is a political, social and economic mode of experience as well as a metaphysical one. Nevertheless, the growth of chance in the mid-part of the twentieth century implicates the idea of freedom in various ways, and, I would argue, specifically reintroduces the cultural shadow left by the Second World War.

In Chapter Three, I sketched the linkage between the existentialist's conception of freedom and possibility with our understanding of chance, and concluded that the post-existential idea of chance was infected with the pessimism of the post-war idea of possibility – an idea that had become heavily ironized. The paradigmatic existentialist idea of freedom was one of literal constraint due to the experience of the war, as demonstrated by Sartre's famous statement in that '[n]ever were we freer than under the German occupation' (Sartre, 2008, p. 3), his point being that, during an occupation, every choice is endowed with, literally, life or death significance, and that this, at least, is one way to escape meaninglessness. The paradoxical association of oppression with freedom has resonance with the existential conception of possibility, and I limn the immediately post-war conception of possibility as a sort of 'negative possibility', as expressed in Beckett's *Watt*. The idea of freedom, and of possibility, cut loose from wartime strictures became not a liberating idea, but a terrifying one. In suggesting this I follow Erich Fromm, whose *The Fear of Freedom* (1942) was one of the most influential and powerful works of mid-twentieth-century psychoanalytical philosophy. Fromm charts the distinction between 'negative' and 'positive' freedom: the former he diagnoses as the wartime reality, and the latter as a possible state to which we might aspire. He uses the fall in Christian theology as the point of beginning for human freedom: '[Man] acts against God's command, he breaks through the state of harmony with nature of which he is a part without transcending it' (Fromm, 2001, p. 28). This is 'sin' from the perspective of the Christian institution. And yet, posits Fromm, 'from the standpoint of man, this is the beginning of human freedom'. However, 'freedom from', we must understand, is not identical with positive freedom, which Fromm calls 'freedom to'. 'Freedom from' is negative freedom, merely existence without instinctive determination of actions. As such, it is perhaps best understood as a condition of being human, to some extent, and amounts to the realization that one's actions are willed and not mere products of mechanistic systems. Negative freedom, in fact, emerges as barely freedom at all; Fromm describes the modern individual as pathetically incapable of meaningful choice. His sketch of modern man, helpless and unfree, amounts to a rebuttal of the perhaps easy assumptions about the empowering potential of choice that the existentialists were making during the same period, and is worth quoting at length:

> The threat of war has also added to the feeling of individual powerlessness. To be sure, there were wars in the nineteenth century too. But since the last the possibilities of destruction have increased so tremendously – the range of people to be affected by war has grown to such an extent as to comprise everybody without exception – that the threat of war has become a nightmare which, though it may not be conscious to many people before their nation is actually involved in the war, has overshadowed their lives and increased their feeling of fright and individual powerlessness. . . . The 'style' of the whole period corresponds to the picture I have sketched. Vastness of cities in which the individual is lost, buildings that are as high as mountains, constant acoustic bombardment by the radio, big headlines changing three times a day and leaving one no choice to decide what is important, shows in which one hundred girls demonstrate their ability with clocklike precision to eliminate the individual and act like a powerful though smooth machine, the beating rhythm of jazz – these and many other details are expressions of a constellation in which the individual is confronted by uncontrollable dimensions in comparison with which he is a small particle. All he can do is fall in step like a marching soldier or a worker on the endless belt. He can act; but the sense of independence, significance, has gone. (ibid., p. 113)

As a possible solution to this circumscribed and stymied existence, Fromm offers the following: 'We believe there is a positive answer, that the process of growing freedom does not constitute a vicious circle, and that man can be free and not alone' (ibid., p. 222). 'Freedom to' is thus the state to which we must aspire, where we are capable of spontaneous acts of true freedom. Fromm's essay is an attempt to define this positive freedom and the ways in which it is stymied by modern life: by commercial, political and economic systems to which the individual, automaton-like, feels he must submit. He continues: 'positive freedom consists in the spontaneous activity of the total, integrated personality' (ibid.). Artists and small children, he suggests, have his essential quality of spontaneity, and it is what we must strive to achieve if we are to escape the automatized actions that come naturally to us in the face of the depersonalized conditions sketched above, and which, without our conscious assent, construct a psychic prison in which most people live their lives. Moreover, 'Love is the foremost component of such spontaneity; not love as the dissolution of the self in another person, not love as the possession of another person, but love as spontaneous affirmation of others' (ibid., p. 225).

This is strikingly similar to Iris Murdoch's prescriptive advocacy of love as a path to the Good. For both Fromm and Murdoch, 'love' is a mode of communion between individuals, not necessarily as in the all-consuming submersion of the self in another as is often implied in modern conceptions of romantic love, but a form of conducting one's relationships to other individuals and the wider society. It consists of appreciating others' individuality and thus maintaining each person's contingency: that is, in respecting another person as an individual site of consciousness as valid as one's own, rather than perceiving them dimly through the refracting lens of one's own ego. By loving in this way, Murdoch argued throughout her oeuvre, we could allow the contingency of character, or that unpredictable aspect of others that is not like ourselves, its full expression. In 'The Sublime and the Beautiful Revisited', Murdoch writes: 'Virtue is not essentially or immediately concerned with choosing between actions or rules or reasons, nor with stripping the personality for a leap. It is concerned with really apprehending that other people exist. This too is what freedom really is' (Murdoch, 1999a, p. 284). She expands on this idea in the essay 'Against Dryness', where she says that character should be thought of as 'substantial, impenetrable, individual, indefinable and valuable' (Murdoch, 1991, p. 16). The ideal character is 'free and separate . . . related to a rich and complicated world from which as a moral being he has much to learn' (ibid., p. 18). This is how contingency, the differentness of the world and others, can help us out of the trap of unfreedom; for evil for Murdoch is done when an individual tries to impose their own ego on the world surrounding them. Fromm's vision of 'spontaneity', in this sense, does a similar job to Murdoch's 'contingency' (and indeed the very word spontaneity comes from the Latin for free will).

As mentioned in Chapter Three, Leland Monk argues that Joyce's *Ulysses* marks the cut-off point of chance's representation in literature because it 'rejoices in things that happen by chance', and the resulting 'undecidability of pleasure' supersedes the authorial will and imposes its own agency on the text – an agency that prioritizes the pleasurable aesthetic of the unpredictable over the aesthetic of authorial will and determination (Monk, 1993, pp. 151, 152). Although *Ulysses* predates the historical period that I have been examining, the idea has a kinship with my central argument that undermines Monk's claim that Joyce represents a watershed for chance. I have suggested that what happened throughout the period was a slow accommodating of the positive aspects of chance, resulting in Murdoch's philosophical rehabilitation of chance in her work under the rubric of contingency as the Good. Accepting chance as the controlling force in the universe endows the individual with an ability to see all events as ultimately forgivable: accidentality allows for a sort of grace. Monk's principle of pleasure perhaps allows for the open-endedness of texts in the same way that the idea espoused by Murdoch and Fromm allows for the open-endedness of persons: form, is, after all, 'the temptation of love and its peril' (Murdoch, 1999a, p. 285). To revel in a lack of form, and to let the pleasurable aesthetic of chance (erratic, whimsical, flirtatious) dominate, is thus instructive. The pleasure of chance was after all that identified by Bergler as 'the one exceptional situation in life *where the reality principle has no advantage over the pleasure principle*. There blind chance rules' (Bergler, 1957, p. 18; my emphasis).

Contingency, and its embracing of character, is thus perhaps the key concept in terms of getting us out of the dead end into which Johnson, and the branch of 1960s' experimental literature that he represents had backed us into; where chance was made to stand in for the idea of artistic authority. An appreciation of contingency allows for pure randomness. It tells us that the world makes no sense. But it also invites us to bear it, to live with it passively. Murdoch articulates and bodies forth this new optimism about contingency in her novels. If contingency can be allied with goodness, then the increasingly neurotic treatment of randomness, the fear of chance and its subversive capabilities, can perhaps be forced into quietude. Murdoch's radicalism lies in her break with the centuries-old apprehension of chance's negative ethical capability. Murdoch believes that mess and muddle are the natural state of the universe when it is perceived by a good, ego-less consciousness that does not seek to distort what it perceives. As a corollary to this, she believes that form is untruthful, a prop for the uncourageous and a sop to the ego-bound who need to believe that they have had a detectable impact on the mess of reality. In this '[thinking] *with* mess as well as *about* it', as David Trotter has it (Trotter, 2000, p. 8), Murdoch tries to let the mess into her novels, allowing the contingency of the self in the form of character to subvert the necessary rigidity of literary form. As such, much of what we find in Murdoch is a rigorous formulation and working out of ideas we saw emerging in Green. That chance came to be, for Green, a mode of existing passively in the world, is systematized in Murdoch into the Good – co-existing with contingency, or being 'good for nothing'. In the Murdoch novels that explore her philosophical ideas about chance, it is eventually chance and contingency that prove redemptive. The submission to them, or the allowance of their potentially transformative natures, is what subverts the deathly pull of necessity in life and the deathless pull of form in art.

Murdoch's transformation of chance into 'positive' chance is thus analogous to Fromm's prescriptive vision of positive freedom twenty years earlier. The formulation of strategies for transforming chance's operations in the text from a difficult, marginal, unrepresentable 'other', has been a largely narratological task, but one that has throughout its history sustained implications for wider ethical questions about society's attitude to determinism and uncertainty. Indeed, mastery over the facts of history has always involved the suppression and undermining of uncertainty, as Monk notes:

> Of course, chance has been marginalized not simply because of some covert and pervasive metaphysical conspiracy but because it is by its very nature eccentric in relation to a central paradigm of action and thought; chance inhabits the periphery of whatever frame of power-knowledge is in place, simultaneously defining and transgressing the borders or limits that constitute that frame. (Monk, 1993, pp. 4–5)

The transformation of chance from an aspect of experience that was marginalized in the novel into a textual trope analogous to positive freedom, and capable of delivering a stark rebuttal to any easy assumptions about deterministic aspects of narrative, is thus no small achievement; even if, as individuals, the authors I have discussed met with varying degrees of success, and are limited by varying degrees of obscurity from being representative of a wider cultural shift towards the acceptance of the more recalcitrant aspects of chance.

The suggestion of an engagement between pure chance and narrative as a positive, text-enhancing mimetic boon is where I part company with certain other critics of chance in the modern novel. Leland Monk argues persuasively that chance *always* becomes fate in narrative, that the steamroller power of a teleological narrative always results in chance's yielding to the demands of the greater good of the novel's causal desire. Possibly it does in terms of technical representation: chance is, and remains, unrepresentable in traditional narrative. But then pure chance in the novel, to my mind, is interesting less for its literal presence or absence in texts than for what it represents to the authors who align themselves with it, and for what it can tell us about their motivations and the wider cultural forces, philosophical shifts of meaning and scientific ideas that inspire it. Writers who either attempt to represent it, or who, by highlighting their inability to do so communicate to us an oblique commentary on its subversive potential, are utilizing Edmund Bergler's understanding of chance as a 'latent rebellion against logic, intelligence, moderation, morality, and renunciation' (Bergler, 1957, p. 18). This is a realization that a recognition of chance contains the potential to disrupt the very form in which they are writing. Chance endows us, as readers, with the knowledge that its insolent, unruly power is capable of empowering texts to have a destructive faculty – an ability, albeit a partial and often subtextual one, to work against their own best interests and stated aims. When we think of Beckett's nightmare reproduction of possibility in *Watt*, Murdoch, working to undo her own crystalline form; Green sitting pickled in his study for twenty years unable to write anything except dialogue for fear of interfering in his character's freedom; and B. S. Johnson, dead by his own hand, aged 42, convinced of his artistic failure to represent the truly random nature of reality – all, in their treatment of chance, replicate this sense of artistic ambition, to incorporate the very aspects of the novel that are intractable; to attempt to accommodate chance into their work, however ceaselessly resistant.

In the serialized version of Joseph Conrad's popular 1913 novel *Chance*, in a passage deleted by the author before it was published as a novel, Conrad wrote:

For most people the pages of life are ruled like the pages of a copybook headed with some sound moral maxim at the top. They can turn them over with the certitude that the very catastrophes shall keep to the traced lines. And it is comforting, in a way, to one's friends and even to one's self to think that one's very misfortunes, if any, will be of the foreseen type. (cited in Monk, 1993, p. 84)

Typographical order, for Conrad, becomes interchangeable with the determinism we appeal to in terms of our own personal teleologies. The organization of our lives is thus inextricable from the organization of their
narrative equivalents: the pages of life are 'like the pages of a copybook'.
Chance events become inevitably assimilated into fate; they become the
narrative fabric of one's life; once they happen, they are retrospectively
recalibrated as 'foreseen type' (by what Leland Monk brilliantly calls the
'narrative engines of recuperation' (ibid., p. 89) and indeed, the impulse
that straightens out the haphazard in narrative certainly resonates as an
image of soothing, of smoothing, of making safe for the predictable movements of causal determinism). Once this sleight of hand has been achieved,
the events of life assume the weight of 'history': how could it have been any
other way? This is what we might call the 'novelization' of life, where we
seek to impose a narrative on random events retrospectively, to attempt to
make sense backwards of what, as lived forwards, is ceaselessly nonsensical.

Throughout this book, I have tried to isolate moments of literary history,
centring on a particular historical period where these questions were pressing, where this inevitable assimilation has been resisted, subverted or at
least postponed. As such, I have been interested in novels and writers who
refuse to acquiesce easily to this vision of the function of narrative, and
rather, choose to embrace the disquieting, disruptive aspects of chance. In
this process I have found a slow movement towards a reconciliation between
chance and narrative, as evinced by all my authors' attempts to represent
chance, and finally as manifested in Iris Murdoch's rehabilitation of chance
in narrative as a philosophically sophisticated ethical prescription for us to
achieve a state analogous to the 'positive' freedom limned by Fromm as our
only escape during the war.

Iris Murdoch's husband, the critic John Bayley, wrote in *The Characters of
Love* (1960), that:

> . . . the greatest English literature is not about the Human Condition.
> We might say that it is about 'Nature', a term which has no equivalent in
> the Franco-American critical vocabulary which is current today. . . .
> It implies, above all, an absence of purpose, of insistence, and of individ-
> ual insight; the portrayal of Nature suggests an almost involuntary fidelity
> to what is constant in human types and human affairs; to the repetition of
> birth and death, joy and sorrow; to the humours of men and women and
> the peculiarities that are at once recognised as universal. It implies a lack
> of pretension – the author gets no particular credit for portraying it well.
> The Human Condition, on the other hand, implies a personal sense of

where life is significant, of where humanity suffers especially or feels intensively; of unusual violence and unusual modes of feeling; of interesting development or of illuminating decay. The subject matter may even be the same, but those who write about the Human Condition take an attitude towards it. (Bayley, 1960, pp. 268–9)

Bayley's expression of a sympathy with 'neutrality' in writing in this passage, with an attempt to quell the author's own attitude towards the world he is attempting to describe, finds allies in Murdoch, and with Green, in particular, but also in Johnson and Beckett. What they all have in common is an attempt to liberate the novel from the strictures that signify meaning. What is natural, unpredictable and contingent, character and the accidental nature of reality, must be allowed to flourish, as difficult as that is, and the temptation of allowing form to suffocate reality must be resisted.

Any study of chance will, I believe, end up insinuating a defence of the superiority of reality over art. An understanding of the tensions and interplay between the random and the man-made necessarily inculcates a vision of chance as striving to undercut our grand schemes and inventions, and recognizes its unique vantage, from which it is able to speak to us of the inadequacy of form, and the limits of art's ability 'to see and to really represent', in James's characteristically neat formula, the human experience.

Notes

Prelims

[1] Monk's study is closest to mine in terms of argument and approach, though we differ in time period and in conclusion. Monk argues persuasively that James Joyce's *Ulysses* represents the cut-off point in terms of chance's possible accommodation within narrative, and that subsequent, 'post-modern' attempts to deal with pure chance are doomed to failure. In some ways the argument I make in this book picks up where Monk's leaves off; where Monk argues that the modernist novel is the apogee of the fictional representation of chance, I seek to demonstrate that it is in the fiction of the mid-twentieth century, and the attempts of certain writers of this later period to assimilate pure chance to the novel form, that we see chance's most successful representations.

Chapter 1

[1] 'The Music of Chance', *The Guardian*, Friday, 16 Jan 2004, p. 10.

[2] For elaboration of this idea, see Adam Phillips, *On Flirtation* (1994) or, for my discussion of it below, Chapter Five.

[3] Gerda Reith's definition of chance is particularly succinct: '. . . the idea that events have no identifiable cause and no particular meaning' (Reith, 1999, p. 157).

[4] Richardson here uses the dramatic examples of the realist works of Thomas Mann, Bernard Shaw and Eugene O'Neill, for which, in terms of the novel, we could exchange Eliot, Dickens and Tolstoy.

[5] Trotter describes Turner's approach to the visual 'lateral rhymes' that invest each everyday activity in a crowd-scene with autonomy, which Trotter suggests was an adoption of technique from Teniers: 'They do not draw attention to themselves. Instead they have to be sought out among the casual arrangements of everyday life, arrangements they do little to disturb. If the rhymes express anything, they express the infiltration of chance into human purpose. They inscribe human presence, but not human meaning, not human value; the nested contingencies they articulate are worlds away from the relation of cause and effect which determines the impact of light on cloud and water, on bodies and equipment. The picture is radically split, into a realm of necessity and a realm of chance' (Trotter, 2000, p. 48).

[6] For discussions of the linguistic roots of chance, see Kavanagh, T. (1993), *Enlightenment and the Shadows of Chance*, p. 4; Reith, G., *The Age of Chance: Gambling in Western Culture*, p. 4.

7 See Lacan, J. (1972), 'Seminar on "The Purloined Letter"', in *French Freud: Structural Studies in Psychoanalysis* Ed., J. Mehlman. New Haven, CT, Yale University Press. He concludes 'A letter always arrives at its destination' (p. 72), denying chance a meaningful role.

8 For a useful discussion of Aristotle's definitions of chance, see Monk, L. (1993), *Standard Deviations: Chance and the Modern British Novel.* Palo Alto, CA, Stanford University Press, pp. 16–18.

9 Interestingly, coincidence's elision with, rather than opposition to, causality has continued into the period that I will be concentrating on. As Arthur Koestler argues, 'the simultaneous occurrence of two meaningfully, but not causally connected events or alternatively as a coincidence in time of two or more causally unrelated events which have the same or similar meanings . . . equal in rank to causality as a principle of explanation' Koestler, A. (1972), *The Roots of Coincidence.* New York, Random House, p. 94.

10 Brenner's first chapter 'The History of Lotteries' has a useful list of Biblical and historical sources, and also see Bolen, D. (1976), 'Gambling: Historical Highlights and Trends and their Implication for Contemporary Society', in *Gambling and Society* Ed. William Eadington. Springfield, IL, Thomas, pp. 7–38.

11 '[C]hance came to indicate, not the favour of the gods, but an absence of knowledge. From being a *sacred,* it now became an *epistemological* category.' Reith argues that this represents the major shift in our understanding chance, as it becomes detached from its religious/magical signifiers. She identifies the second half of the seventeenth century as the crucial period for this transformation (Reith, 1999, p. 13).

12 Though mentioned in most books that examine the history of the concept of chance, I owe my specific understanding of the significance of this incident to Gerda Reith in her seminal work *The Age of Chance.* See p. 25 for her commentary on Pascal's wager.

13 The parallel between games of chance and religious belief has been widely recognized, and perhaps the most complete discussion of the parallels can be found in Csikszentmihalyi, M. and Csikszentmihalyi, S. Bennet (1971), 'An explanatory model of play', *American Anthropologist,* 73 (1), 45–58; and David, F. N. (1969), *Games, Gods and Gambling: A History of Probability and Statistical Ideas.* London, Griffin. Both of these texts argue that games of chance are exercises in relationships with the supernatural, which is an analysis that is also pursued by Gerda Reith, who argues that the 'coincidental or unlikely was interpreted for a more profound meaning from the realm of the sacred through divination or augury in the classical, ancient and "primitive" worlds' (Reith, 1999, p. 13). The subsequent link between probabilism and atheism is often implied by the condemnation from the religious that the new attitude to chance inspired.

14 Kavanagh on chance and the Enlightenment: 'Rather than examine the polarities traditionally to define the Enlightenment . . . I suggest we look at another opposition: that between everything the terms "reason" and "nature" came to signify and the recalcitrant challenge of chance' (ibid., p. 4).

15 Freud ultimately discredited this theory in a letter to Theodor Reik; see Reik, T. (1942), *Thirty Years with Freud.* London, The Hogarth Press, pp. 155–6. For a summary of psychological interpretations, still relying on Freud's initial insights,

see Kusyszyn, I. (1984), 'The psychology of gambling', *Annals of the American Academy of Social and Political Science*, no. 474. For the psychology of gambling in general see Bergler, E. (1957), *The Psychology of Gambling*. New York, Hill and Wang.

[16] For instance, if we look at a roulette wheel, we would imagine that it is entirely random; the results, after all, are unpredictable in the basic sense. And yet, Chaos Theory has given us a means of explaining why tiny outside influences have disproportionate effects. If we could re-create the exact same throw of the ball at the exact same moment as the exact same spin of the wheel then, theoretically, the ball would land in the same slot. Chaotic systems explain why outside slight perturbations have irregular effects, but they have been caused, and they are predictable. Therefore chance has, perhaps, stopped operating. Ian Stewart provides a very clear elaboration of these ideas in *Does God Play Dice? The Amazing Science of the Unpredictable* (1989); for a scientific definition of randomness, see p. 280; for further discussion of the tension between chaos and stochastic behaviour, see p. 283.

Chapter 2

[1] As Patrick Swinden has suggested, Beckett's fame in Britain reignited the experimental tradition when in 1956 *Waiting for Godot* made the translation of *The Trilogy* into English necessary: 'the link with Joyce' he explained, 'had been reforged' (Swinden, 1984, p. 64).

[2] This interview with Terry Southern was originally published in *The Paris Review*, in 1958.

[3] Treglown sees the most overt parallels with Samuel Beckett in *Party Going*: 'Samuel Beckett was born only a year after Henry Green, and there are resemblances between their work, especially in *Party Going*'s emphasis on obsession, loneliness, and the impossibility of truly communicating with or knowing anything certain about other people' (Treglown, 2000, p. 111).

[4] Green's first two novels, *Blindness* and *Living*, are too early to be of real interest for this project, and his last two, *Nothing* and *Doting*, are less substantial than those of his middle period.

[5] For more on the decline of the novel form during the war years, see Mengham, R., *Reading The Lull*, p. 456.

[6] See Chapter 1. Leland Monk also draws an association between the etymological roots of chance as falling and the importance of the observer's perspective in the novel: 'the fall implies a position and a situation, a horizon of experience and a horizontality into which the vertical movement of the chance occurrence falls unexpectedly. The abandonment of a god's-eye view of narrative events and the increasing concern with perspective in the post-Victorian novel therefore provides a helpful index to the influence of chance upon modernist narrative forms' (Monk, 1993, p. 76).

[7] It is worth noting that Summers works at a parabolam factory, and thus literally fulfils the Freudian motif of turning shit into precious metal.

Chapter 3

[1] Hazel Barnes makes clear the closeness between the ideas of possibility and chance: 'Like uncertainty, [possibility] simply means that something is not yet decided, that the future is open' (Barnes, 1959, p. 365).

[2] Coincidence is, of course, merely randomness that has been brought to our attention, or chance made narrative, but as mentioned, its utilization as a narrative device normally heralds a hidden significance, and always, once it appears, inevitably becomes subsumed as 'plot'.

[3] Barnes takes her title from the central tenet of the Italian existentialist Nicola Abbagnano, who argued that possibility is central to any conception of freedom, and that the popular formulation of one being 'condemned to freedom' was thus disingenuous.

[4] Briony Fer, in her book on abstract art in the twentieth century, describes Arp's commitment to the aleatorical expression of form in his own work: 'His formal language . . . [consists of] a set of curved, amorphous and apparently random forms – configurations which are contrasted with the geometric, the grid, and the straight line.' He belonged, along with his friend Blossfeldt, to the group and journal *Abstraction-Creation* from 1932–36, which Fer describes as the mouthpiece for those avant-garde artists who were in part in opposition to Surrealism (Fer, 1977, p. 56ff).

[5] For an approachable and full introduction to this often forbidding subject, see Gleick, J. (1988), *Chaos: Making a New Science*. London, Heinemann.

[6] What was being replaced can be described as the general scientific dogma, stretching back to Aristotle, that each event will generate predictable effects, and that each effect will have a related cause, even if hidden. Hume makes an interesting point that 'Every effect presupposes a cause; effect being a relative term, of which cause is the correlative. But this does not prove that every being must be preceded by a cause; no more than it follows, because every husband have a wife, that therefore every man must be married' (Hume, 1888, p. 128).

[7] Indeed Beckett went as far to disavow the existentialist theories of being, in an interview with Tom Driver: 'When Heidegger and Sartre speak of a contrast between being and existence, they may be right, I don't know, but their language is too philosophical for me. I am not a philosopher' (Driver, 1961, p. 22). Edith Kern makes a useful summary of critical linkages made between Beckett and philosophy: she argues that he defies philosophical pigeonholing, yet his work abound with references, if mocking ones. Descartes was the protagonist of 'Whoroscope', Geulincx is mentioned in *Murphy* and *The End*. Kern finds common ground between Beckett and Sartre in the concept of the Self and the Sartrean *pour-soi*, and Michael Collins also relates *Waiting For Godot* to Existentialism. Eric P. Levy argues that *Molloy* represents a rejection of the Sartrean notion of freedom. Kern points out the uncomfortable fact that in Beckett's denial of allegiance to philosophy there is something profoundly Kierkegaardian, in that Kierkegaard railed frequently against the idea of philosophical system, and argued instead that one must merely represent true, lived experience. See Levy, E. P. (2001), 'Living without a life: the disintegration of the Christian

Humanist synbook in *Molloy*. *Studies in the Novel*, 33:1; Kern, E. (1970), *Existential Thought and Fictional Technique: Kierkegaard, Sartre, Beckett*. New Haven, CT, Yale University Press, p. 167.

8 The argument against this development I have attributed to Kavanagh, but it is also a widely held view of the nineteenth-century novel, the type that Beckett would be self-consciously kicking against, that it concentrates on explanatory, psychological motivations.

9 Richardson also argues this, but for *Molloy*. Richardson argues that by deferring the causal connections, Beckett leaves us with a 'mere collocation of fragmentary episodes' (Richardson, 1992, p. 71).

10 The association between possibility and despair is clarified by Sartre in the short, explanatory book *Existentialism and Humanism*: 'As for "despair," the meaning of this expression is very simple. It merely means that we limit ourselves to a reliance upon that which is within our wills, or within the sum of probabilities which render our actions feasible. Whenever one wills anything, there are always these elements of probability. If I am counting on a visit from a friend, who may be coming by train or by tram, I presuppose that the train will arrive at the appointed time, or that the tram will not be derailed. I remain in the realm of possibilities' (Sartre, 1980, p. 39).

11 This mathematically informed deliberation anticipates Molloy's calculations of his number of farts ('extraordinary how mathematics helps you to know yourself'), and the famous 16 sucking stones in the four pockets of his greatcoat, both from *Molloy* (Beckett, 1994, pp. 30, 69).

12 This is different to the view, which I share with Reith, Kavanagh and Hacking, and that I argued for in Chapter One, where chance is not given full status but instead perceived as an ontological lack. Before the explosion of probability theory in the seventeenth century, references to chance had become interchangeable with those to ignorance, and it was widely understood that if something happened by 'chance', it was merely an event whose cause or the machinery that brought it into being had not yet been revealed to us. Bennett elides this Humean 'indifference' with this idea of insufficient knowledge, a blurring I would not endorse merely on the grounds she gives, that is, their shared 'subjectivity'.

13 This association of a rapprochement with contingency as a path to happiness is a tantalizingly early example of contingency and chance as an ethical 'Good': an association that, I go on to argue, becomes systematic in the work of Iris Murdoch.

14 Interestingly, this quote will later become a talisman of the chance-obsessed strand of the British avant-garde of the 1950s and 1960s that idolized Beckett. B. S. Johnson repeated this quote often and let it inspire his paean to randomness of form, the 1969 'novel in a box' *The Unfortunates*. See Coe, J. (2004), *Like A Fiery Elephant: The B. S. Johnson Story*. London, Picador. I deal with this link in more detail in Chapter Four.

15 '[T]he novel came to identify itself with an ability to evoke, yet limit, chance's power to disrupt narratives of mastery and reason' (Kavanagh, 1993, p. ix).

16 The arbitrary nature of the relationship between language and the things to which it refers seems almost a (postmodern) cliché now, but it certainly wasn't then – although Eliot among others had had a modernist preoccupation with the disjunction between language and reality.

[17] This is obviously, for an Irishman, not a purely philosophical position.

[18] And, in fact, when Beckett talks of 'chaos' (as he does, for instance, in the quote from his interview with Driver, above) this is certainly what he means by it – the parallel I drew with modern Chaos Theory in respect to the butterfly effect and wildly disproportionate narrative aetiology is not meant to suggest that Beckett, or any of his contemporaries, would have been aware of this level of meaning. The idea of classical chaos is nevertheless an important one, and a useful meta-phorization of either the 'mess', that recurring Beckettian idea, or of the expansion of possibility in the existential sense that Watt, and *Watt*, are both at supreme pains to curtail.

[19] Kavanagh's conclusion to his analysis of Voltaire's *Candide* also elided an aware-ness of the power of chance with the failure of language: 'Pangloss's defence of a liberty compatible with necessity enunciates the ultimate cacophony of language, the bankruptcy of man's attempts to represent reality, to offer anything more elo-quent than silence as a way of making sense of what happens in the world.' Anything else will be 'a fragile crust of language proclaiming its categories of good and evil, knowledge and ignorance, causality and rationality, over a volcano of chance poised to contradict and abolish them' (Kavanagh, 1993, p. 168).

[20] An idea which has an antecedent in Hume: 'To form a clear idea of anything is an undeniable argument for its possibility' (Hume, 1888, p. 136).

Chapter 4

[1] The conservative tendency of the immediately post-war years in Britain I under-stand to be embodied by writers as diverse as Graham Greene, Patrick Hamilton, Evelyn Waugh, and in certain respects, Henry Green.

[2] Leland Monk's excellent work *Standard Deviations* (1993) follows a similar line of argument to mine up until this point; he argues that 'chance *always* takes on a necessarily fateful quality once it is represented in narrative' (2), and that 'it is in the nature of narrative to render chance as fate so that "what happens" in a story becomes indistinguishable from the more evaluative "what was meant to hap-pen"' – a point on which we agree. However he goes on to suggest that 'I am not . . . interested in describing anything like "pure" chance in the novel or celebrat-ing moments of "radical" "subversive" "freedom"' (8). As such his examination ends with Joyce, who Monk believes reached the limits of how far chance could be assimilated into narrative: 'chance *always* gets read as fate, and this inevitabil-ity is characteristic of *any* narrative' (Monk, 1993, p. 10).

[3] Probability's relation to the novel would take up another book, but two excellent studies that deal with it specifically are Patey, D. L. (1984), *Probability and Literary Form: Philosophic Theory and Literary Practice in the Augustan Age*. Cambridge, Cambridge University Press; and Newsom, R. (1988), *A Likely Story: Probability and Play in Fiction*. Rutgers, NJ, Rutgers University Press.

[4] Similarly, Daniel Albright in his book *Modernism and Music* defines 'postmodern-ism' as a loose collection of tendencies. Two of these are *bricolage* and *randomness*. Bricolage: 'the jury-rigging of art, the assembling of the art object, in a denatured and desecrated fashion, in order to expose the purely arbitrary nature of the

signs that all artists, past and present, employ' (Albright, 2004, p. 12). His definition of randomness is equally apposite for my purposes, describing it as he does as: 'a technique for depersonalizing the artist, for demonstrating the transcendental anonymity of the work of art. If artistic decisions are governed by the rolling of dice, then the artwork is liberated from human responsibility' (ibid., p. 13).

[5] For more on their relationship see Joseph, B. W. (2003), *Random Order: Robert Rauschenberg and the Neo-Avant-Garde.* Cambridge, MA, MIT Press.

[6] Although 'rebirth' is perhaps misleading, as certain Dadaists were still producing original work, indeed, Duchamp himself was part of the group to which art historians attach the epithet 'neo-Dada'.

[7] Brandon Joseph, in his authoritative work on Robert Rauschenburg, defines the neo-Dadaists as overlapping loosely with, or including, those artists at the symposium for the exhibition *The Art of Assemblage* at the Museum of Modern Art in New York in 1961. Amongst these were Robert Rauschenberg, Roger Shattuck, Richard Huelsenbeck and Marcel Duchamp (Joseph, 2003).

[8] The association between the natural world – between dirt, mud and rock – and chance composition continued, as Masters relates: 'Richard Long was another artist interested in exploring the idea of sculpture which was not dependent on a conventional notion of artistic skill. His art works were often ephemeral and open to the vagaries of time where the weather or another person might change what he has created. His *A Line in Ireland* (1974), is just that. It consists of a low-lying row of rocks pulled together from the bleak and craggy surroundings to form a line. The landscape asserts its own sense of order into which Long has subtly intervened' (Masters, 2000, p. 215).

[9] Sterne was in fact, one of Johnson's holy triumvirate of the only authors he believed to be exemplary; the other two were Joyce and Beckett.

[10] As recounted in the introduction to 'Aren't You Rather Young to be Writing Your Memoirs?'. This essay, originally written in 1973, stands as Johnson's most extensive and concise exposition of his artistic philosophy.

[11] Tredell argues that the hole in the page represents, eventually, a false prolepsis: 'an arousing in a narrative, by selective or distorted anticipation, of reader expectations that are subsequently, to a greater or lesser extent, disconfirmed' (Tredell, 1985, p. 67).

[12] Johnson would have been aware of both William Burroughs' experiments with 'cut-up', and the Oulipo group in France's interest in randomness under constraint. He certainly would have been familiar with the Dadaists' earlier aleatorical poetry, and with Samuel Beckett's 1969 prose-poem *Lessness*. Marc Saporta's *Composition One* had also worked on a similar principle as *The Unfortunates*. Although it is not clear whether Johnson was aware of this novel as it was never published in English.

[13] Due to the unique problems posed by the pagination of *The Unfortunates*, I have resorted to the inelegant but practical solution of identifying the individual chapters by their opening two words; the opening and closing chapters are exempt from this, as they were labelled as such by Johnson, and will therefore be referred to as 'first' and 'last'.

Chapter 5

1 '[F]lirtation is among other things a way of acknowledging the contingency of our lives – their sheer unpredictability, how accident-prone we are – without at the same time turning this uncertainty into a new kind of master-plot. Flirtation confirms the connection between excitement and uncertainty, and how we make uncertainty possible by making it exciting' (Phillips, 1994, p. xii).

2 'But the hardest thing of all to think about is chance, which denies the very form and purpose of thought itself' (Trotter, 2000, p. 10). Also, 'few concepts are as alien to human thought as the notion of pure chance – the idea that events have no identifiable cause and no particular meaning' (Reith, 1999, p. 157).

3 'The artist, like the God of the creation, remains within or behind or beyond or above his handiwork, invisible, refined out of existence, indifferent, paring his fingernails' (Joyce, 1992, p. 215).

4 For more on Murdoch's recourse to the figure of the saint, and his relation in her work to the idea of the artist, see Conradi, P. (1986), *Iris Murdoch: The Saint and the Artist*. London, Macmillan.

5 The argument of Gordon's excellent *Fables of Unselfing* could be summed up as follows: 'the central moral imperative of her work is the imperative of unselfing, the overcoming of self-centredness that prevents us from loving others as separate existences . . . Solipsism is for her our moral burden, as unselfing is our moral task' (Gordon, 1995, p. 7).

6 For Murdoch, 'misreadings' are an exertion of one's ego onto the neutral and blameless truthful messy information that the world is actually offering. One's perception, when distorted by ego, is capable of knocking perception askew; and this, she suggests, is how evil manifests itself: as a refusal to truthfully accept the world for what it is.

Bibliography

Albright, D. (Ed.) (2004), *Modernism and Music: An Anthology of Sources*. Chicago, University of Chicago Press.

Alvarez, A. (1973), *Beckett*. London, Fontana.

Arnheim, R. (1971), *Entropy and Art*. Berkeley, CA, University of California Press.

Arnheim, R. (1972), *Towards a Psychology of Art*. Berkeley, CA, University of California Press.

Auden, W. H. (1963), *The Dyer's Hand*. London, Faber & Faber.

Auerbach, E. (1953), *Mimesis*, Trans. W. R. Trask. Princeton, NJ, Princeton University Press.

Bakhtin, M. (1999), *Problems of Dostoevsky's Poetics*, Trans. C. Emerson. Minneapolis, MI, University of Minneapolis Press.

Baldanza, F. (1974), *Iris Murdoch*. New York, Twayne.

Bardin, J. (1951), 'Fire and flight'. *The Freeman*, 7 May, 9–10.

Barnes, H. E. (1959), *The Literature of Possibility: A Study in Humanistic Existentialism*. Lincoln, NB, University of Nebraska Press.

Barrows, J. (1961), 'Iris Murdoch'. *John O'London's*, 4 May, 498.

Barthes, R. (1977), 'The Death of the Author'. *Image, Music, Text*, Trans. S. Heath. London, Fontana.

Bayley, J. (1960), *The Characters of Love: A Study in the Literature of Personality*. London, Constable.

Beckett, S. (1931), *Proust*. London, Chatto & Windus.

—. (1976), *Watt*. London, John Calder.

—. (1984), 'Lessness'. *Collected Shorter Prose, 1945–80*. London, John Calder.

—. (1993), *Murphy*. London, John Calder.

—. (1994), *Molloy, Malone Dies, The Unnamable*. London, John Calder.

—. (1995), 'First Love'. In S. E. Gontarski (Ed.), *The Complete Short Prose, 1929–1989*. New York, Grove Press.

Bell, D. F. (1993), *Circumstances: Chance in the Literary Text*. Lincoln, NB, University of Nebraska Press.

Bennett, D. (1998), *Randomness*. Cambridge, MA, Harvard University Press.

Bergler, E. (1957), *The Psychology of Gambling*. New York, Hill and Wang.

Bergonzi, B. (1970), *The Situation of the Novel*. London, Macmillan.

—. (1993), *Wartime and its Aftermath: English Literature and its Background, 1939–1960*. Oxford, Oxford University Press.

Bergson, H. (1910), Trans. Pogson, F. L., *Time and Free Will*. London, Macmillan.

Bloom, C. and Day, G. (Eds.) (2000), *Literature and Culture in Modern Britain, Volume Three: 1956–1999*. London, Longman.

Boethius (1969), Trans. Watts, V. E., *Consolations of Philosophy*. London, Penguin.

Bolen, D. W. (1976), 'Gambling: Historical Highlights and Trends and Their Implication for Contemporary Society'. In Eadington, W. (Ed.), *Gambling and Society*. Springfield, IL., Thomas.

Bowen, E. (1942), 'Contemporary', Review of *In My Good Books* by V. S. Pritchett. *New Statesman*, 23 May 1942.

Brannigan, J. (2002), *Literature, Culture and Society in Postwar England, 1945–65*. Lewiston, NY, New Mellen Press.

Brenner, R. and Brenner, G. A. (1990), *Gambling and Speculation: A Theory, a History, and a Future of Some Human Decisions*. Cambridge, Cambridge University Press.

Brienza, S. and Brater, E. (1976), 'Chance and choice in Beckett's *Lessness*'. *ELH*, 43, 244–58.

Bronfen, E. and Goodwin, S. W. (Eds.) (1994), *Death and Representation*, Baltimore, MA, Johns Hopkins University Press.

Burgin, V. (1986), 'The Absence of Presence'. *The End of Art Theory – Criticism and Postmodernity*. London, Macmillan.

Burroughs, W. (1986), 'The Fall of Art', in *The Adding Machine*. New York, Seaver.

Buttner, G. (1984), *Samuel Beckett's Novel* Watt. Philadelphia, University of Pennsylvania Press.

Cabanne, P. (1967), *Entretiens avec Marcel Duchamp*. Paris, Edition Pierre Belfond.

Cage, J. (1961), 'Where Are We Going? And What Are We Doing?'. In *Silence: Lectures and Writings*. Middletown, CT, Wesleyan University Press.

—. (1961a), 'Experimental Music'. In *Silence: Lectures and Writings*. Middletown, CT, Wesleyan University Press.

—. (1961b), 'To Describe the Process of Composition Used in *Music of Changes* and Imaginary Landscape No. 4'. In *Silence: Lectures and Writings*. Middletown, CT, Wesleyan University Press.

—. (1961c), 'On Robert Rauschenberg, Artist, and His Work'. In *Silence: Lectures and Writings*. Middletown, CT, Wesleyan University Press.

Camus, A. (1955), *The Myth of Sisyphus*, Trans. J. O'Brien. London, Hamish Hamilton.

Capel, H. W. (Ed.) (1995), *Chance and Uncertainty: Their Role in Various Disciplines*. Amsterdam, Vossiuspers.

Carroll, L. (2000), *Poetry for Young People*. London, Sterling Publishing.

Coe, J. (2004), *Like a Fiery Elephant: The B.S. Johnson Story*. London, Picador.

Cohen, J. (1964), *Behaviour in Uncertainty*. New York, Basic.

Conradi, P. (1986), *Iris Murdoch: The Saint and the Artist*. London, Macmillan.

—. (2001), *Iris Murdoch: A Life*. London, HarperCollins.

Csikszentmihalyi, M. and S. B. Csikszentmihalyi (1971), 'An exploratory model of play'. *American Anthropologist*, 73, 45–58.

Cunningham, V. (1988), *British Writers of the Thirties*. Oxford, Oxford University Press.

Darwin, C. (2003), *On the Origin of the Species By Means of Natural Selection*. London, Broadview Press.

Daston, L. (1988), *Classical Probability in the Enlightenment*. Princeton, NJ, Princeton University Press.

David, F. N. (1969), *Games, Gods and Gambling: A History of Probability and Statistical Ideas*. London, Griffin.

Dearlove, J. E. (1982), *Accommodating the Chaos: Beckett's Nonrelational Art*. Durham, Duke University Press.

Deleuze, G. (1983), *Nietzsche and Philosophy*, Trans. H. Tomlinson. New York, Columbia University Press.

Derrida, J. (2007), 'My Chances/*Mes Chances*', in *Psyche: Inventions of the Other*, Ed. Peggy Kamuf and Elizabeth Rottenberg. Stanford, Stanford University Press.

Dickens, C. (1989), *Hard Times*. London, Penguin.

Diderot, D. (1875), *Jacques le fataliste*. Paris, Hermann.

—. and J. D'Alembert (1969), *Encyclopedie*. New York, Readex Microprint.

Dipple, E. (1982), *Iris Murdoch: Work for the Spirit*. London, Methuen.

Dostoevsky, F. (1972), *Notes from the Underground*, Trans. J. Coulson. Harmondsworth, Penguin.

Dostoevsky, F. (1992), *The Gambler*, Trans. J. Kentish. Oxford, Oxford University Press.

Driver, T. F. (1961), 'Beckett by the Madeleine'. *Columbia University Forum*, IV, 22–3.

Earnshaw, S. (2000), 'Literature and Culture in Modern Britain, Volume Three: 1956–1999'. In Day, C. B. and Gary Day (Eds.) London, Longman.

Ehrenberg, W. (1977), *Dice of the Gods: Causality, Necessity and Chance*. London, Birkbeck University Press.

Ellmann, R. (1982), *James Joyce*. Oxford, Oxford University Press.

Epstein, R. A. (1977), *The Theory of Gambling and Statistical Logic*. New York, London Academic Press.

Fer, B. (1977), *On Abstract Art*. New Haven, CT, Yale University Press.

Fourny, J.-F. and C. D. Minahen (Eds.) (1997), *Situating Sartre in Twentieth-Century Thought and Culture*. London, Macmillan.

Franklin, J. (1999), *Serious Play: The Cultural Form of the Nineteenth-Century Realist Novel*. Philadelphia, University of Philadelphia Press.

Freud, S. (1928), 'Dostoevsky and Parricide'. In Strachey, J. (Ed. and Trans.), *Collected Papers*. London, The Hogarth Press.

—. (1957), 'Leonardo Da Vinci: A Memory of His Childhood'. In Strachey, J. (Ed. and Trans.), *The Standard Edition of the Complete Psychological Works of Sigmund Freud*, Vol. 11. London, The Hogarth Press.

—. (1966), *The Psychopathology of Everyday Life*. London, Benn.

Fromm, E. (2001), *The Fear of Freedom*. London, Routledge & Kegan Paul.

Gibson, A. (1984), 'Henry Green as experimental novelist'. *Studies in the Novel*, 16, 197–214.

Gigerenzer, G., Swijtink, Z., Porter, T., Daston, L., Beatty, J. and L. Kruger (1989), *The Empire of Chance: How Probability Changed Science and Everyday Life*. Cambridge, Cambridge University Press.

Gleick, J. (1988), *Chaos: Making a New Science*. London, Heinemann.

Goodwin, S. W. and E. Bronfen (Eds.) (1993), *Death and Representation*. Baltimore, MD, The Johns Hopkins University Press.

Gordon, D. J. (1995), *Iris Murdoch's Fables of Unselfing*. Columbia, MO, University of Missouri Press.

Graver, L. and R. Federman (Eds.) (1997), *Samuel Beckett: The Critical Heritage*. London, Routledge & Kegan Paul.

Green, H. (1940), *Pack My Bag*. London, Hogarth Press.

—. (1943), *Caught*. London, Hogarth Press.

—. (1946), *Back*. London, Hogarth Press.

—. (1950), 'The English novel of the future'. *Contact* I, 20–24.

—. (1992), 'The Art of Fiction'. In Yorke, M. (Ed.), *Surviving: The Uncollected Writings of Henry Green*. London, Chatto & Windus.

Greene, B. (2004), *The Fabric of the Universe: Space, Time, and the Texture of Reality*. London, Penguin.

Greene, G. (1951), *The End of the Affair*. London, Heinemann.

Gribbin, J. (1985), *In Search of Schrödinger's Cat*. London, Corgi.

Hacking, I. (1975), *The Emergence of Probability*. London, Cambridge University Press.

—. (1990), *The Taming of Chance*. Cambridge, Cambridge University Press.

Halliday, J. and P. Fuller (Eds.) (1974), *The Psychology of Gambling*. London, Allen Lane.

Harrisson, T. and C. Madge (Eds.) (1940), *War Begins at Home*. London, Chatto & Windus.

Hesla, D. (1963), 'The shape of chaos: a reading of Beckett's *Watt*'. *Critique*, 85–105.

—. (1971), *The Shape of Chaos: An Interpretation of the Art of Samuel Beckett*. Minneapolis, University of Minnesota Press.

Hobson, H. (1962), 'Lunch with Iris Murdoch'. *The Sunday Times*, 11 March.

Huizinger, J. (1998), *Homo Ludens: A Study of the Play Element in Culture*. London, Routledge & Kegan Paul.

Hume, D. (1888), *Treatise of Human Nature*. Oxford, Clarendon Press.

—. (1902), *Enquiries Concerning the Human Understanding and Concerning the Principles of Morals*. Oxford, Oxford University Press.

Hunter, J. P. (1994), 'From Typology to Type'. In Ezell, M. J. M. and K. O. B. O'Keeffe (Eds.), *Cultural Artifacts and the Production of Meaning: The Page, the Image and the Body*. Ann Arbor, MI, University of Michigan Press.

James, H. (1934), *The Art of the Novel: Critical Prefaces*. New York, Scribner.

—. (1996), *What Maisie Knew*. London, Penguin.

Johnson, B. S. (1964), *Albert Angelo*. Constable, London.

—. (1975), 'Fat Man on a Beach'. In Gordon, G. (Ed.), *Beyond the Words: Eleven Writers in Search of a New Fiction*. London, Hutchinson.

—. (1985), 'Aren't you rather young to be writing your memoirs?' *Review of Contemporary Fiction*, 5, 4–13.

—. (1999), *The Unfortunates*. London, Picador.

—. (2004), *Trawl*, in *Omnibus*. London, Picador.

Joseph, B. W. (2003), *Random Order: Robert Rauschenberg and the Neo-Avant-Garde*. Cambridge, MA, MIT Press.

Joyce, J. (1992), *Portrait of the Artist as a Young Man*. London, Penguin.

Judson, R. L. (1986), *Aristotle on Necessity, Chance and Explanation*. Oxford, University of Oxford Press.

Kavanagh, T. (1993), *Enlightenment and the Shadows of Chance: The Novel and the Culture of Gambling in Eighteenth Century France*. Baltimore, The Johns Hopkins University Press.

Kermode, F. (1963), 'House of fiction: interviews with seven English novelists'. *Partisan Review*, 30, 61–82.

—. (1971), *Modern Essays*. London, Fontana.

—. (2004), 'Retripotent'. *London Review of Books*, 5 August 2004.

Kern, E. (Ed.) (1962), *Sartre: A Collection of Critical Essays*. Englewood Cliffs, NJ, Prentice-Hall.

—. (1970), *Existential Thought and Fictional Technique: Kierkegaard, Sartre, Beckett*. New Haven, CT, Yale University Press.

Koestler, A. (1972), *The Roots of Coincidence*. New York, Random House.

Kusyszyn, I. (1984), 'The psychology of gambling'. *Annals of the American Academy of Social and Political Science*, 474 (July), 133–45.

Lacan, J. (1972), 'Seminar on "The Purloined Letter"'. In Mehlman, J. (Ed.), *French Freud: Structural Studies in Psychoanalysis*. New Haven, Yale University Press.

Laing, S. (1983), *Society and Literature 1945–1970*. In Sinfield, A. (Ed.), London, Methuen.

Laplace, P. S. (1830), *The System of the World*, Trans. H. H. Harte. Dublin, Longman.

—. (1951), *A Philosophical Essay on Probabilities*, Trans. F. W. Truscott and F. L. Emory. New York, Dover Publications.

Lee, R. A. (Ed.) (1996), *The Beat Generation Writers*. London, Pluto Press.

Lessing, D. (1962), *The Golden Notebook*. London, Michael Joseph.

Levy, E. P. (2001), 'Living without a life: the disintegration of the Christian Humanist synthesis in *Molloy*'. *Studies in the Novel*, 33, 80–94.

Lodge, D. (1969), 'The novelist at the crossroads'. *Critical Quarterly*, 2, 105–32.

—. (1979), *Language of Fiction: Essays in Criticism and Verbal Analysis of the English Novel*. London, Routledge & Kegan Paul.

Lowry, R. (1989), *The Architecture of Chance*. London, Oxford University Press.

Magny, C. E. (1962), 'The Duplicity of Being'. In Kern, E. (Ed.), *Sartre: A Collection of Critical Essays*. Englewood Cliffs, NJ, Prentice-Hall.

Mallarmé, S. (1966), *Collected Poems*, Trans. H. Weinfield. Berkeley, CA, University of California Press.

Masters, D. (2000), 'British Art'. In Day, G. and C. Bloom (Eds.), *Literature and Culture in Modern Britain, Volume Three: 1956–1999*. London, Longman.

Matthews, J. H. (1991), *The Surrealist Mind*. Selinsgrove, PA, Susquehanna University Press.

Maynard, J. (2000), 'British Poetry 1956–1999'. In Day, G. and C. Bloom (Eds.), *Literature and Culture in Modern Britain, Volume Three: 1956–1999*. London, Longman.

McBride, W. (Ed.) (1977), *Sartre and Existentialism: The Development and Meaning of Twentieth Century Existentialism*. New York, Garland.

McCarthy, P. A. (Ed.) (1986), *Critical Essays on Samuel Beckett*. Boston, G. K. Hall.

Mellor, D. (1971), *The Matter of Chance*. London, Cambridge University Press.

Mengham, R. (1982), *The Idiom of the Time: The Writings of Henry Green*. Cambridge, Cambridge University Press.

—. (1983), 'Reading *The Lull*'. *Twentieth-Century Literature*, 29, 455–70.

—. and Reeve, N. H. (Eds.) (2001), *The Fiction of the 1940s: Stories of Survival*. Basingstoke, Palgrave.

Merkel, B. (1987), *The Concept of Freedom and the Development of Sartre's Early Political Thought*. New York, Garland.

Miller, K. (Ed.) (1968), *Writing in England Today: The Last Fifteen Years*. London, Penguin.

Moivre, A. de. (1756), *The Doctrine of Chances*. London.

Monk, L. (1993), *Standard Deviations: Chance and the Modern British Novel*. Palo Alto, CA, Stanford University Press.

Monod, J. (1972), *Chance and Necessity: An Essay of the Natural Philosophy of Modern Biology*, Trans. A. Wainhouse. London, Collins.

Montmort, P. R. de. (1713), *Essai d'analyse sur le jeux de hazard*, Paris.

Morin, E. (1983), 'Beyond determinism: the dialogue of order and disorder'. *SubStance*, 40, 22–35.

Motherwell, R. (Ed.) (1989), *The Dada Painters and Poets: An Anthology*, 2 Ed. Cambridge, MA. Belknap Press of Harvard University Press.

Murdoch, I. (1959), 'The Sublime and the Good'. *Chicago Review*, 13, 42–55.

—. (1961), 'Against Dryness'. *Encounter*, 16 (January), 16–20.

—. (1970a), *The Sovereignty of Good*. London, Routledge & Kegan Paul.

—. (1970b), 'Existentialists and Mystics'. In Robson, W. W. (Ed.), *Essays and Poems Presented to Lord David Cecil*. London, Constable.

—. (1975), *The Black Prince*. London, Penguin.

—. (1987), *Sartre, Romantic Rationalist*. New York, Viking.

—. (1992), *Metaphysics as a Guide to Morals*. London, Chatto & Windus.

—. (1999a), 'The Sublime and the Beautiful Revisited'. In Conradi, P. (Ed.), *Existentialists and Mystics: Writings on Philosophy and Literature*. London, Penguin.

—. (1999b), *The Sea, the Sea*. London, Vintage.

—. (2001), *A Fairly Honourable Defeat*. London, Vintage.

—. (2003a), *The Time of the Angels*. London, Vintage.

—. (2003b), *An Accidental Man*. London, Vintage.

Nehring, N. (1993), *Flowers in the Dustbin: Culture, Anarchy and Postwar England*. Ann Arbor, MI, University of Michigan Press.

Newsom, R. (1988), *A Likely Story: Probability and Play in Fiction*. New Brunswick, NJ, Rutgers University Press.

Nicholls, P. (1995), *Modernisms: A Literary Guide*. London, Macmillan.

Nietzsche, F. (1982), *Daybreak*, Trans. R. J. Hollingdale. Cambridge, Cambridge University Press.

Nietzsche, F. (1982), *Thus Spoke Zarathustra*, Trans. R. J. Hollingdale. Harmondsworth, Penguin.

North, M. (1984), *Henry Green and the Writing of His Generation*. Charlottesville, VA, University Press of Virginia.

Nussbaum, M. (1986), *The Fragility of Goodness: Luck and Ethics in Greek Tragedy and Philosophy*. Cambridge, Cambridge University Press.

Orwell, G. (1968), 'The Lion and the Unicorn'. In Orwell, S. and I. Angus (Eds.), *Collected Essays, Journalism and Letters of George Orwell*. London, Secker & Warburg.

Patey, D. L. (1984), *Probability and Literary Form: Philosophic Theory and Literary Practice in the Augustan Age*. Cambridge, Cambridge University Press.

Peirce, C. S. (1932), 'The Doctrine of Necessity Examined'. In Hartstone, C. and P. Weiss (Eds.), *The Collected Papers of Charles Sanders Peirce*. Cambridge, MA, Harvard University Press.

—. (1932), 'A Reply to the Necessitarians'. In Hartstone, C. and P. Weiss (Eds.), *The Collected Papers of Charles Sanders Peirce*. Cambridge, MA, Harvard University Press.

Peterson, E. (1971), *Tristan Tzara*. New Brunswick, NJ, Rutgers University Press.

Phillips, A. (1994), *On Flirtation*. London, Faber & Faber.

Pilling, J. (1997), *Beckett before Godot*. Cambridge, Cambridge University Press.

Plank, W. (1981), *Sartre and Surrealism*. Ann Arbor, MI, UMI Research Press.

Plato, (1987), 'The Statesman'. *The Dialogues of Plato*. Oxford, Oxford University Press.

Poisson, S. D. (1837), *Recherches sur la probabilité des jugements en matière criminelle et un matière civile*. Paris, Bachelier.

Pope, A. (1950), *Essay on Man*, Ed., M. Mack. London, Methuen.

—. (1999), *The Dunciad in Four Books*. Harlow, Longman.

Popper, K. (1956), *The Open Universe: An Argument for Indeterminism*. Towota, NJ, Rowman & Littlefield.

Rauschenberg, R. (1963), 'Random order'. *Location*, 1, (1), 27–31.

Reik, T. (1942), *Thirty Years with Freud*. London, The Hogarth Press.

Reith, G. (1999), *The Age of Chance: Gambling in Western Culture*. London, Routledge & Kegan Paul.

Richardson, B. (1992), 'Causality in *Molloy*: philosophic theme, narrative transgression, and metafictional paradox'. *Style*, 26, 66–78.

—. (1997), *Unlikely Stories: Causality and the Nature of Modern Narrative*. Cranbury, NJ, Associated University Presses.

Richter, H. (1971), *Hans Richter*. New York, Holt, Rhinehart and Winston.

Robbe-Grillet, A. (1965), *Snapshots and Towards a New Novel*, Trans. B. Wright. London, Calder & Boyars.

Rorty, R. (1989), *Contingency, Irony, and Solidarity*. London, Cambridge University Press.

Rousseau, J. J. (1953), *Confessions*, Trans. J. M. Cohen. London, Penguin.

Rubner, A. (1966), *The Economics of Gambling*. London, Macmillan.

Ruelle, D. (1991), *Chance and Chaos*. London, Penguin.

Russell, J. (1960), *Nine Novels and an Unpacked Bag*. New Brunswick, NJ, Rutgers University Press.

Saporta, M. (1963), Howard, R., *Composition No. 1*. New York, Simon & Schuster.

Sartre, J. P. (1939), 'M. François Mauriac et la liberté', *La Nouvelle Revue Française*, 305 (February), 212–32.

—. (1950), 'Situation of the Writer in 1947'. In *What is Literature?*, Trans. B. Frechtman. London, Methuen.

—. (1962), Introduction to 'Les Temps Modernes'. In Weber, E. (Ed.), *Paths to the Present: Aspects of European Thought From Romanticism to Existentialism*. New York, Dodd, Mead and Company.

—. (1965), *Nausea*, Trans. R. Baldick. London, Penguin.

—. (1974), *The Writings of Jean-Paul Sartre*, Trans. R. McLeary. Evanston, Northwestern University Press.

—. (1980), *Existentialism and Humanism*, Trans. P. Mairet. London, Methuen.

—. (1992), *Notebooks for an Ethics*, Trans. D. Pellauer. Chicago, University of Chicago Press.

—. (1993), *Quiet Moments in a War: The Letters of Jean-Paul Sartre to Simone de Beauvoir 1940–63*, Trans. L. Fahnestock and N. MacAfee. London, Hamish Hamilton.

—. (2002), *Being and Nothingness*, Trans. H. E. Barnes. London, Routledge & Kegan Paul.

—. (2008), *The Aftermath of War*, Trans. C. Turner. London, Seagull Books.

Shakespeare, W. (1988), *Richard III; King Lear*. In Stanley Wells, G. T., John Jowett, William Montgomery (Eds.), *The Complete Works*. Oxford, Clarendon Press.

Sharples, R. W. (1983), *Alexander of Aphrodisias on Fate*. London, Duckworth.

Shenker, I. (1956), 'Moody Man of Letters'. *New York Times*, 6 May, 2: 2.

Sinfield, A. (Ed.) (1983), *Society and Literature 1945–1970*, London, Methuen.

Sophocles (1982), *The Three Theban Plays*, Trans. R. Fagles. London, Allen Lane.

Spender, S. (1978), 'September Journal', in *The Thirties and After*. London, Fontana.

Sterne, L. (1997), *The Life and Opinions of Tristram Shandy, Gentleman*. London, Penguin.

Stewart, I. (1989), *Does God Play Dice?: The New Mathematics of Chaos*. London, Penguin.

Stokes, E. (1959), *The Novels of Henry Green*. London, Hogarth Press.

Stonebridge, L. (2001) 'Bombs and Roses: The Writing of Anxiety in Henry Green's *Caught*'. In Mengham, R. and N. H. Reeve (Eds.), *The Fiction of the 1940s: Stories of Survival*. Basingstoke, Palgrave.

Swinden, P. (1973), *Unofficial Selves: Character in the Novel from Dickens to the Present Day*. London, Macmillan.

—. (1984), *The English Novel of History and Society, 1940–1980*. London, Macmillan.

Taylor, D. S. (1965), 'Catalytic rhetoric: Henry Green's theory of the novel'. *Criticism: A Quarterly for Criticism and the Arts*, VII (Winter), 81–99.

Tennyson, A. (1995), *In Memoriam*. In Jump, J. D. (Ed.), *In Memoriam, Maud and Other Poems*. London, Everyman.

Thielemans, J. (1985), '*Albert Angelo* or B.S. Johnson's paradigm of truth'. *Review of Contemporary Fiction*, 5, 81–87.

Tippet, L. J. C. (1927), *Random Sampling Numbers*. London, Cambridge University Press.

Tredell, N. (1985a), 'The truths of lying: *Albert Angelo*'. *Review of Contemporary Fiction*, 5, 64–70.

—. (1985b), 'Telling life, telling death: *The Unfortunates*'. *Review of Contemporary Fiction*, 5, 4–41.

Treglown, J. (2000), *The Life and Work of Henry Green*. London, Faber & Faber.

Trotter, D. (2000), *Cooking with Mud: The Idea of Mess in Nineteenth-Century Art and Fiction*. Oxford, Oxford University Press.

Van Ghent, D. (1987), On *Tristram Shandy*. In Bloom, H. (Ed.), *Laurence Sterne's Tristram Shandy*. New York, New Haven, Philadelphia, Chelsea House.

Voltaire (1990), *Candide and Other Stories*, Trans. R. Pearson. Oxford, Oxford University Press.

Voogd, P. J. de (1985), 'Laurence Sterne, the marbled page, and "the use of accidents"'. *Word & Image*, 1, 279–87.

Waldrop, R. (1971), *Against Language?* The Hague, Mouton.

Walpole, H. (1857), *The Letters of Horace Walpole, Earl of Orford*. Edited by Peter Cunningham, London, Richard Bentley.

Ward, K. (1996), *God, Chance and Necessity*. Oxford, One World.

Warner, W. B. (1986), *Chance and the Text of Experience: Freud, Nietzsche, and Shakespeare's Hamlet*. Ithaca and London, Cornell University Press.

Watts, H. A. (1975), *Chance: A Perspective on Dada*. Ann Arbor, MI, UMI Research Press.

Waugh, E. (1961), *Unconditional Surrender*. London, Chapman & Hall.

Waugh, P. (1995), *Harvest of the Sixties: British Literature and its Background 1960–1990*. Oxford, Oxford University Press.

Weatherhead, K. (1959), 'Structure and texture in Henry Green's latest novels'. *Accent*, 111–22.

Wesley, J. (1989), *The Works of John Wesley*. Abingdon, The Abingdon Press.

Wiener, N. (1954), *The Human Use of Human Beings: Cybernetics and Society*. London, Eyre & Spottiswoode.

Wilson, A. (1983), 'Living and loving'. *Twentieth Century Literature*, 29, 384–86.

Woolf, V. (1932), *The Common Reader: Second Series*. London, Hogarth Press.

Index